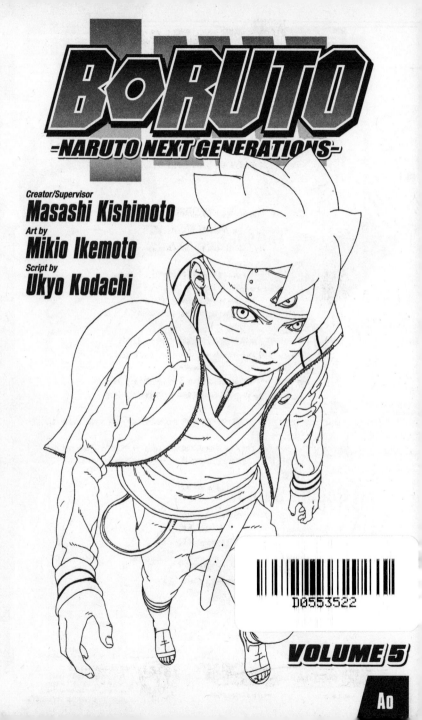

BORUTO
—NARUTO NEXT GENERATIONS—

Creator/Supervisor
Masashi Kishimoto

Art by
Mikio Ikemoto

Script by
Ukyo Kodachi

D0553522

VOLUME 5

Ao

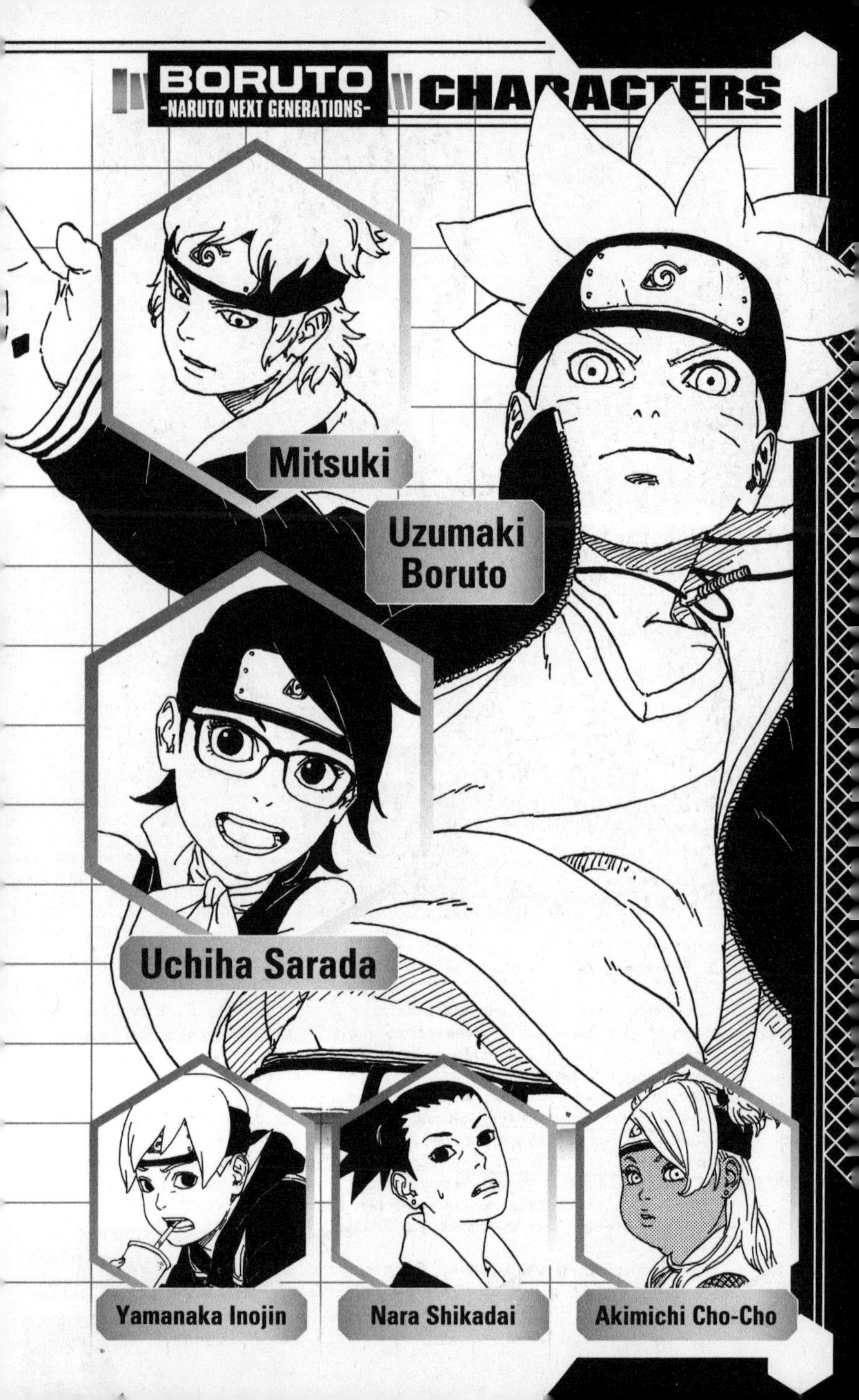
BORUTO
-NARUTO NEXT GENERATIONS-
CHARACTERS
Mitsuki
Uzumaki Boruto
Uchiha Sarada
Yamanaka Inojin
Nara Shikadai
Akimichi Cho-Cho

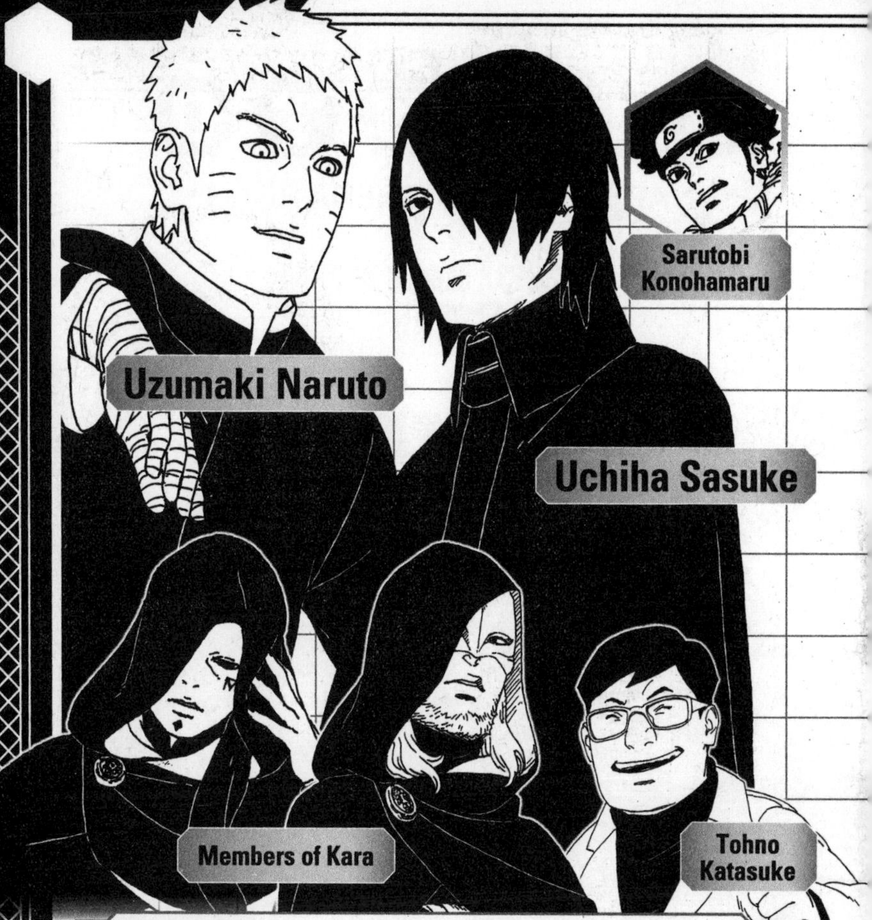

Sarutobi Konohamaru
Uzumaki Naruto
Uchiha Sasuke
Members of Kara
Tohno Katasuke

STORY

The Great Ninja War that shook the world and shed much blood is now history. Naruto has become the Seventh Hokage, and the people of Konohagakure Village are enjoying peace. Yet Naruto's son Uzumaki Boruto has a glum life, perhaps due to his father's too-great influence.

Rebelling against Naruto while simultaneously craving his praise, Boruto decides to enter the Chunin Exam along with his teammates Sarada and Mitsuki.

However, the exam is more intense than Boruto has imagined. Boruto ends up secretly using a prohibited Scientific Ninja Tool and is stripped of his shinobi status by his father.

Just then, members of the Ohtsutsuki Clan attack the arena! Boruto faces off against them alongside Naruto, Sasuke, and others, and they achieve victory with a Rasengan that father and son weave together. However, Otsutsuki leaves behind ominous parting words: "Those blue eyes shall eventually take everything from you..." In addition, a strange mark appears on Boruto's right palm...

Later, with a new resolve to become a ninja, Boruto successfully protects the Daimyo's son from a ring of robbers. However, its leader's words reveal the existence of a mysterious group called Kara...

BORUTO
-NARUTO NEXT GENERATIONS-

VOLUME 5
AO

CONTENTS

Number 16: **The Vessel** ············· 7

Number 17: **Ao** ············· 51

Number 18: **The Hand** ············· 95

Number 19: **Puppets** ············· 139

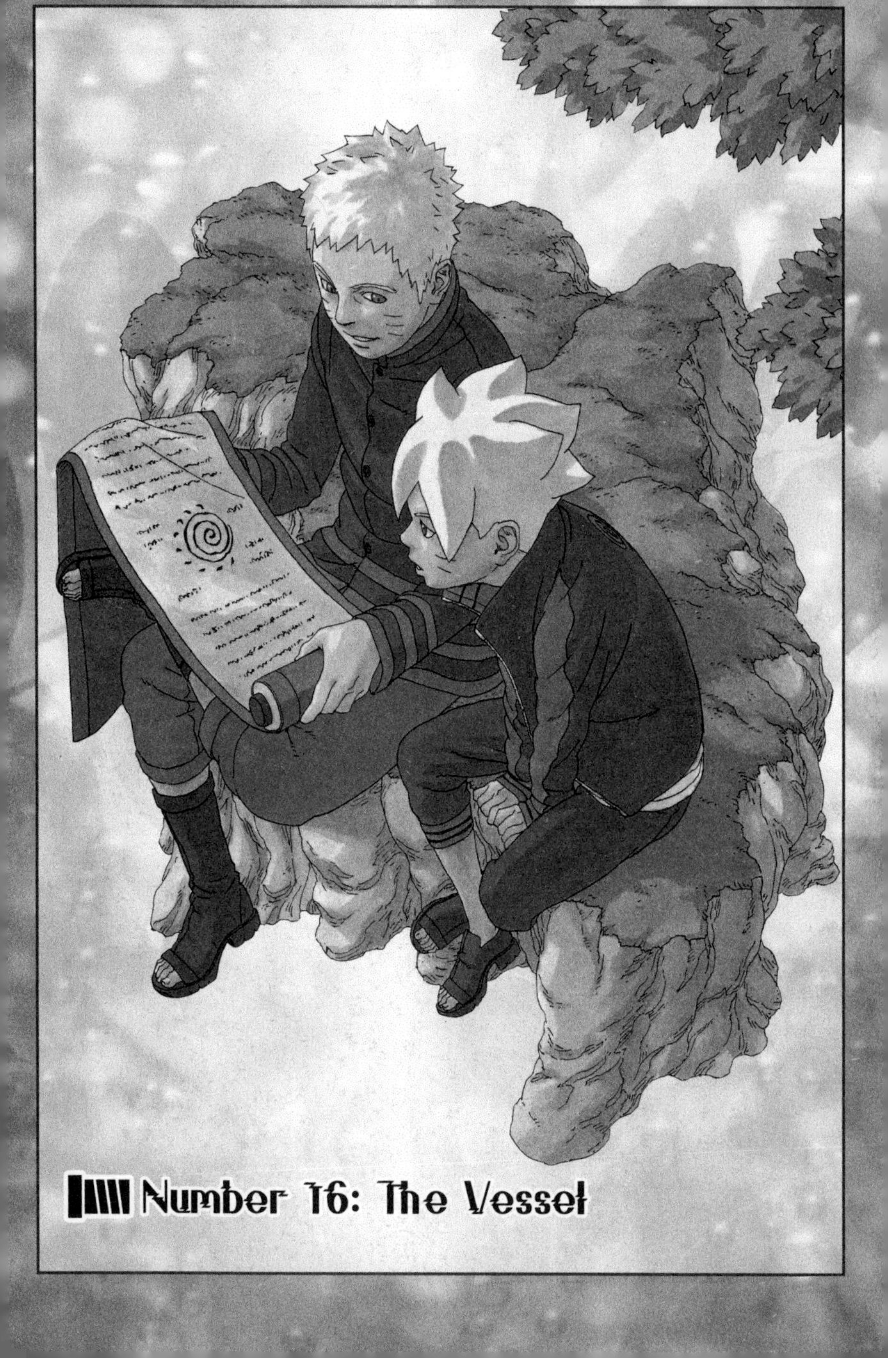

Number 16: The Vessel

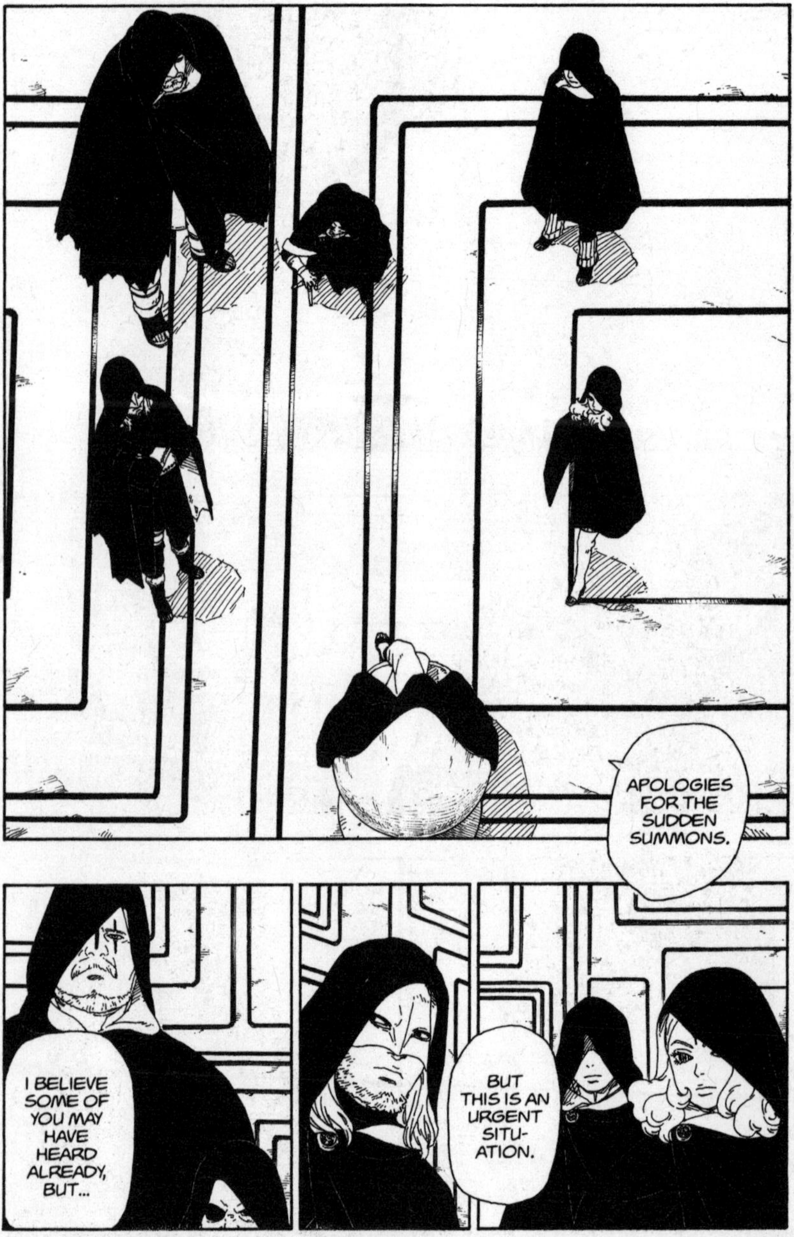
APOLOGIES FOR THE SUDDEN SUMMONS.
BUT THIS IS AN URGENT SITU-ATION.
I BELIEVE SOME OF YOU MAY HAVE HEARD ALREADY, BUT...

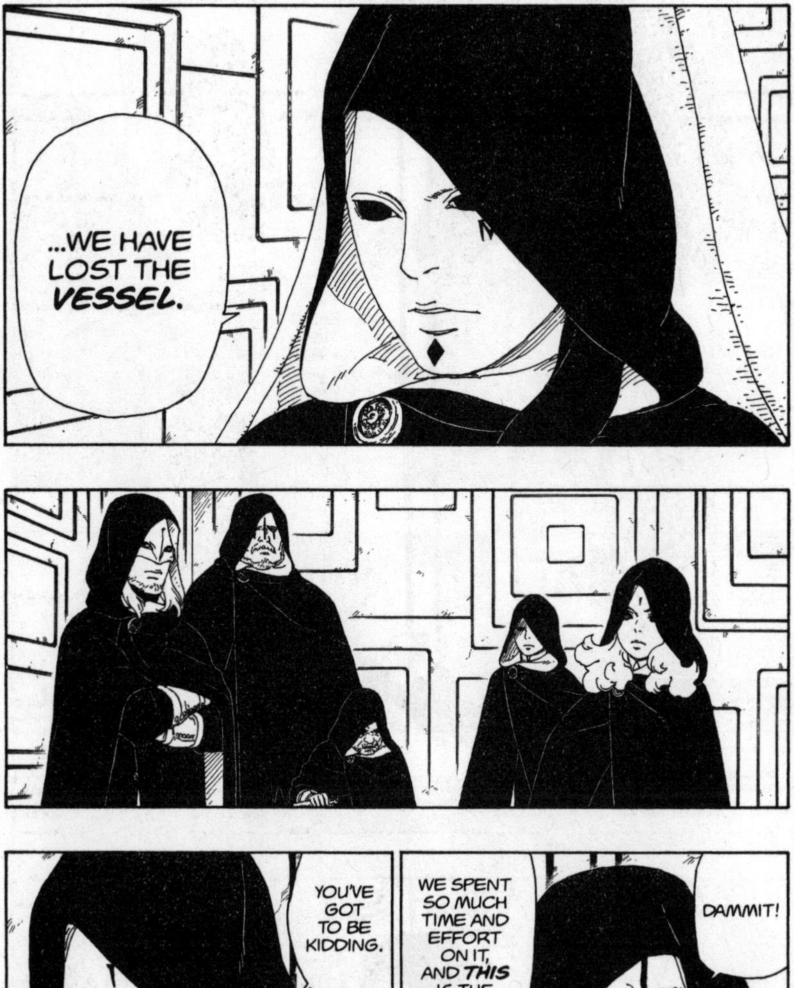
...WE HAVE LOST THE *VESSEL.*
DAMMIT!
WE SPENT SO MUCH TIME AND EFFORT ON IT, AND *THIS* IS THE RESULT?
GREAT, JUST GREAT.
YOU'VE GOT TO BE KIDDING.
ARE YOU SAYING WE FLUSHED ENOUGH MONEY TO BUY A NATION DOWN THE TOILET?

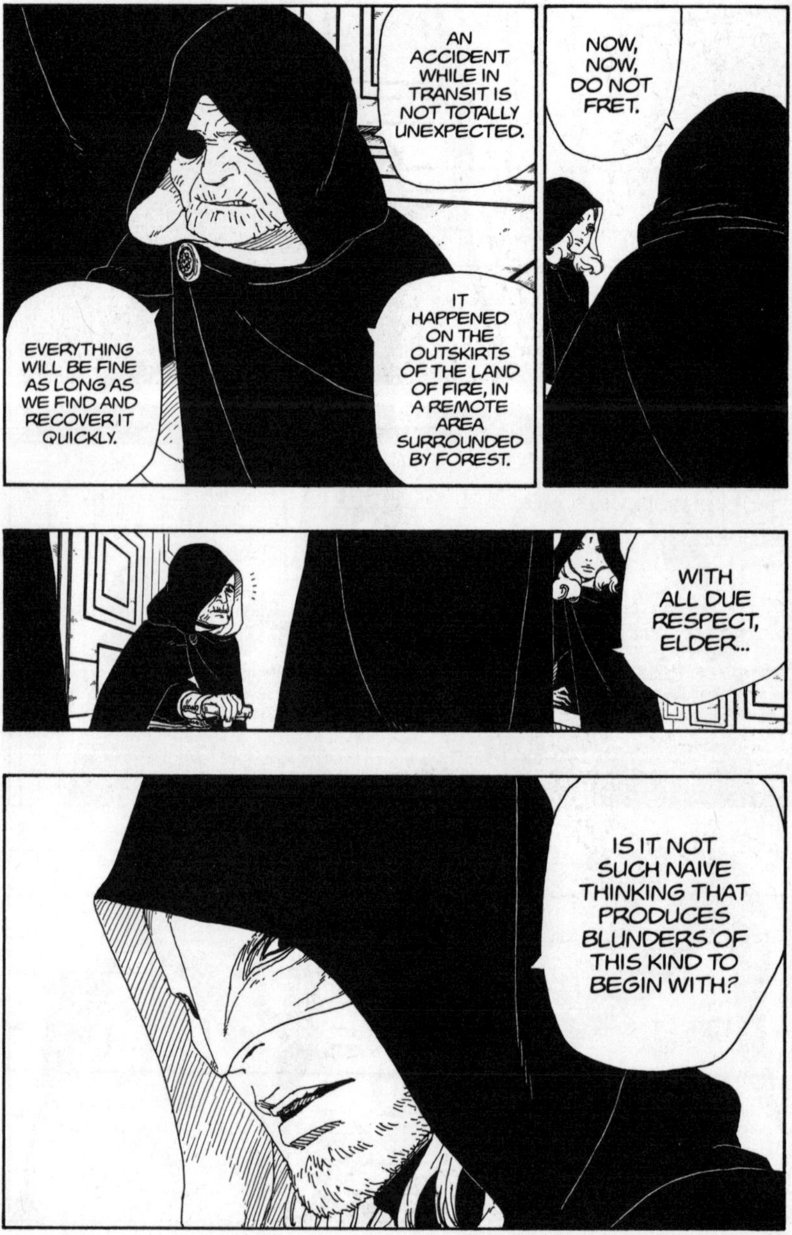
NOW, NOW, DO NOT FRET.
AN ACCIDENT WHILE IN TRANSIT IS NOT TOTALLY UNEXPECTED.
IT HAPPENED ON THE OUTSKIRTS OF THE LAND OF FIRE, IN A REMOTE AREA SURROUNDED BY FOREST.
EVERYTHING WILL BE FINE AS LONG AS WE FIND AND RECOVER IT QUICKLY.
WITH ALL DUE RESPECT, ELDER...
IS IT NOT SUCH NAIVE THINKING THAT PRODUCES BLUNDERS OF THIS KIND TO BEGIN WITH?

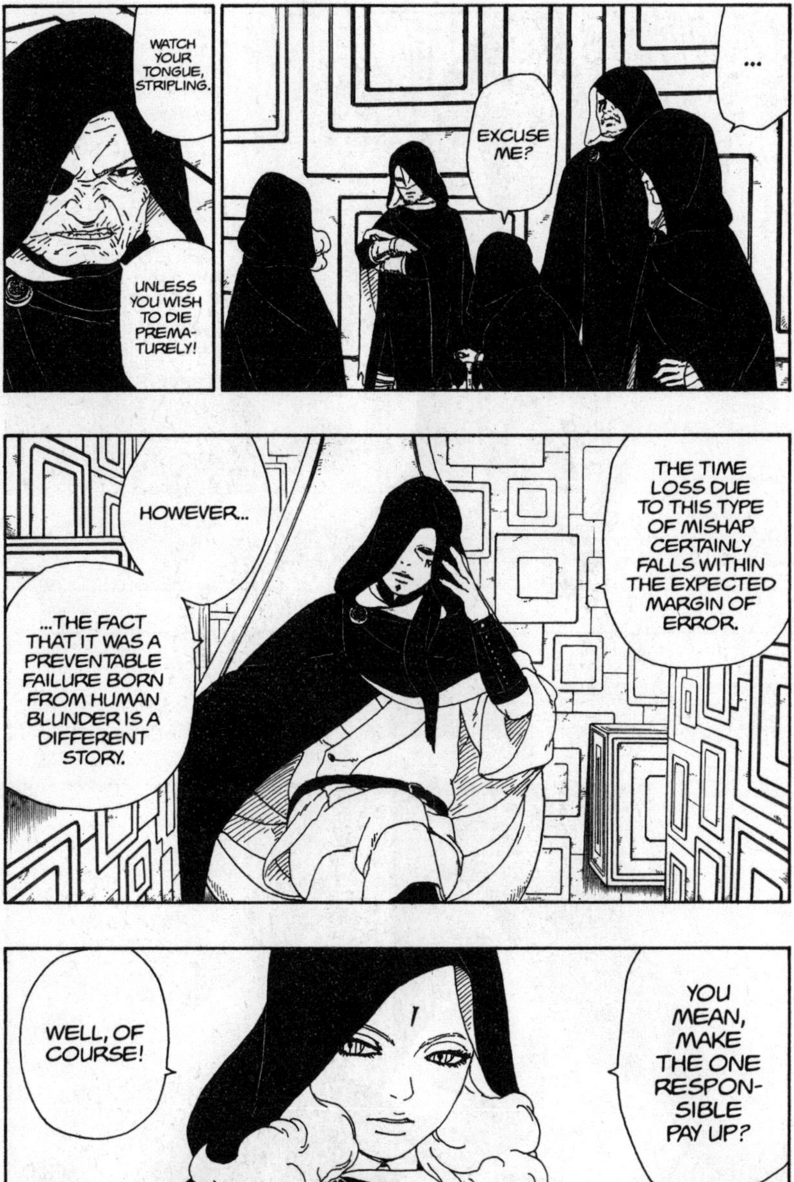
...
EXCUSE ME?
WATCH YOUR TONGUE, STRIPLING.
UNLESS YOU WISH TO DIE PREMATURELY!
THE TIME LOSS DUE TO THIS TYPE OF MISHAP CERTAINLY FALLS WITHIN THE EXPECTED MARGIN OF ERROR.
HOWEVER...
...THE FACT THAT IT WAS A PREVENTABLE FAILURE BORN FROM HUMAN BLUNDER IS A DIFFERENT STORY.
YOU MEAN, MAKE THE ONE RESPONSIBLE PAY UP?
WELL, OF COURSE!

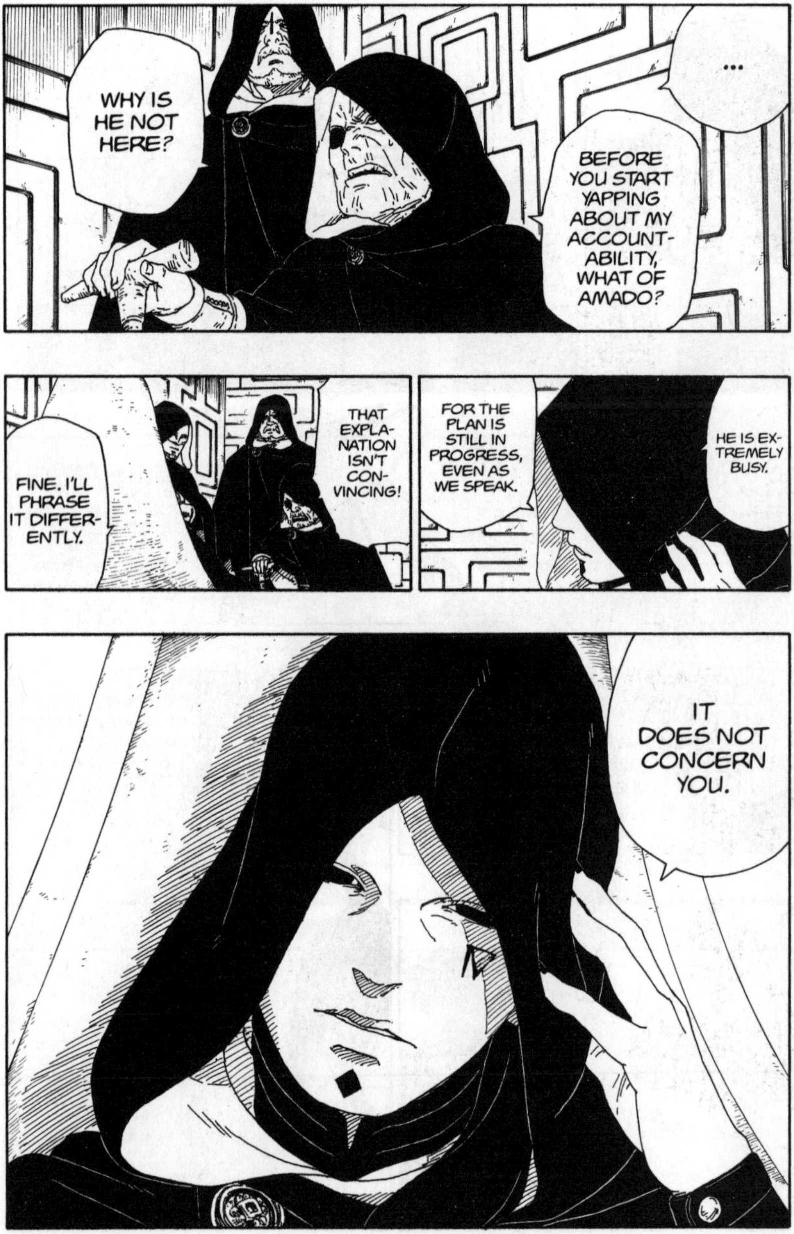
...
BEFORE YOU START YAPPING ABOUT MY ACCOUNT-ABILITY, WHAT OF AMADO?
WHY IS HE NOT HERE?
HE IS EX-TREMELY BUSY.
FOR THE PLAN IS STILL IN PROGRESS, EVEN AS WE SPEAK.
THAT EXPLA-NATION ISN'T CON-VINCING!
FINE. I'LL PHRASE IT DIFFER-ENTLY.
IT DOES NOT CONCERN YOU.

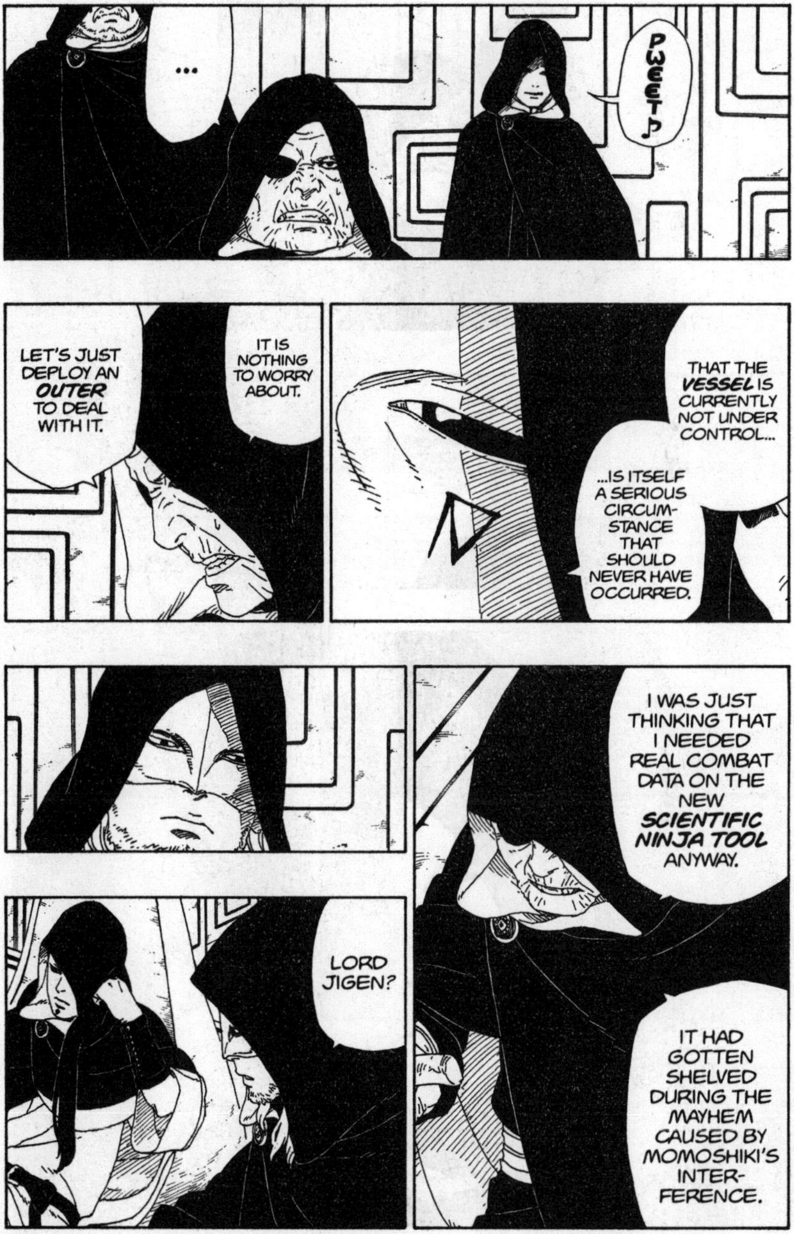
PWEET♪
...
THAT THE VESSEL IS CURRENTLY NOT UNDER CONTROL...
...IS ITSELF A SERIOUS CIRCUMSTANCE THAT SHOULD NEVER HAVE OCCURRED.
IT IS NOTHING TO WORRY ABOUT.
LET'S JUST DEPLOY AN OUTER TO DEAL WITH IT.
I WAS JUST THINKING THAT I NEEDED REAL COMBAT DATA ON THE NEW SCIENTIFIC NINJA TOOL ANYWAY.
IT HAD GOTTEN SHELVED DURING THE MAYHEM CAUSED BY MOMOSHIKI'S INTER-FERENCE.
LORD JIGEN?

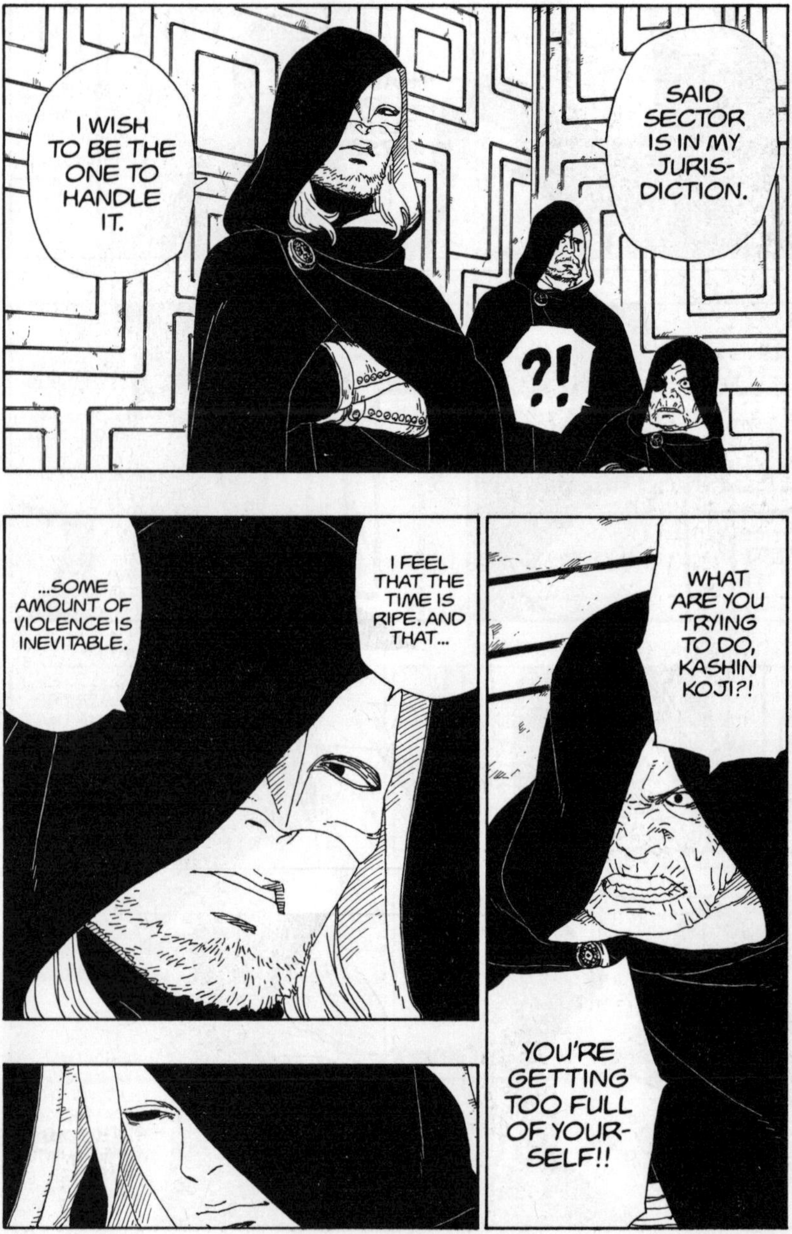
SAID SECTOR IS IN MY JURIS-DICTION.
I WISH TO BE THE ONE TO HANDLE IT.
?!
WHAT ARE YOU TRYING TO DO, KASHIN KOJI?!
YOU'RE GETTING TOO FULL OF YOUR-SELF!!
I FEEL THAT THE TIME IS RIPE. AND THAT...
...SOME AMOUNT OF VIOLENCE IS INEVITABLE.

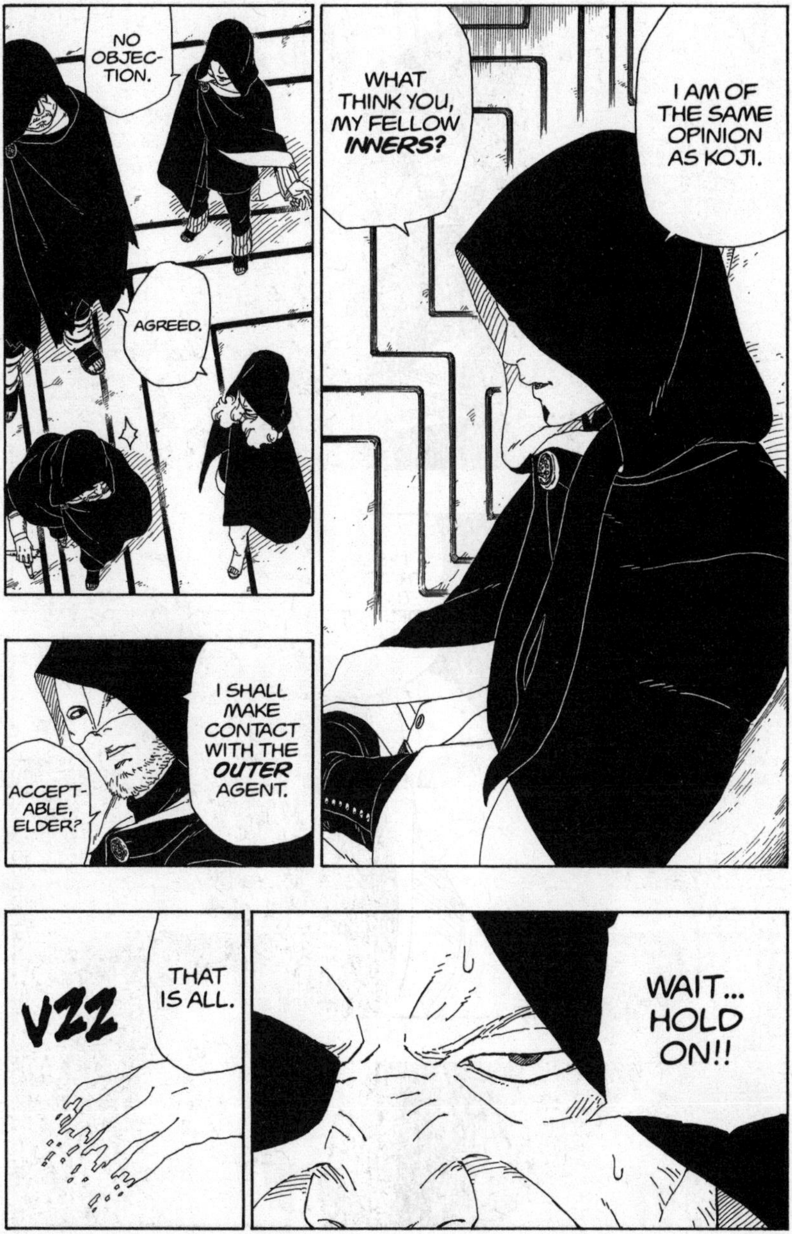
I AM OF THE SAME OPINION AS KOJI.
WHAT THINK YOU, MY FELLOW **INNERS?**
NO OBJECTION.
AGREED.
I SHALL MAKE CONTACT WITH THE **OUTER** AGENT.
ACCEPTABLE, ELDER?
WAIT... HOLD ON!!
THAT IS ALL.
VZZ

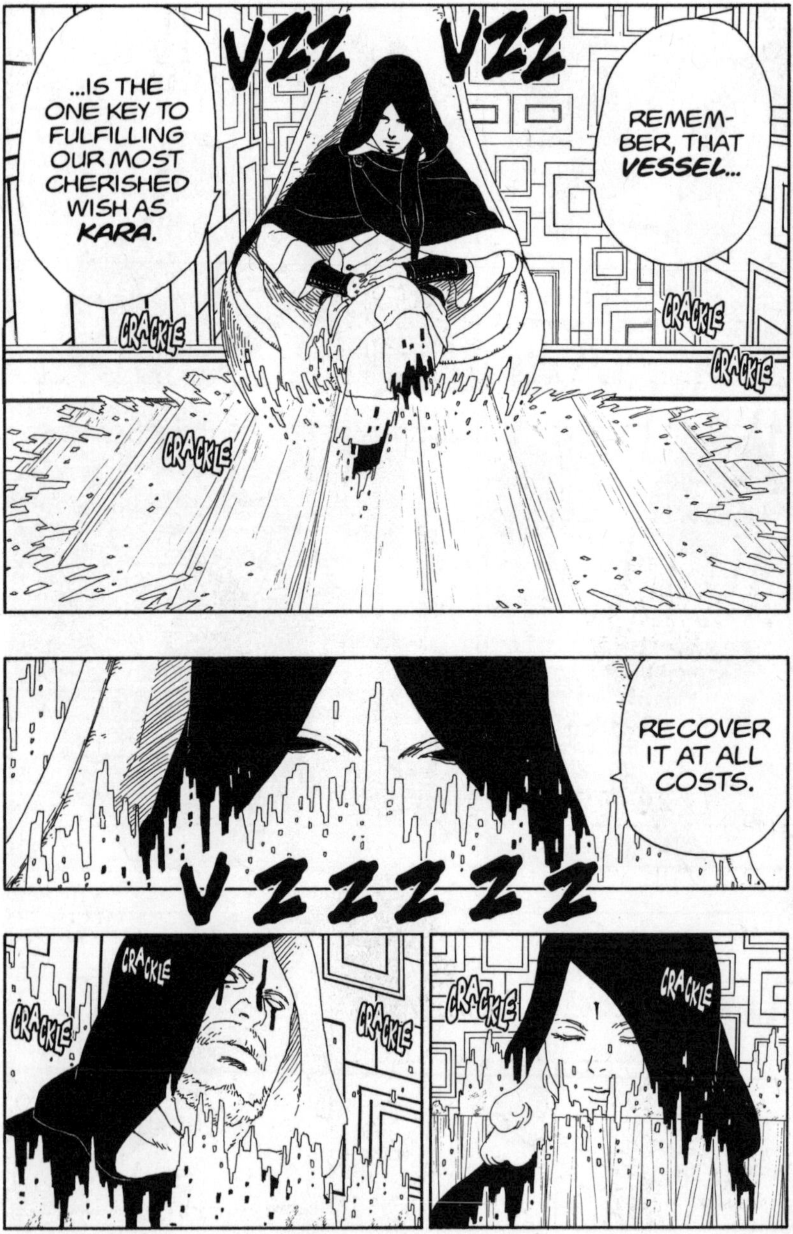
REMEM-BER, THAT VESSEL...
VZZ VZZ
...IS THE ONE KEY TO FULFILLING OUR MOST CHERISHED WISH AS KARA.
CRACKLE
CRACKLE
CRACKLE
CRACKLE
RECOVER IT AT ALL COSTS.
VZZZZZZ
CRACKLE
CRACKLE
CRACKLE
CRACKLE
CRACKLE

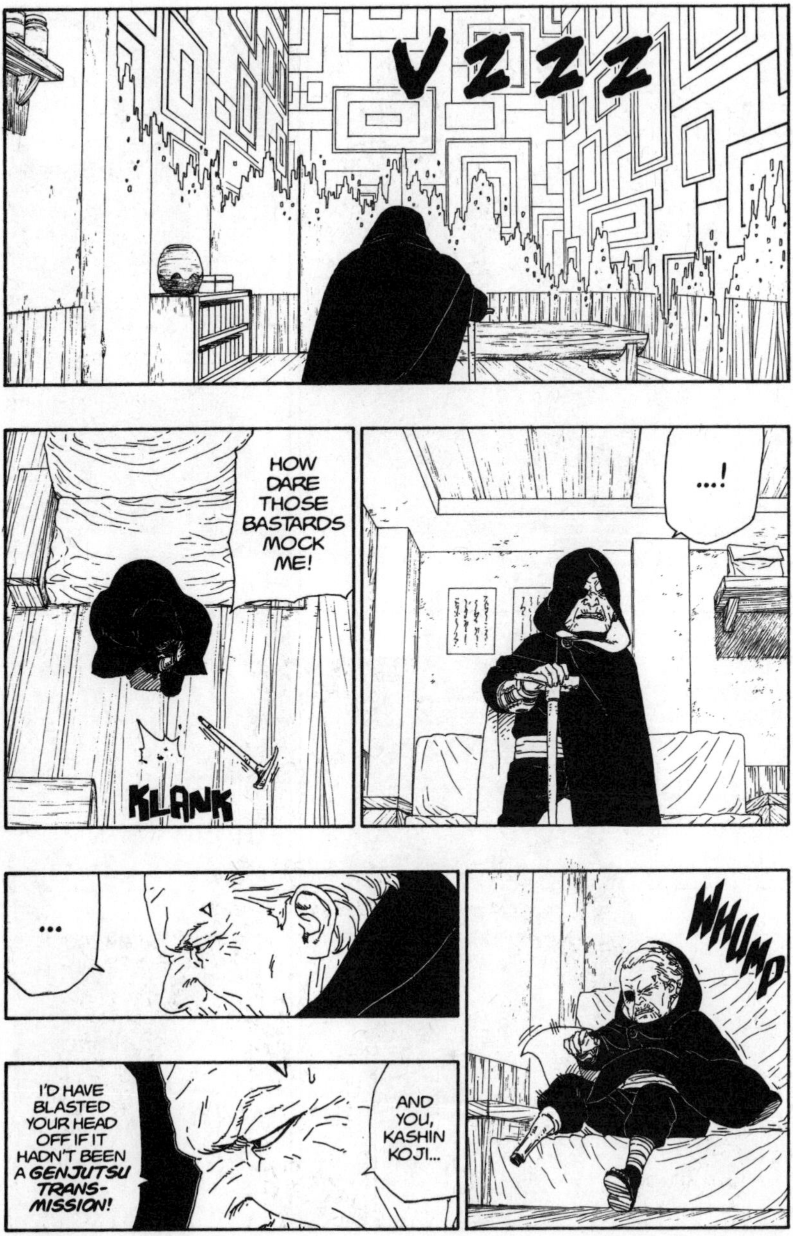
VZZZ
...!
HOW DARE THOSE BASTARDS MOCK ME!
KLANK
WHUMP
...
AND YOU, KASHIN KOJI...
I'D HAVE BLASTED YOUR HEAD OFF IF IT HADN'T BEEN A *GENJUTSU TRANSMISSION*!

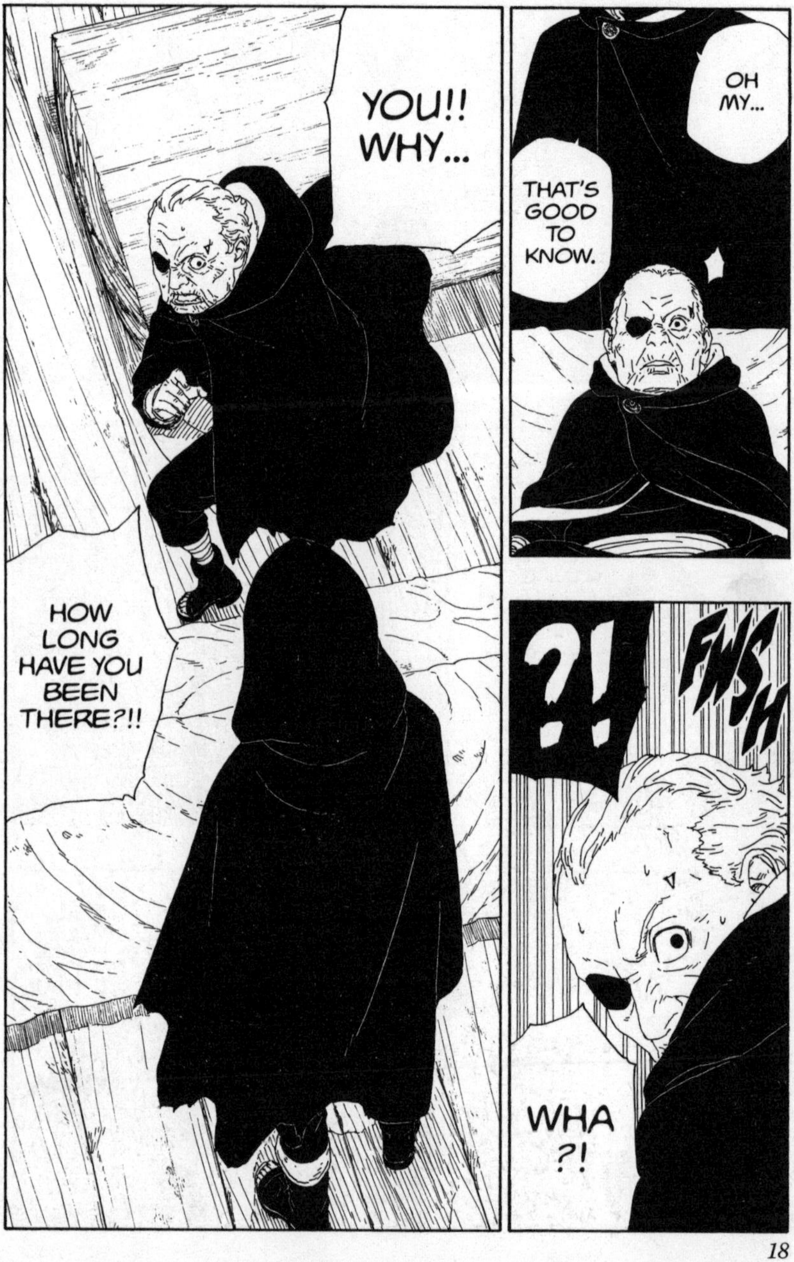
OH MY...
THAT'S GOOD TO KNOW.
?!
FWSH
WHA ?!
YOU!! WHY...
HOW LONG HAVE YOU BEEN THERE?!!

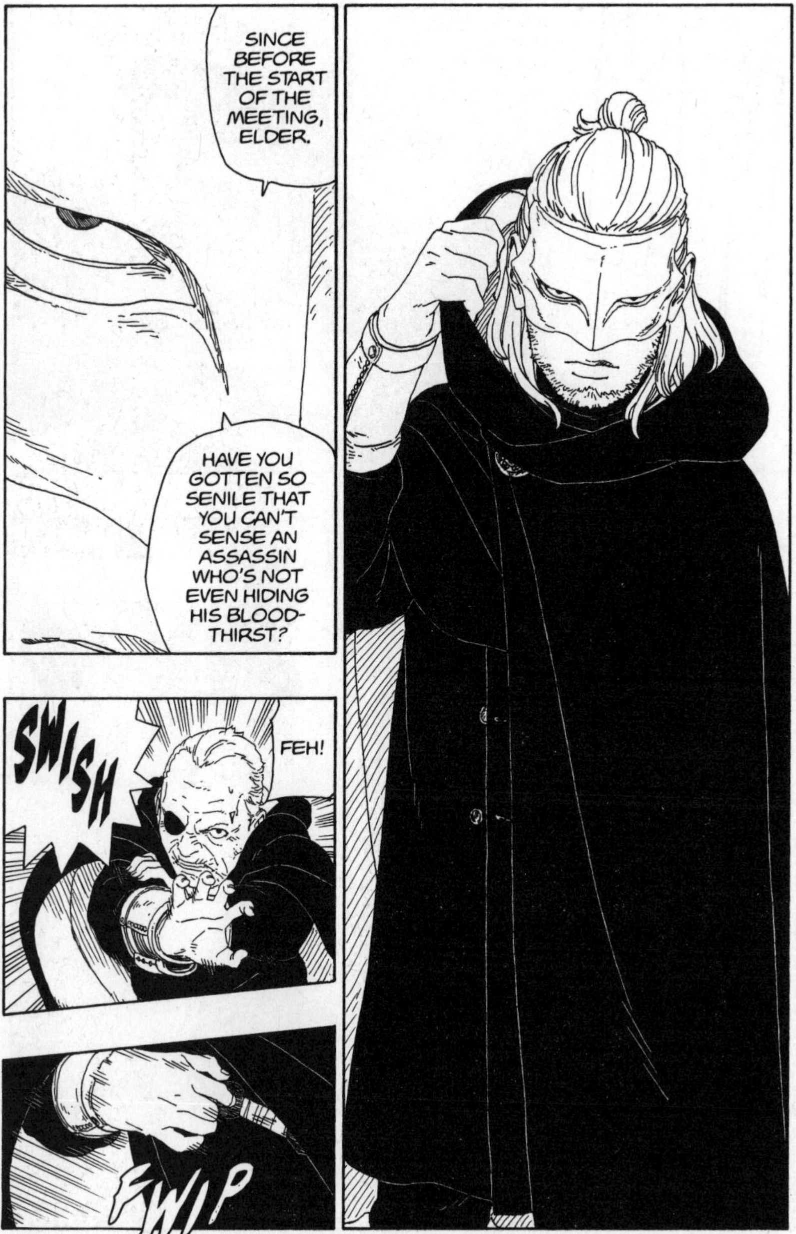
SINCE BEFORE THE START OF THE MEETING, ELDER.
HAVE YOU GOTTEN SO SENILE THAT YOU CAN'T SENSE AN ASSASSIN WHO'S NOT EVEN HIDING HIS BLOOD-THIRST?
FEH!
SWISH
FWIP

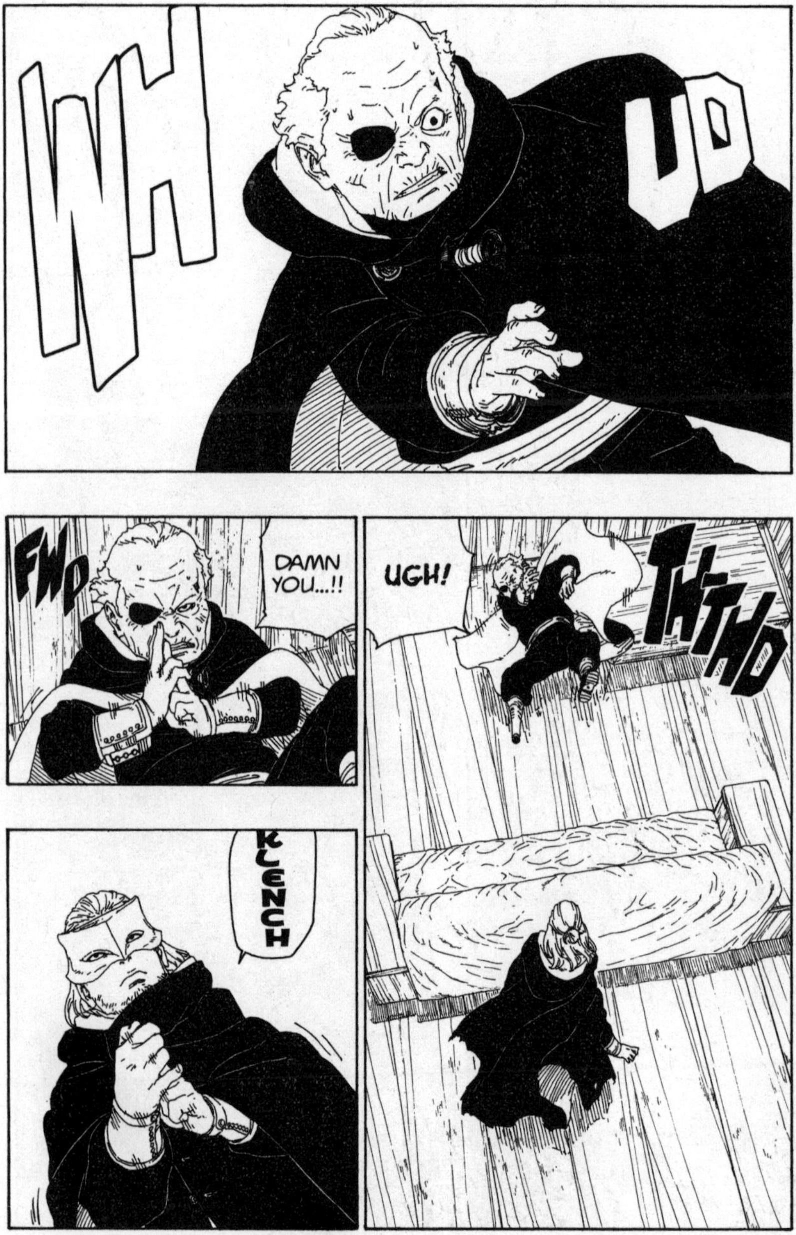
WHUD
UGH!
TH-THD
FWP
DAMN YOU...!!
KLENCH

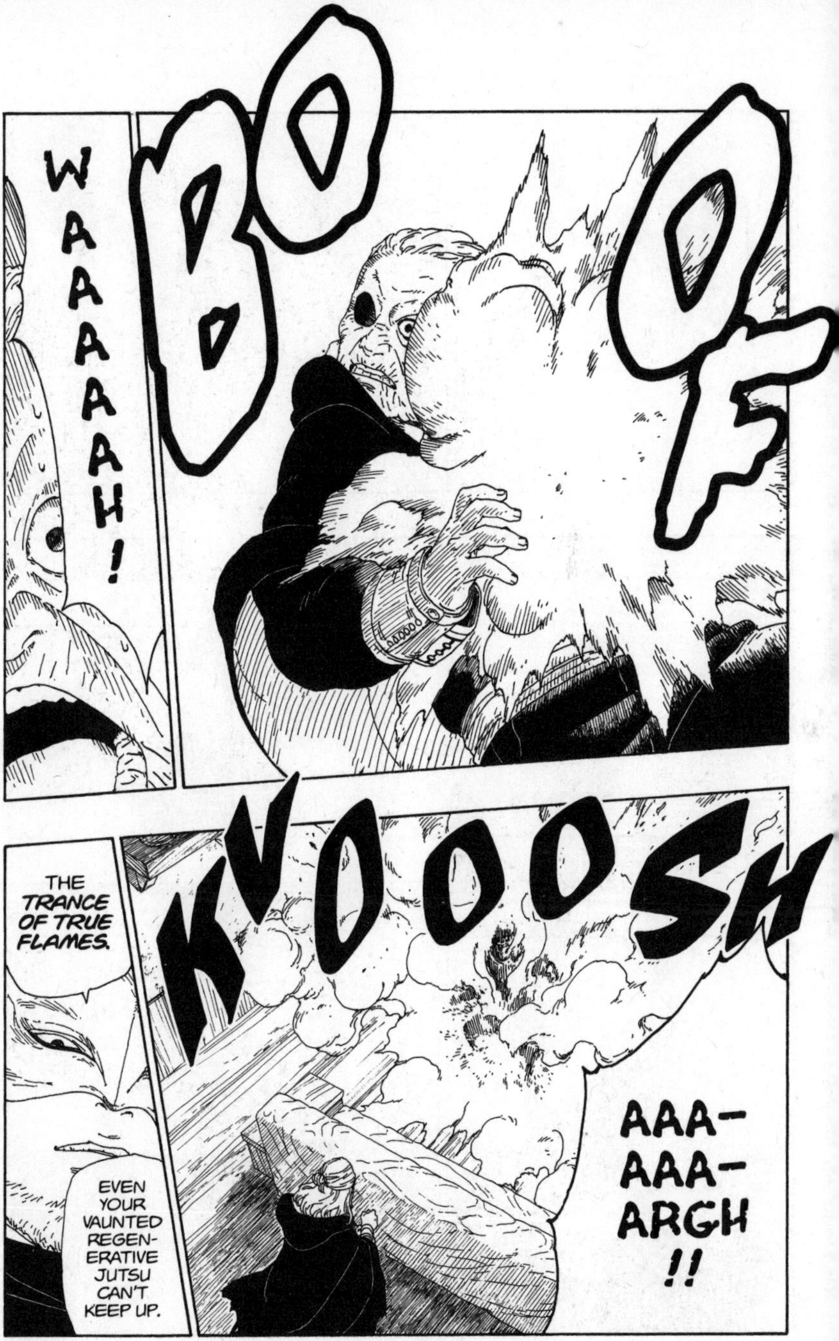
BOOOF
WAAAAAAH!
KVOOOSH
AAA-AAA-ARGH!!
THE *TRANCE OF TRUE FLAMES.*
EVEN YOUR VAUNTED REGENERATIVE JUTSU CAN'T KEEP UP.

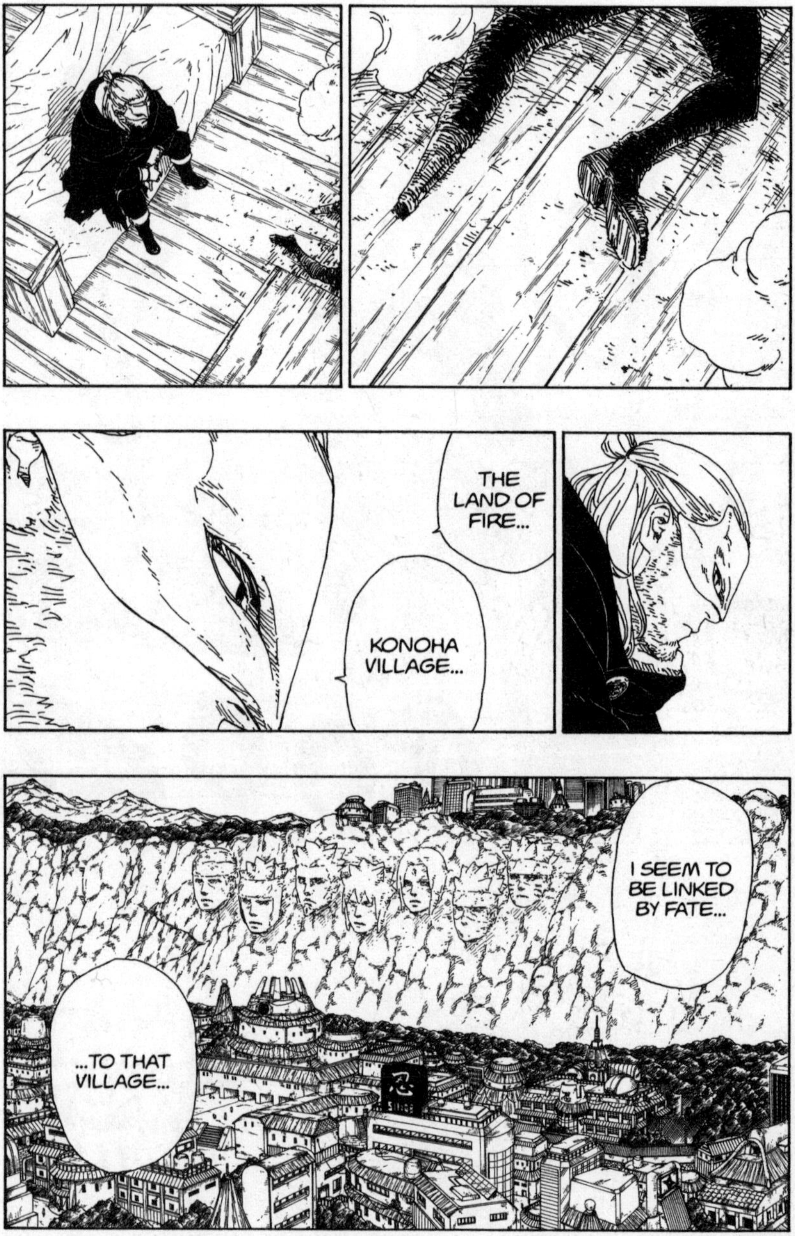
THE LAND OF FIRE...
KONOHA VILLAGE...
I SEEM TO BE LINKED BY FATE...
...TO THAT VILLAGE...

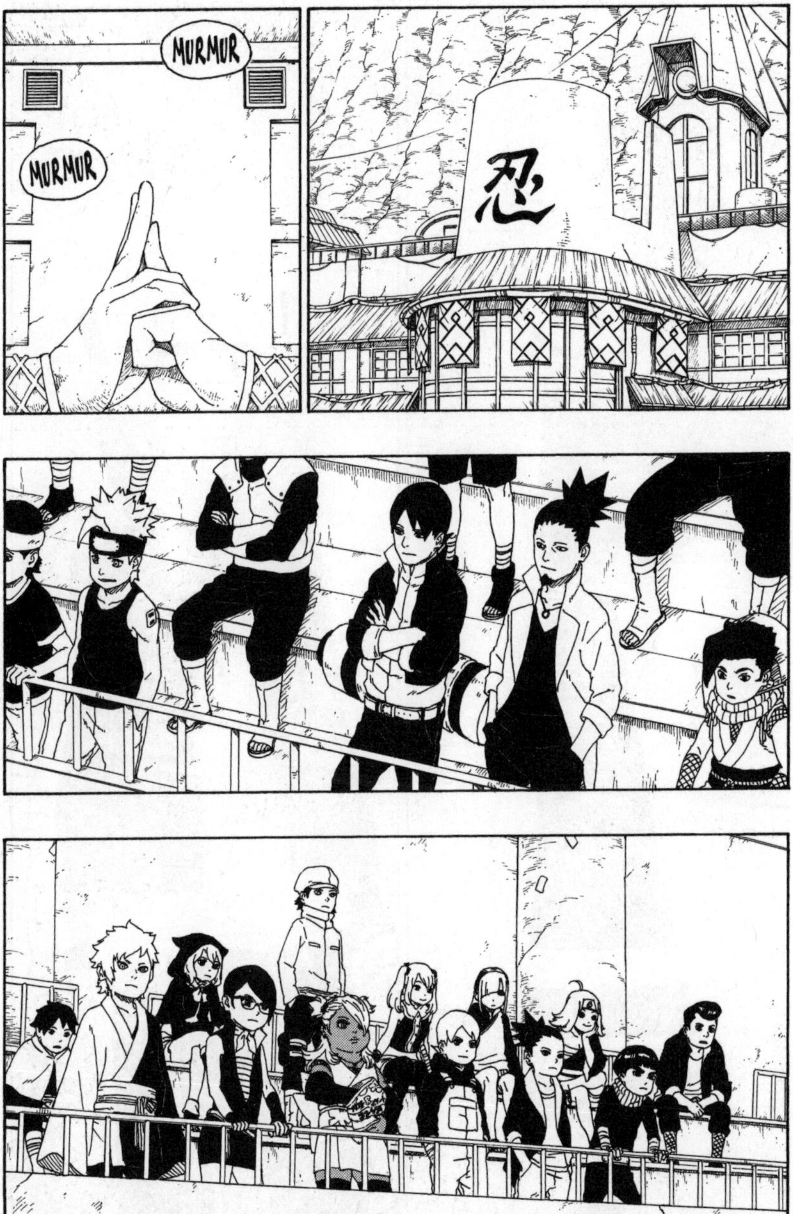
忍
MURMUR
MURMUR

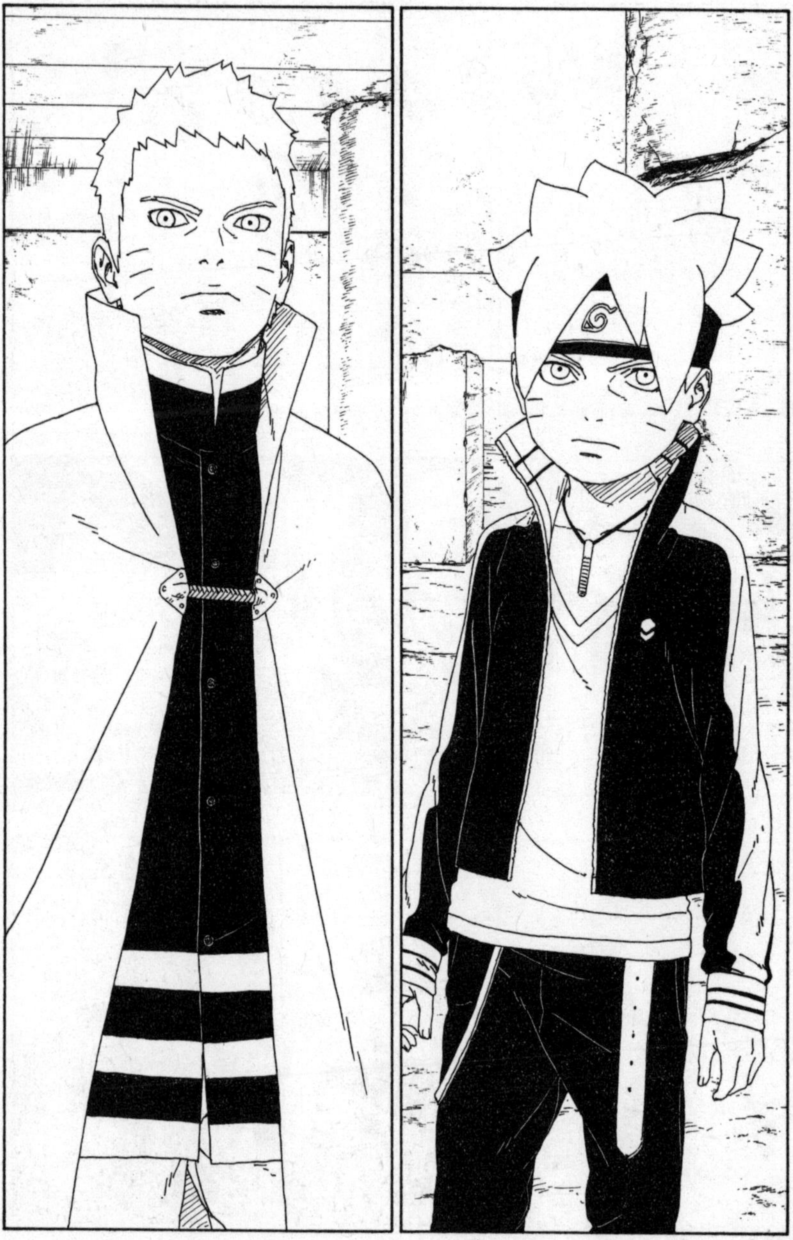

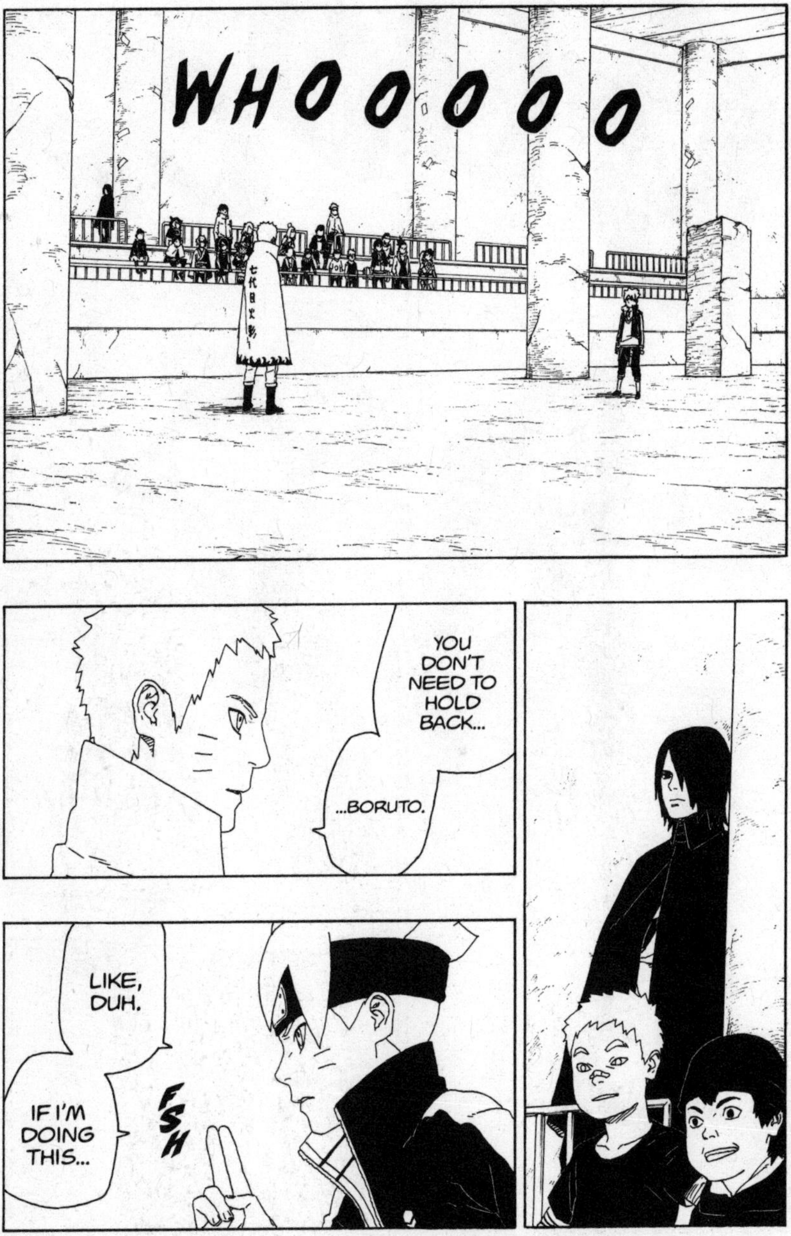
WHOOOOO
七代目火影
YOU DON'T NEED TO HOLD BACK...
...BORUTO.
LIKE, DUH.
FSH
IF I'M DOING THIS...

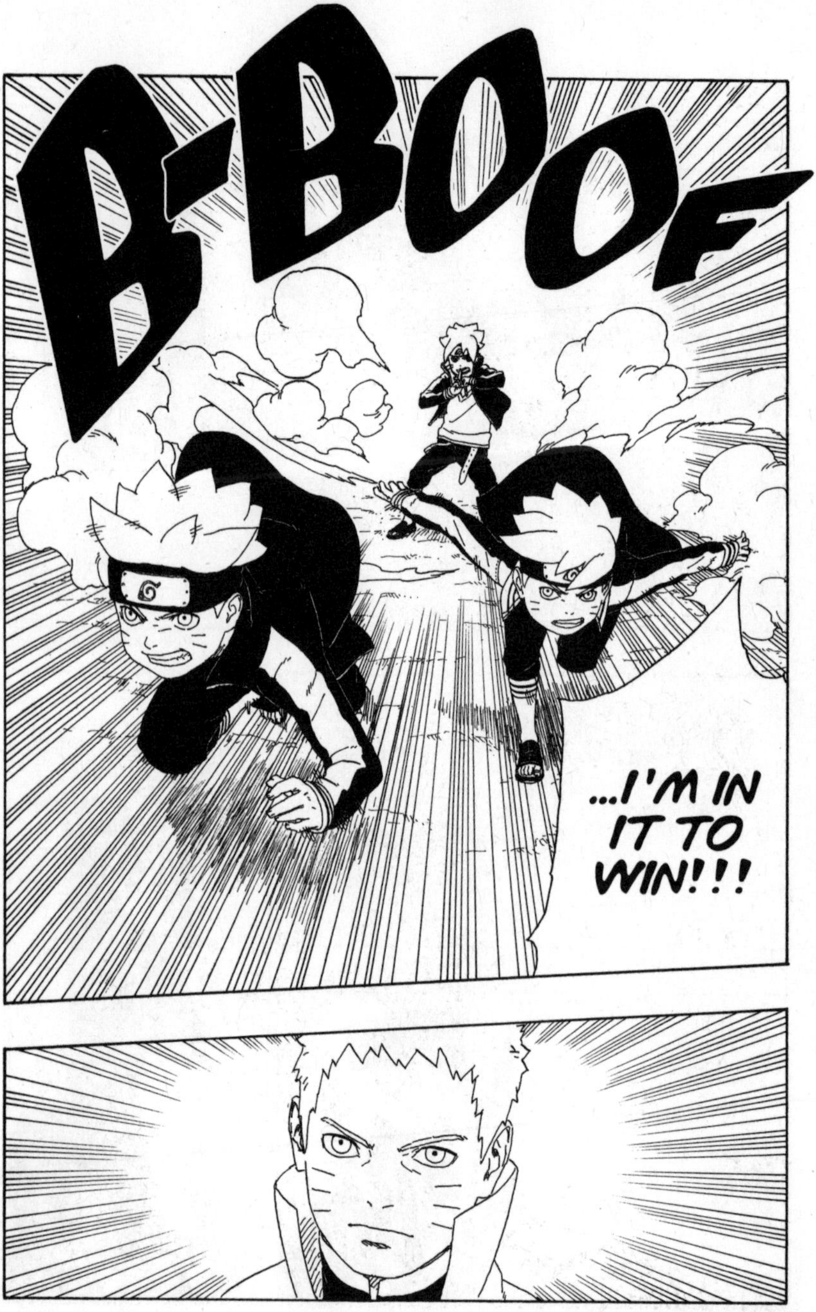
B-BOOF
...I'M IN IT TO WIN!!!

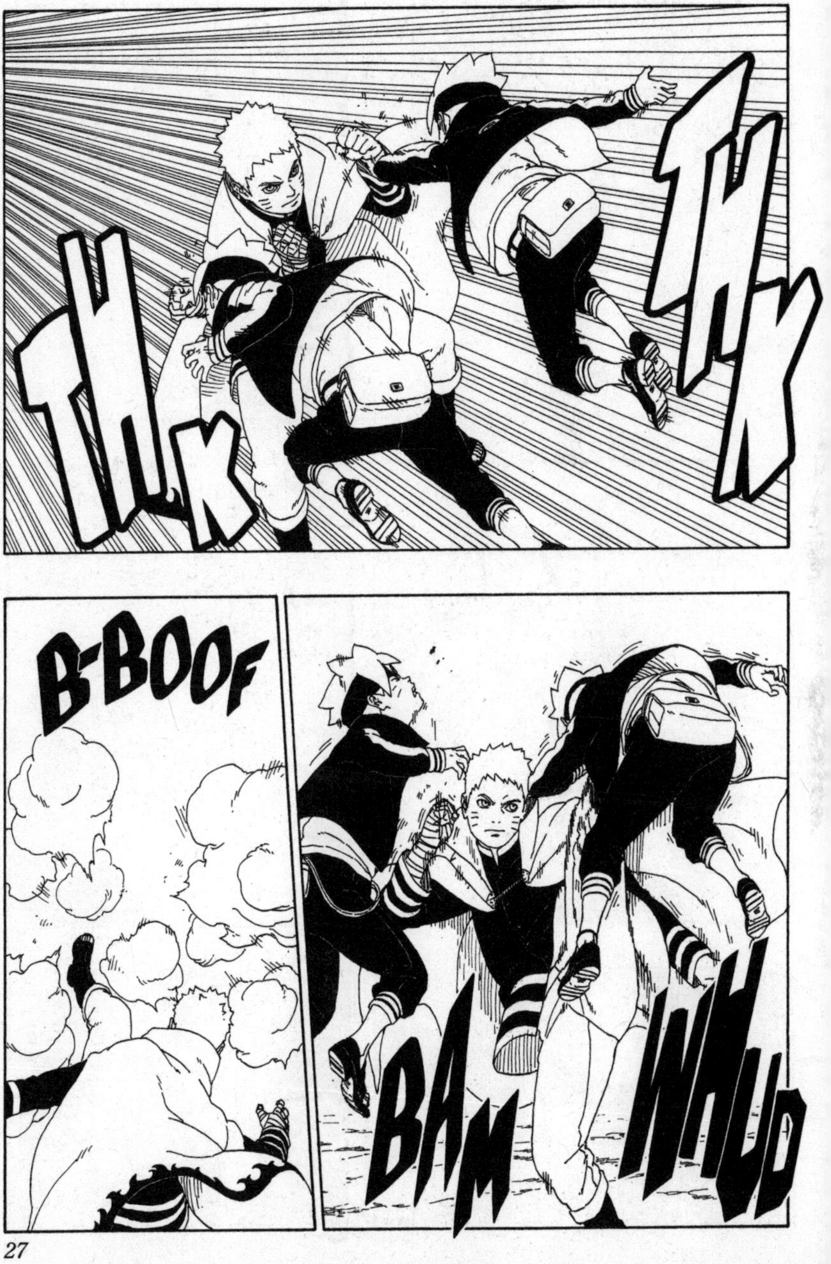
THUNK
THUNK
WHUD
BAM
B-BOOF

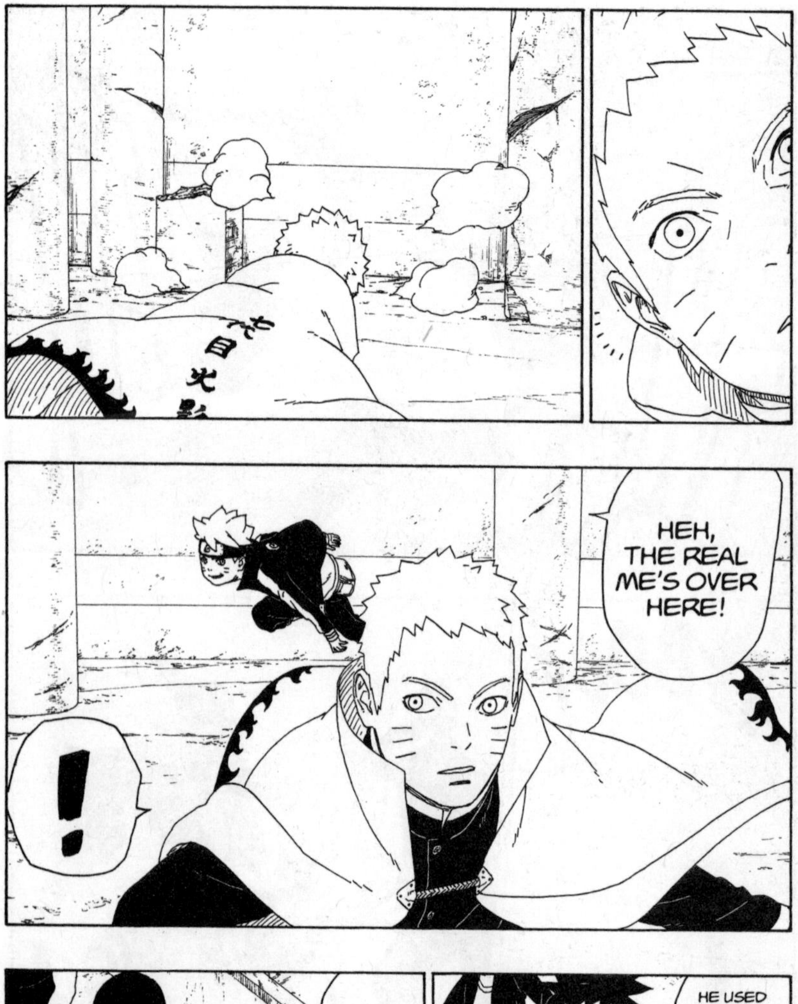
HEH, THE REAL ME'S OVER HERE!
!
HE USED HIS SHADOW DOPPEL-GANGERS AS DECOYS TO SNEAK BEHIND NARUTO, EH!
NICE WORK.
INDEED. HE'S GOT BALLS...
...TO TAKE NARUTO'S REAR.
...

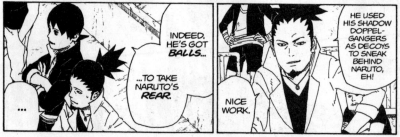

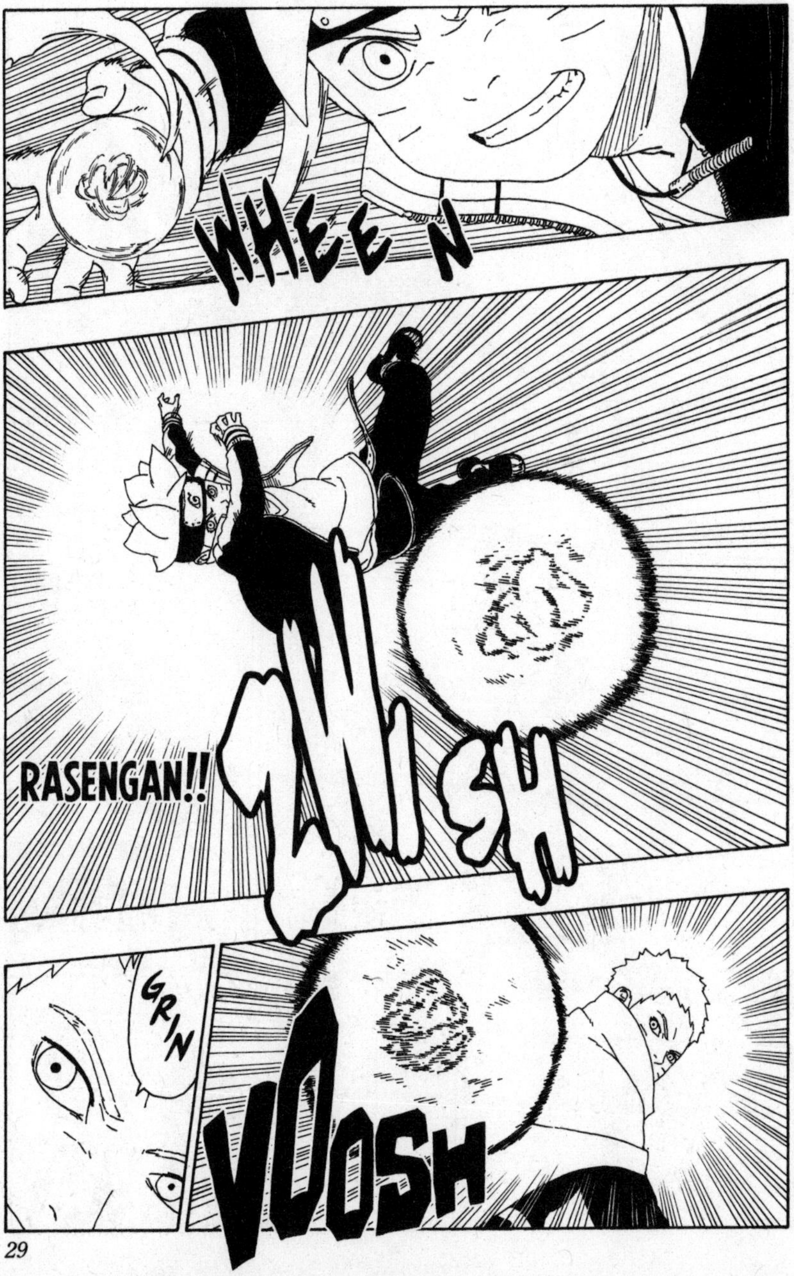
WHEE N
ZWISH
RASENGAN!!
VOOSH
GRIN

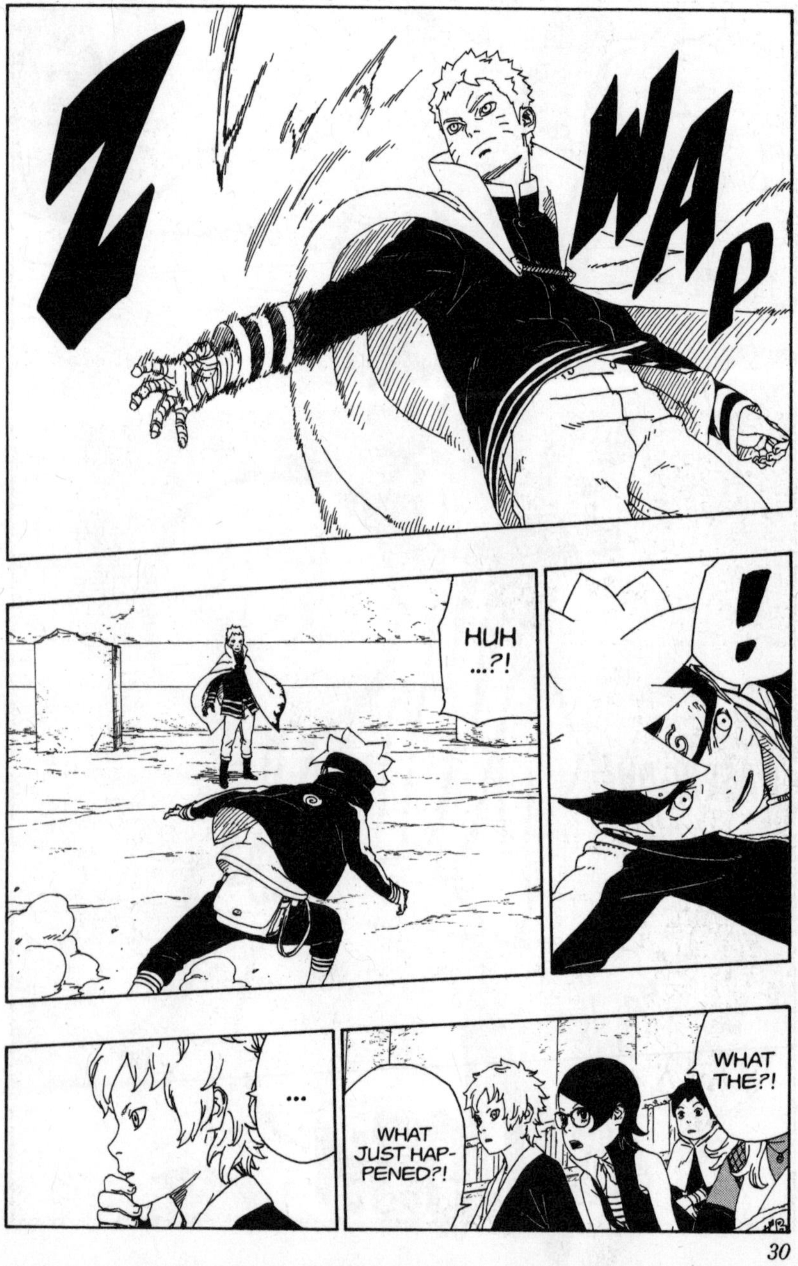
ZWAP
!
HUH ...?!
WHAT THE?!
WHAT JUST HAP-PENED?!
...

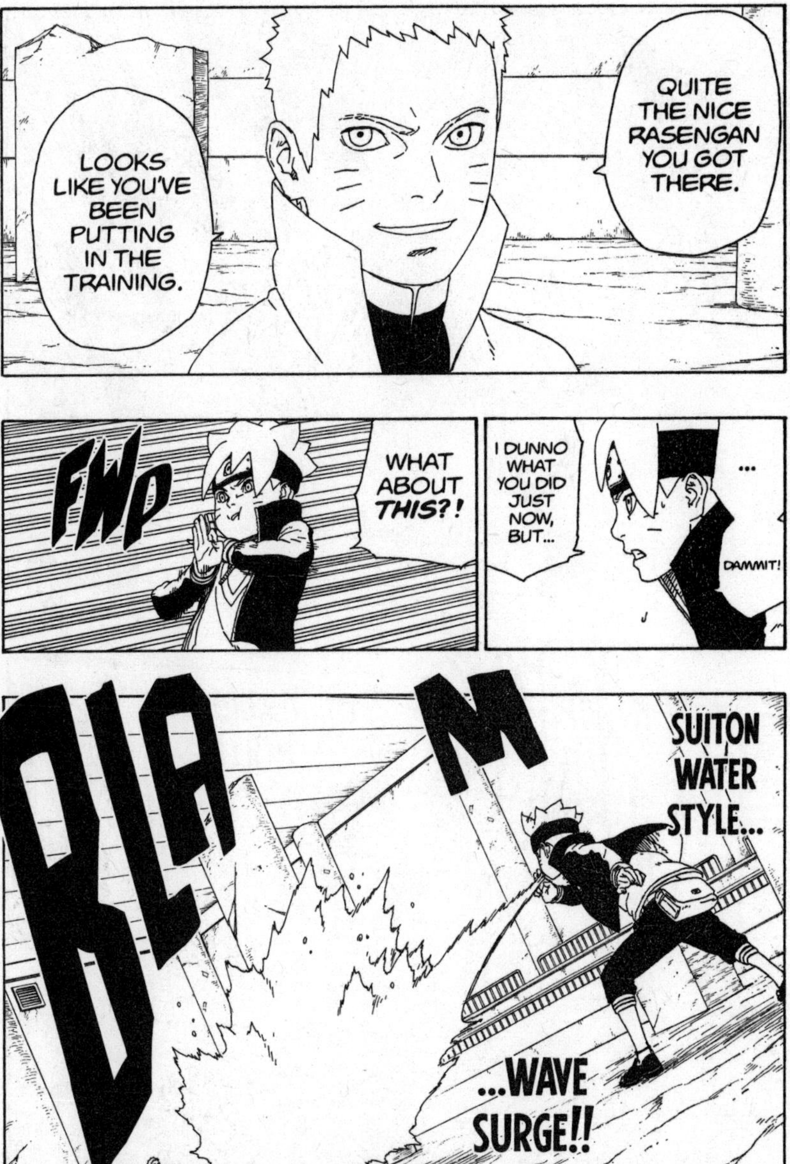
QUITE THE NICE RASENGAN YOU GOT THERE.
LOOKS LIKE YOU'VE BEEN PUTTING IN THE TRAINING.
...
I DUNNO WHAT YOU DID JUST NOW, BUT...
DAMMIT!
WHAT ABOUT *THIS?!*
FWP
SUITON WATER STYLE...
BLAM
...WAVE SURGE!!

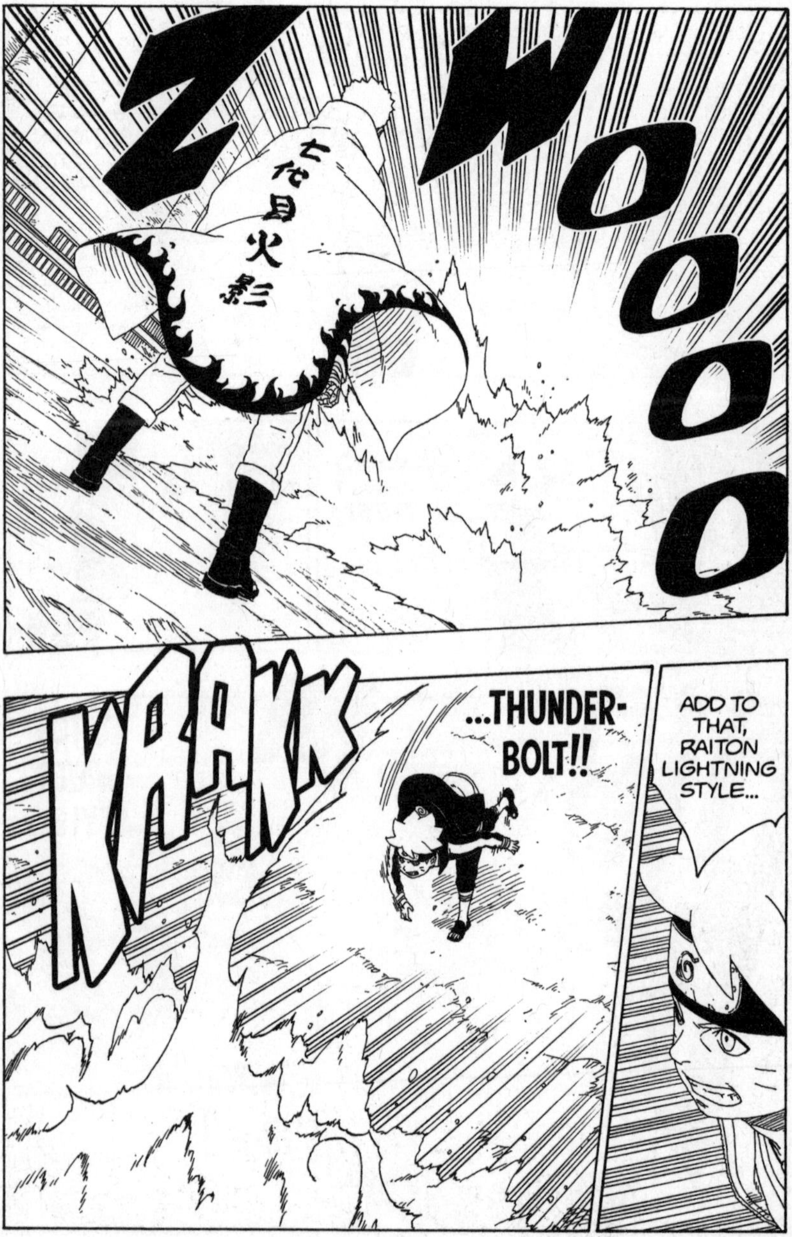
ZWOOOO
七代目火影
ADD TO THAT, RAITON LIGHTNING STYLE...
...THUNDER-BOLT!!
KRAKK

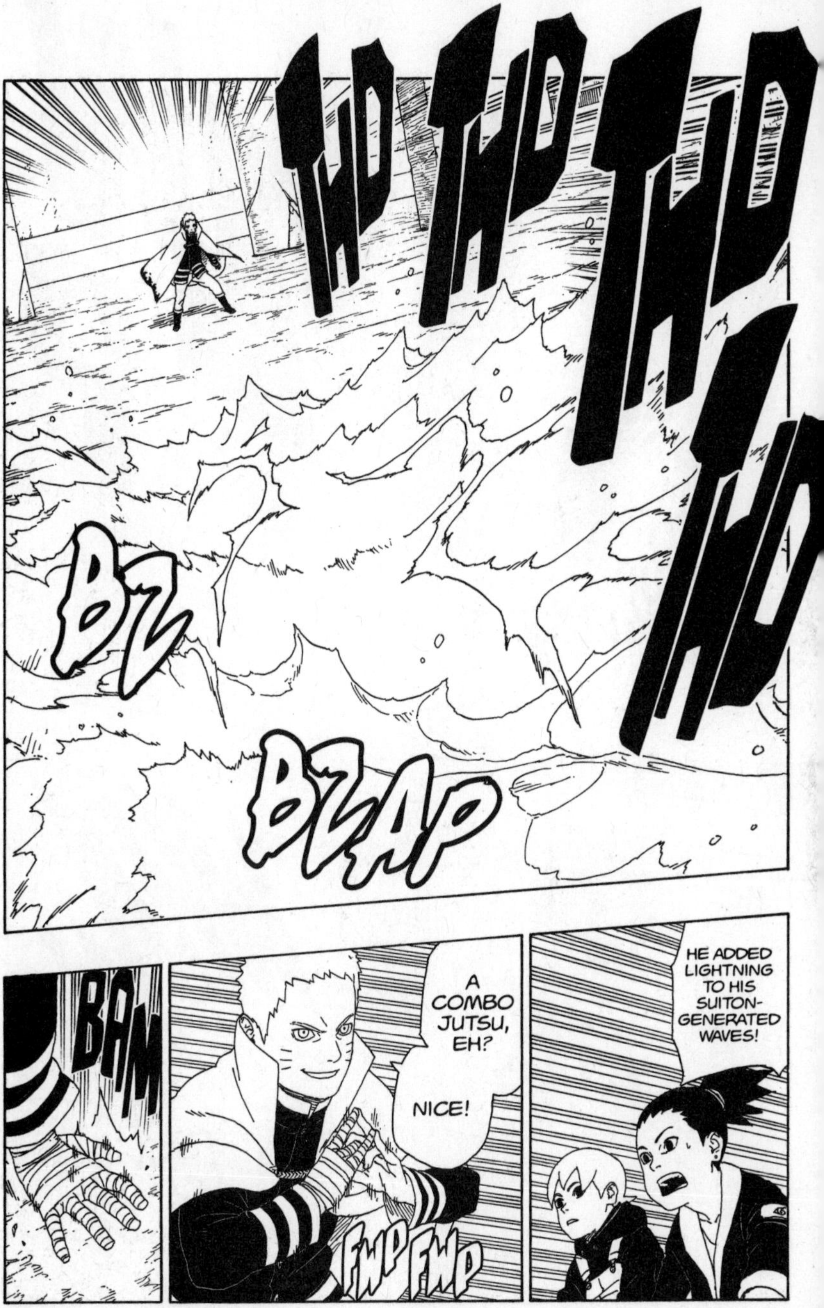
THD THD THD THD THD
BZ
BLAP
HE ADDED LIGHTNING TO HIS SUITON-GENERATED WAVES!
A COMBO JUTSU, EH?
NICE!
FWP FWP
BAM

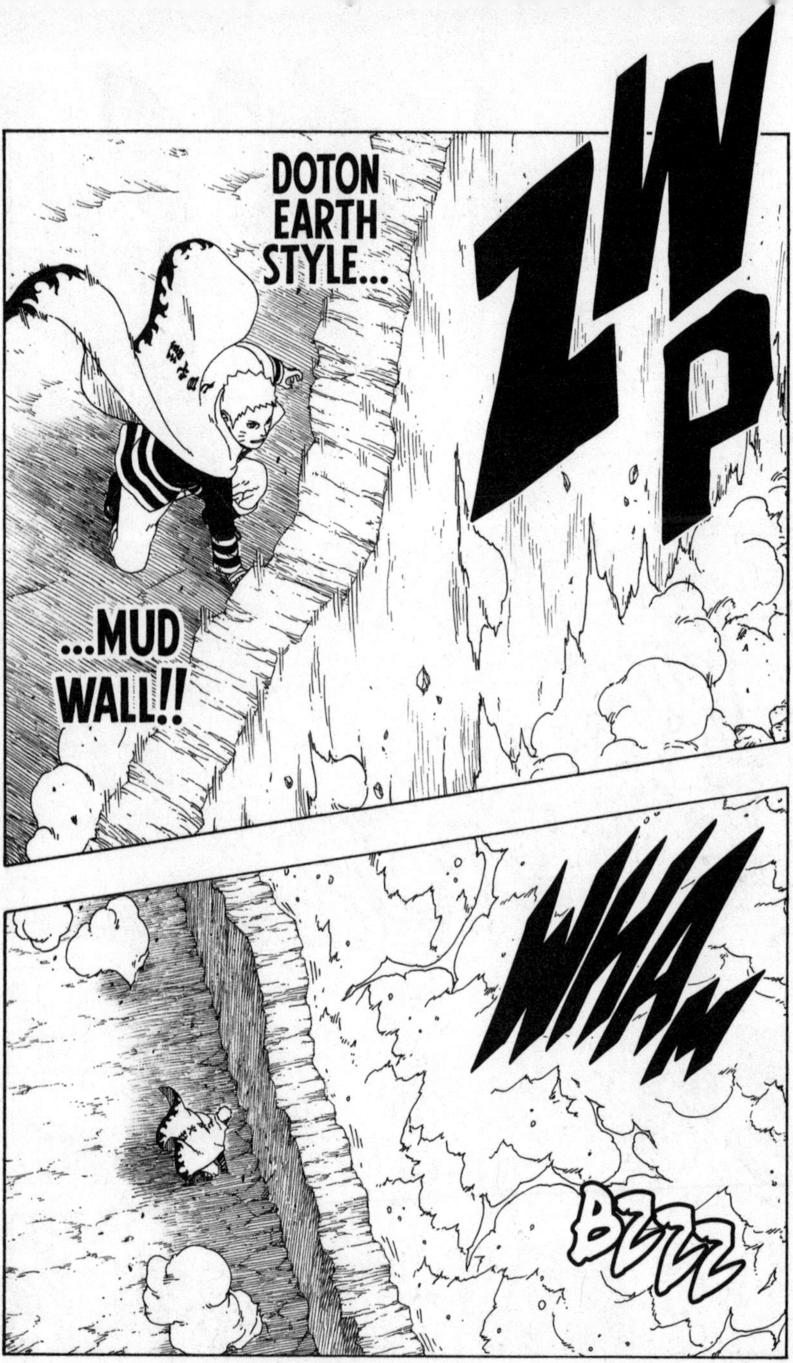
ZWP
DOTON EARTH STYLE...
...MUD WALL!!
WHAM
BZZZ

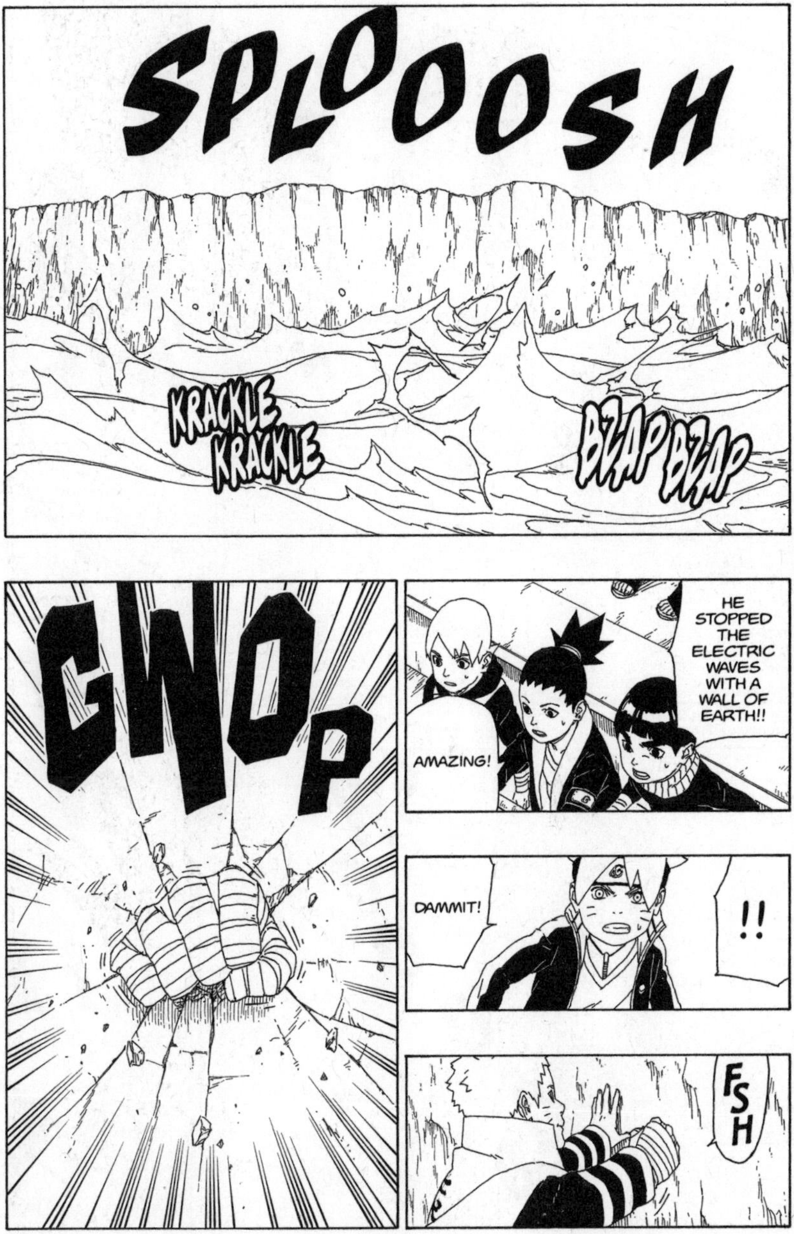
SPLOOOSH
BZAP BZAP
KRACKLE KRACKLE
HE STOPPED THE ELECTRIC WAVES WITH A WALL OF EARTH!!
AMAZING!
!!
DAMMIT!
FSH
GWOP

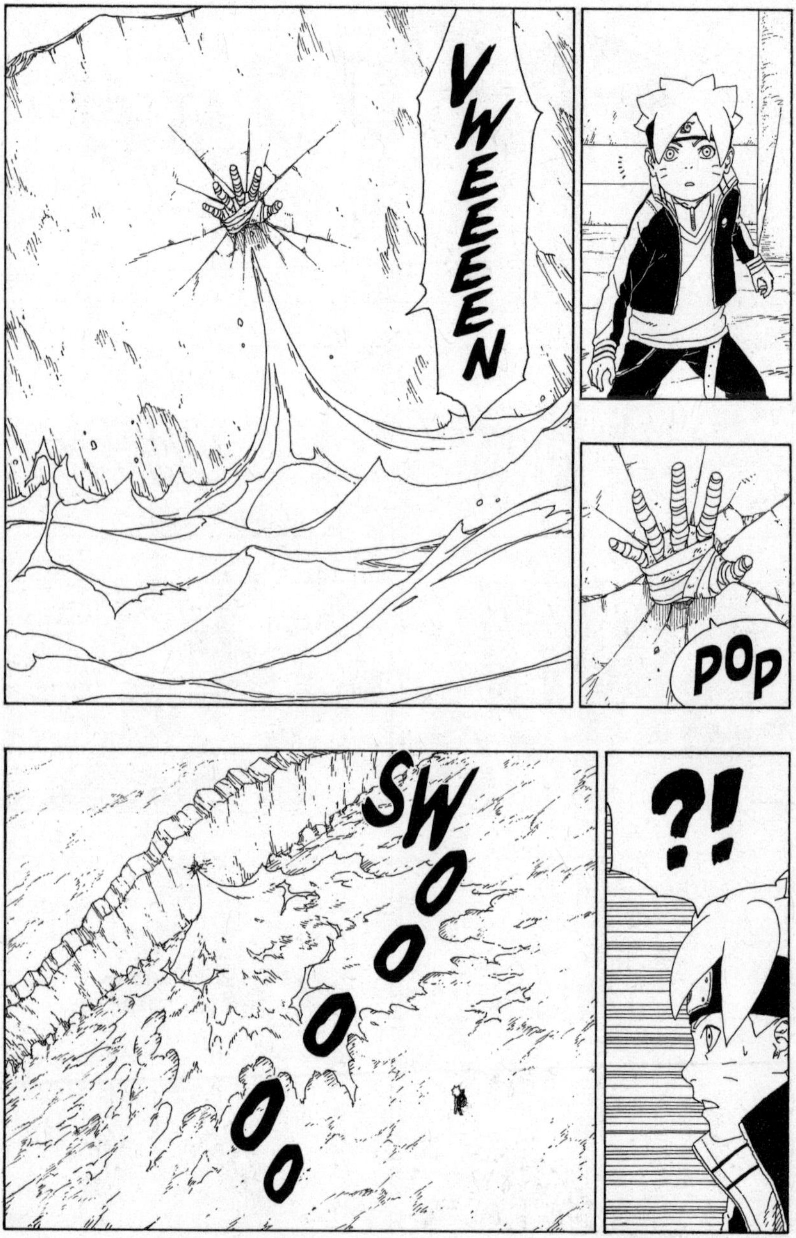
POP
VWEEEEEN
?!
SWOOOOOO

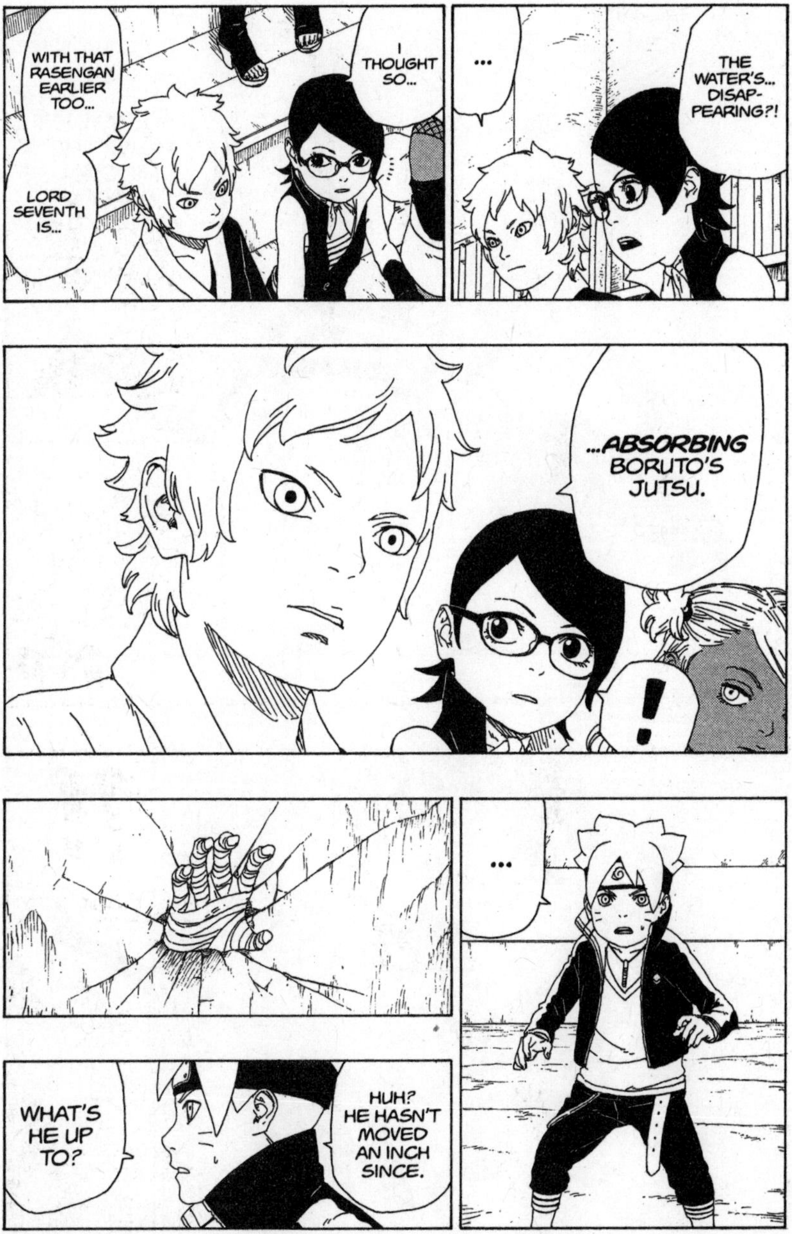
THE WATER'S... DISAPPEARING?!
...
I THOUGHT SO...
WITH THAT RASENGAN EARLIER TOO...
LORD SEVENTH IS...
...ABSORBING BORUTO'S JUTSU.
!
...
HUH? HE HASN'T MOVED AN INCH SINCE.
WHAT'S HE UP TO?

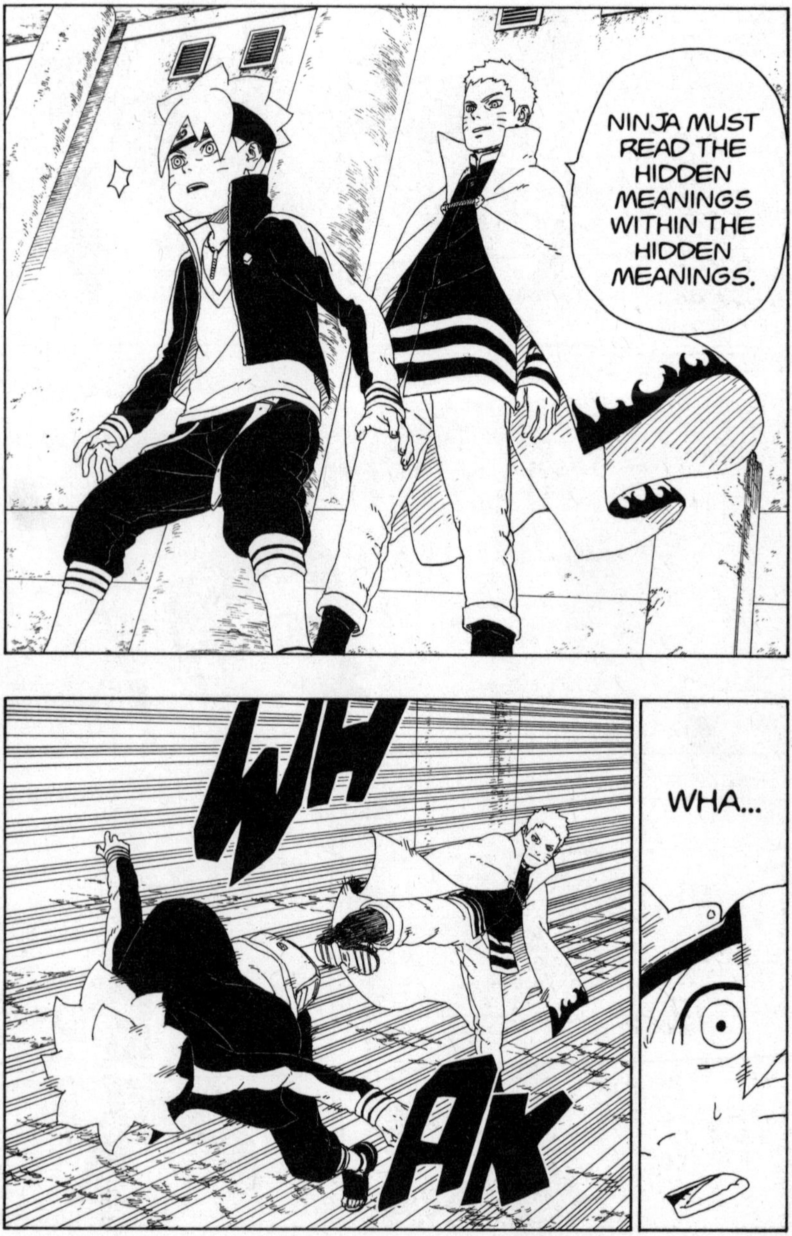
NINJA MUST READ THE HIDDEN MEANINGS WITHIN THE HIDDEN MEANINGS.
WHA...
WHAK

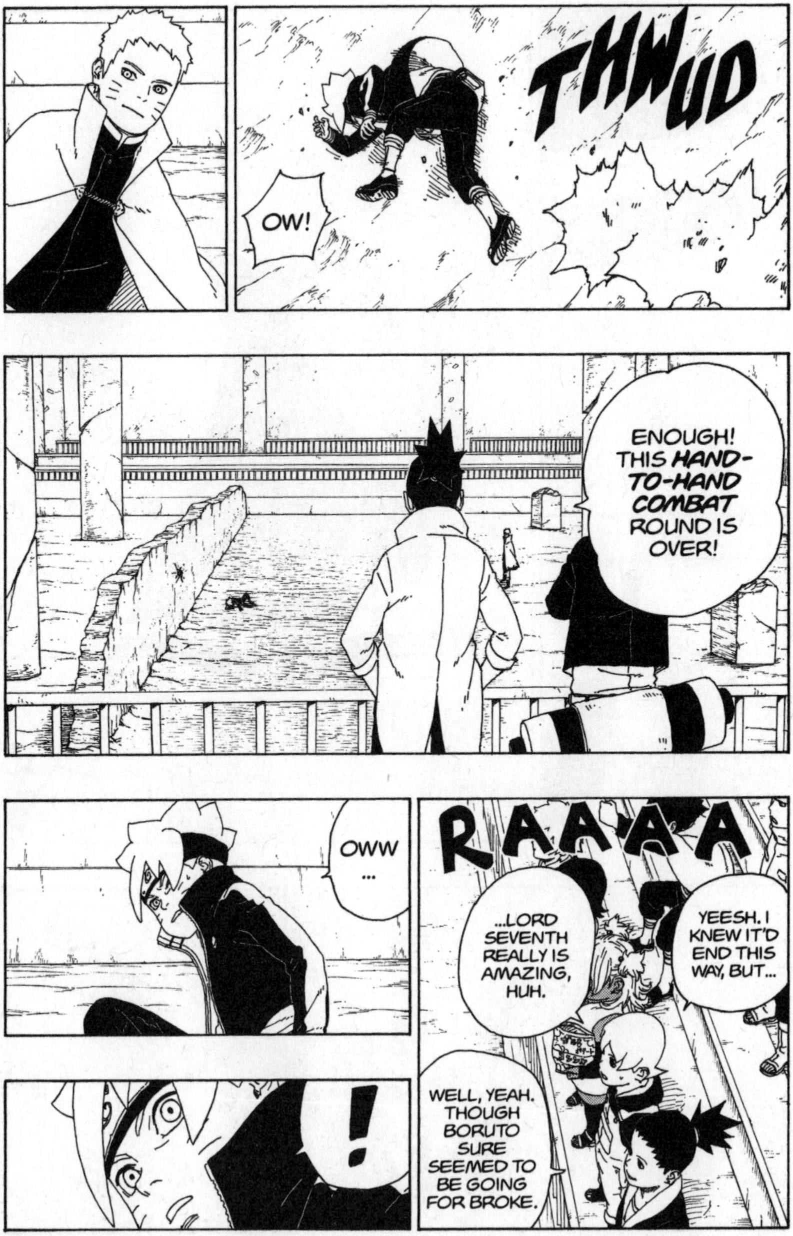
THWUD
OW!
ENOUGH! THIS HAND-TO-HAND COMBAT ROUND IS OVER!
RAAAA
YEESH. I KNEW IT'D END THIS WAY, BUT...
...LORD SEVENTH REALLY IS AMAZING, HUH.
WELL, YEAH. THOUGH BORUTO SURE SEEMED TO BE GOING FOR BROKE.
OWW ...
!

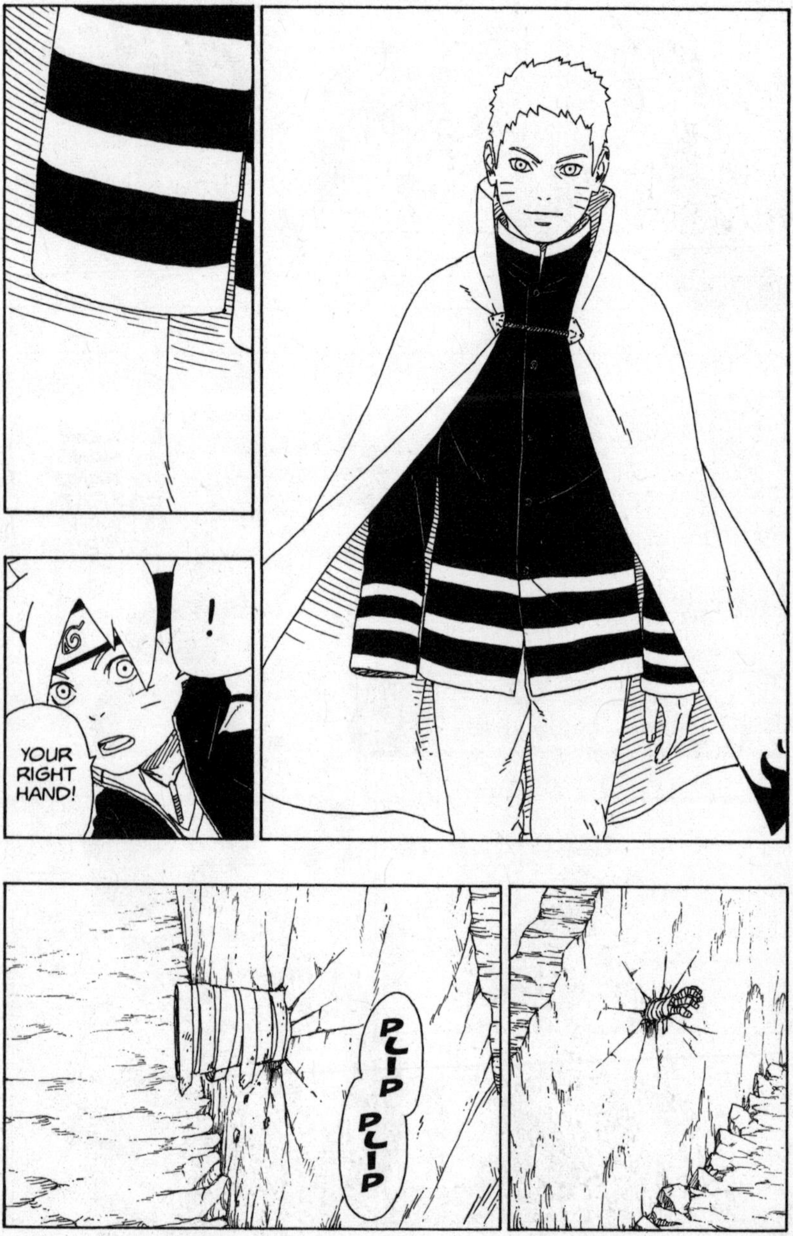
!
YOUR RIGHT HAND!
PLIP PLIP

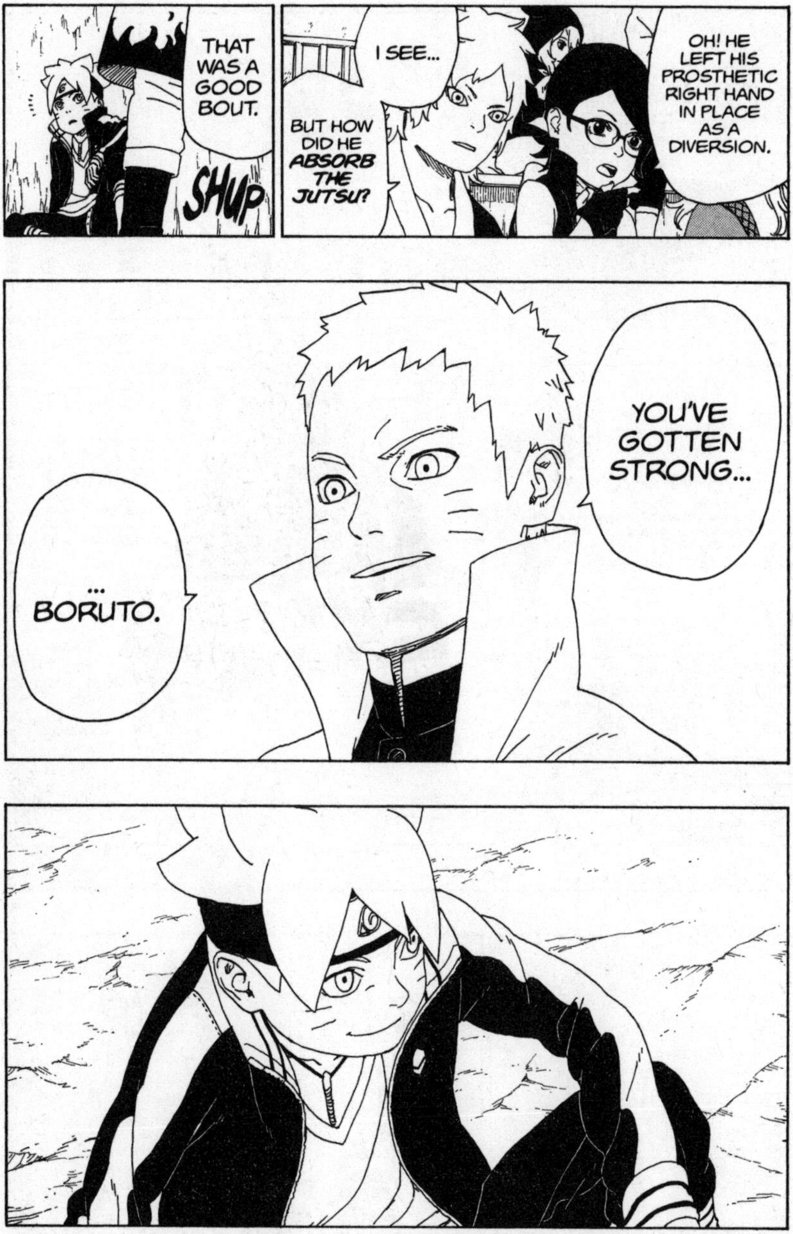
OH! HE LEFT HIS PROSTHETIC RIGHT HAND IN PLACE AS A DIVERSION.
I SEE...
BUT HOW DID HE ABSORB THE JUTSU?
THAT WAS A GOOD BOUT.
SHUP
YOU'VE GOTTEN STRONG...
... BORUTO.

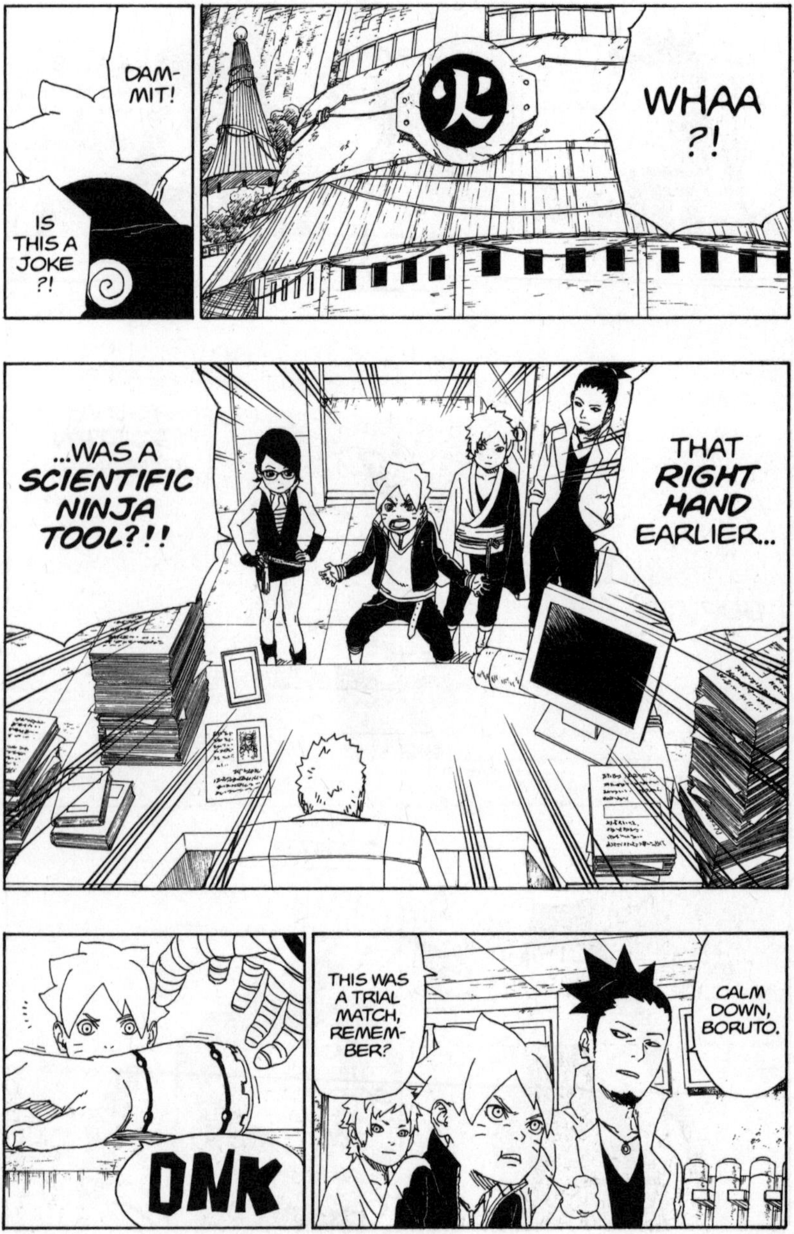
WHAA ?!
DAM-MIT!
IS THIS A JOKE ?!
THAT RIGHT HAND EARLIER...
...WAS A SCIENTIFIC NINJA TOOL?!!
CALM DOWN, BORUTO.
THIS WAS A TRIAL MATCH, REMEMBER?
DNK

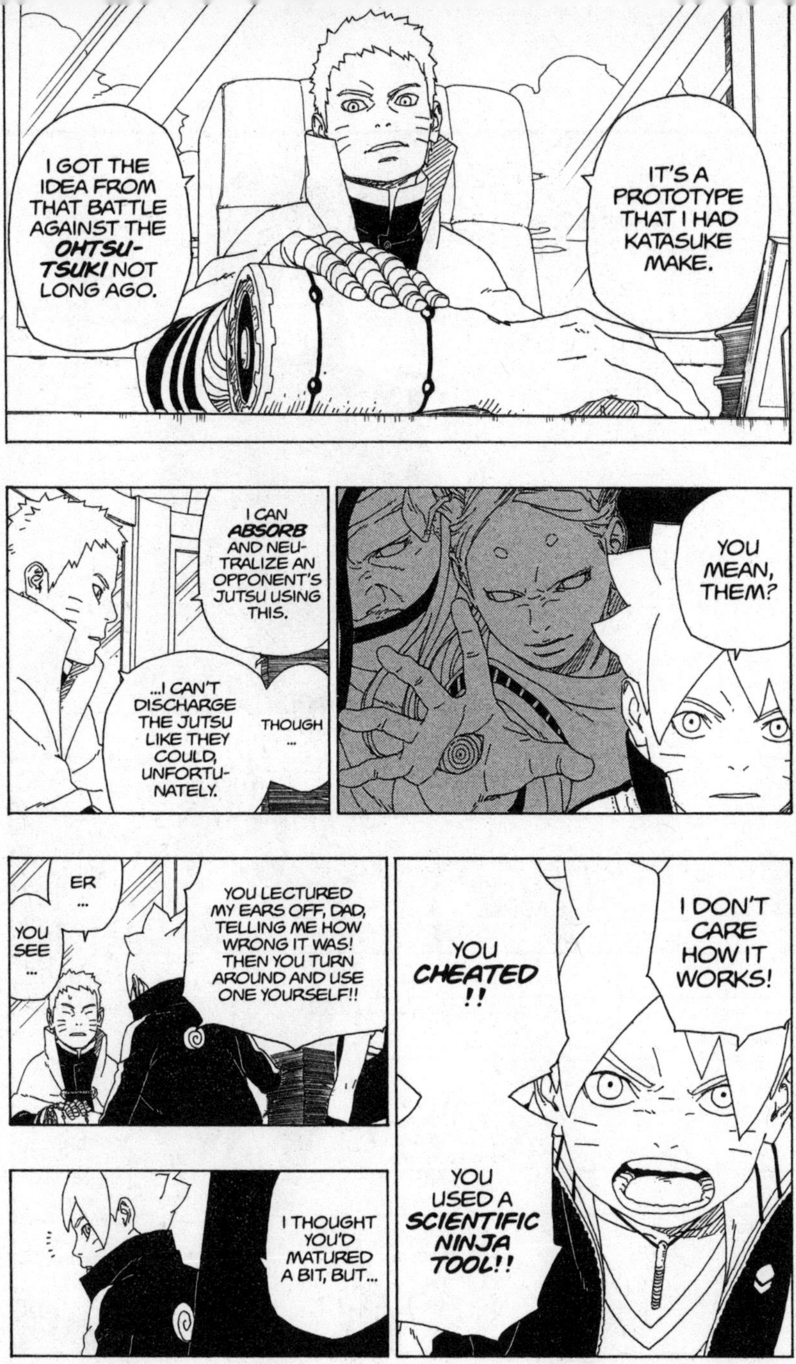
IT'S A PROTOTYPE THAT I HAD KATASUKE MAKE.
I GOT THE IDEA FROM THAT BATTLE AGAINST THE ***OHTSUTSUKI*** NOT LONG AGO.
YOU MEAN, THEM?
I CAN ***ABSORB*** AND NEUTRALIZE AN OPPONENT'S JUTSU USING THIS.
THOUGH ...
...I CAN'T DISCHARGE THE JUTSU LIKE THEY COULD, UNFORTUNATELY.
I DON'T CARE HOW IT WORKS!
YOU ***CHEATED!!***
YOU USED A ***SCIENTIFIC NINJA TOOL!!***
YOU LECTURED MY EARS OFF, DAD, TELLING ME HOW WRONG IT WAS! THEN YOU TURN AROUND AND USE ONE YOURSELF!!
ER ...
YOU SEE ...
I THOUGHT YOU'D MATURED A BIT, BUT...

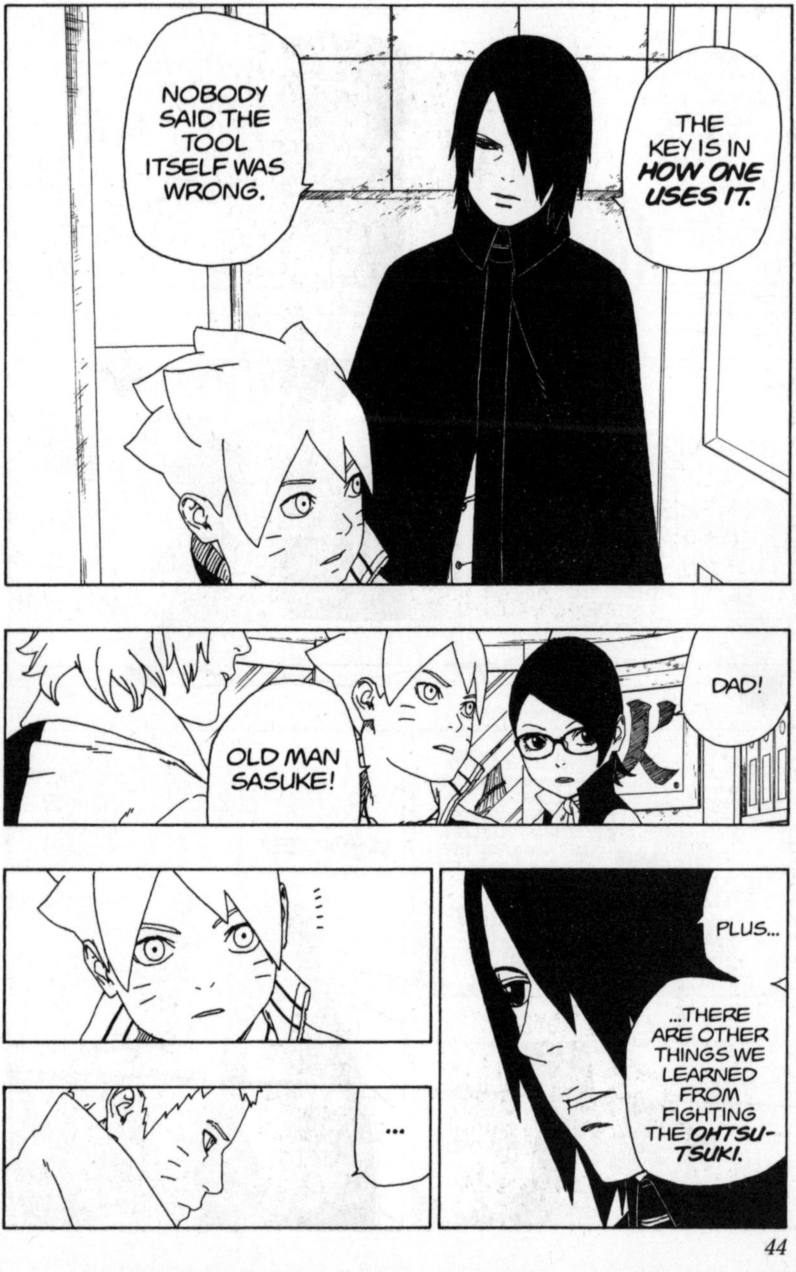
THE KEY IS IN *HOW ONE USES IT.*
NOBODY SAID THE TOOL ITSELF WAS WRONG.
DAD!
OLD MAN SASUKE!
PLUS...
...THERE ARE OTHER THINGS WE LEARNED FROM FIGHTING THE *OHTSUTSUKI.*
...

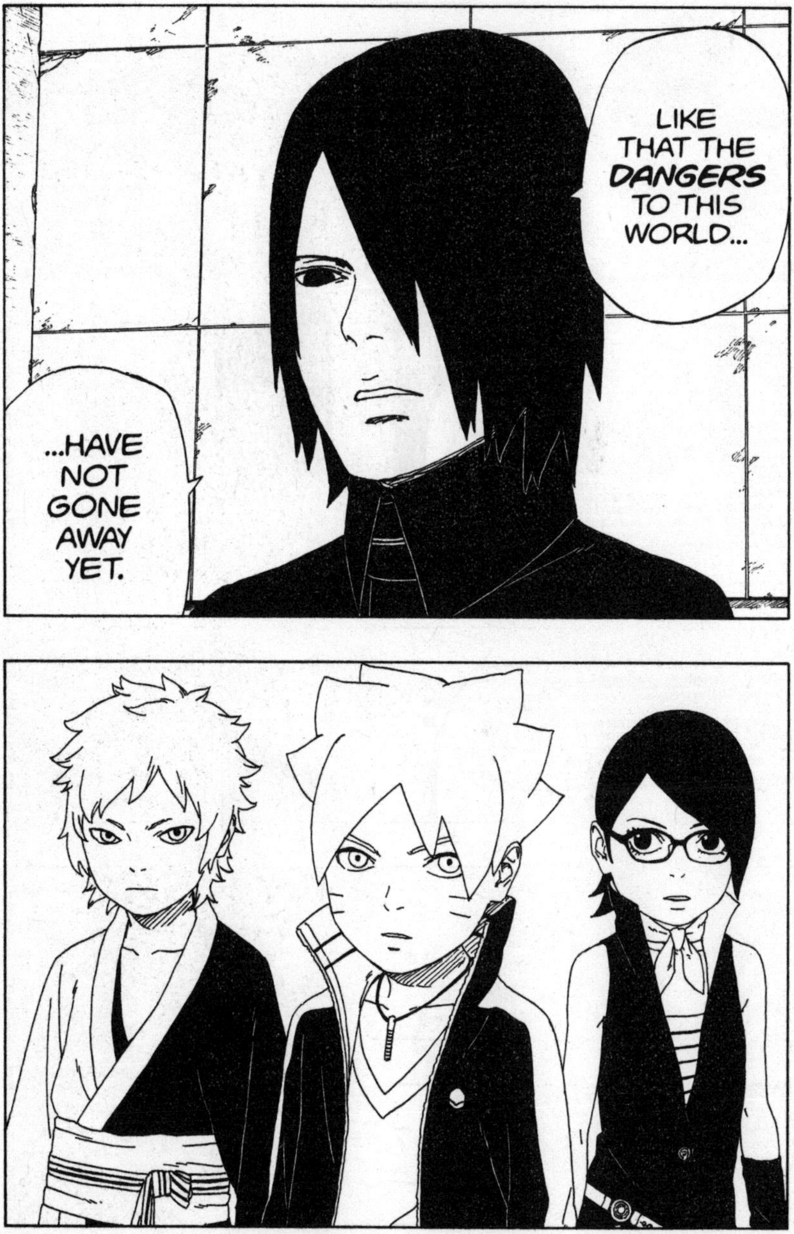
LIKE THAT THE DANGERS TO THIS WORLD...
...HAVE NOT GONE AWAY YET.

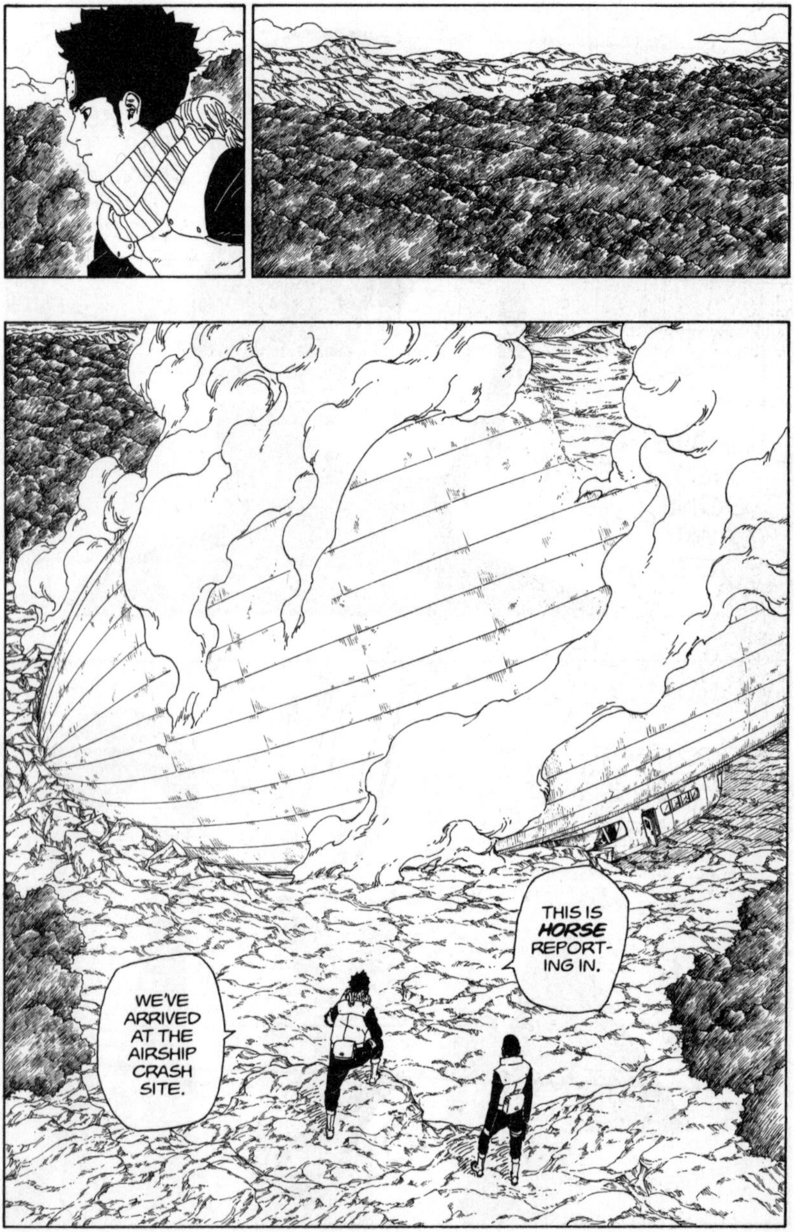
THIS IS HORSE REPORTING IN.
WE'VE ARRIVED AT THE AIRSHIP CRASH SITE.

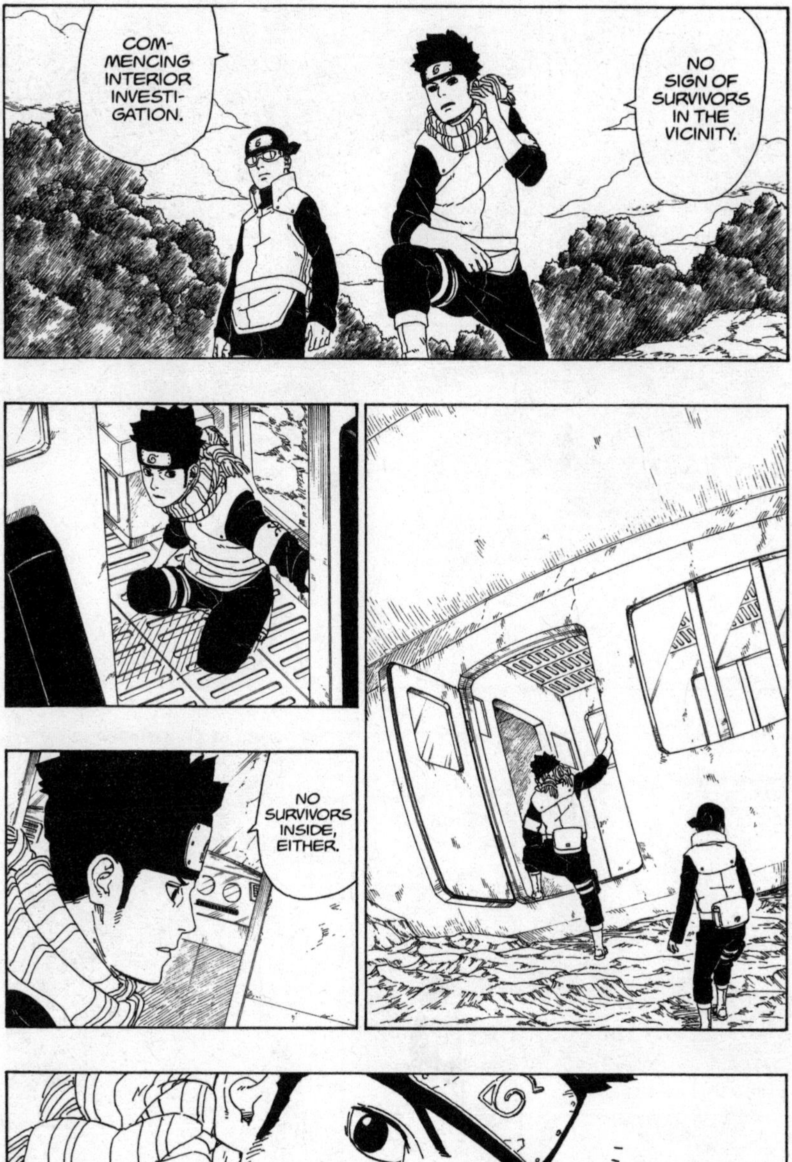
NO SIGN OF SURVIVORS IN THE VICINITY.
COM-MENCING INTERIOR INVESTI-GATION.
NO SURVIVORS INSIDE, EITHER.

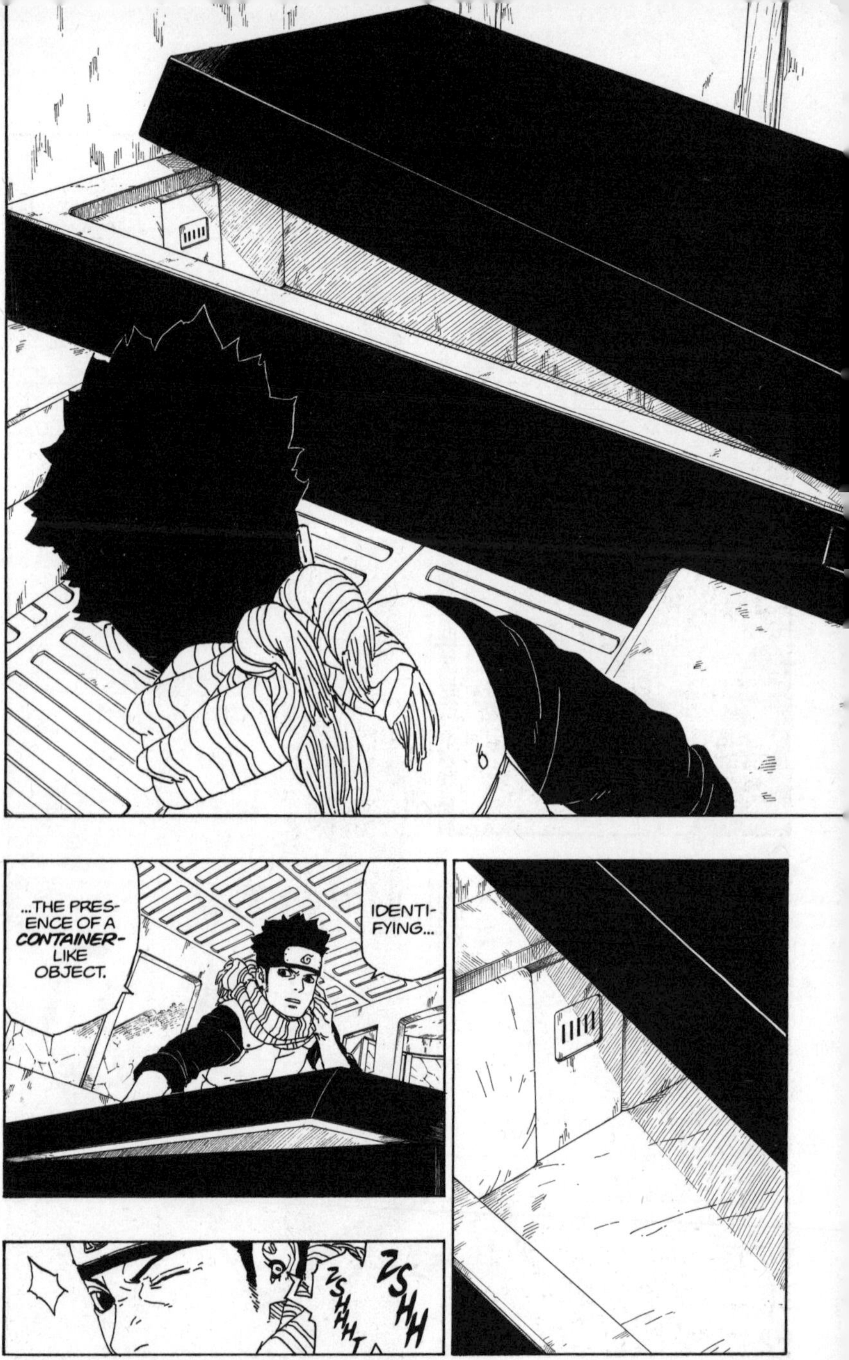
IDENTI-FYING...
...THE PRESENCE OF A CONTAINER-LIKE OBJECT.
ZSHH
ZSHHT

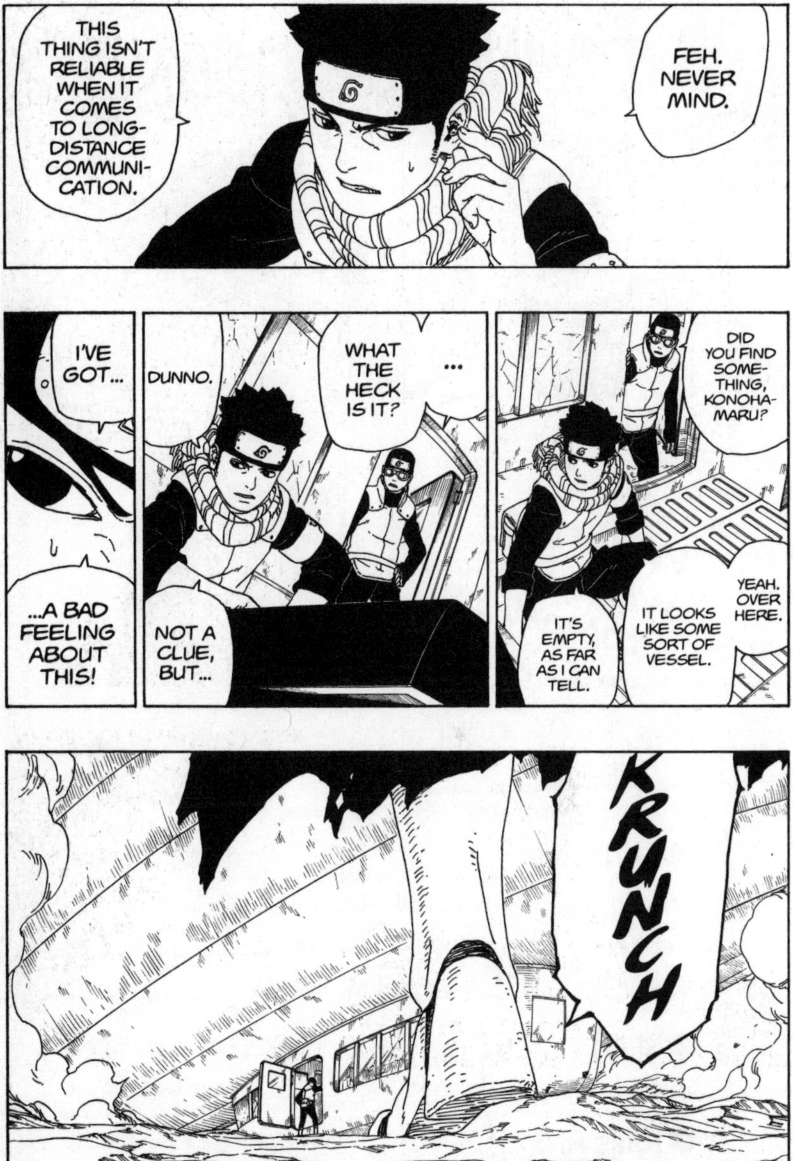
FEH. NEVER MIND.
THIS THING ISN'T RELIABLE WHEN IT COMES TO LONG-DISTANCE COMMUNICATION.
DID YOU FIND SOMETHING, KONOHAMARU?
YEAH. OVER HERE.
IT LOOKS LIKE SOME SORT OF VESSEL.
IT'S EMPTY, AS FAR AS I CAN TELL.
...
WHAT THE HECK IS IT?
DUNNO.
NOT A CLUE, BUT...
I'VE GOT...
...A BAD FEELING ABOUT THIS!
KRUNCH

NINJA ENCYCLOPEDIA · ENTRY 13

TOHNO KATASUKE

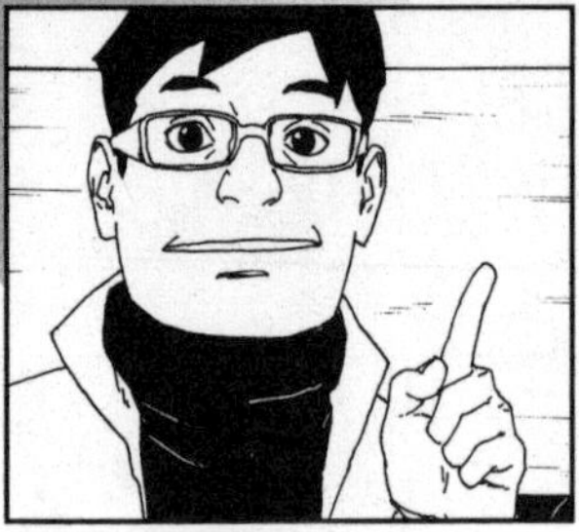

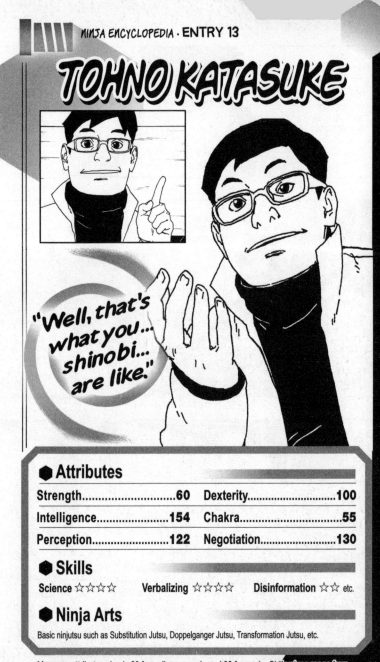

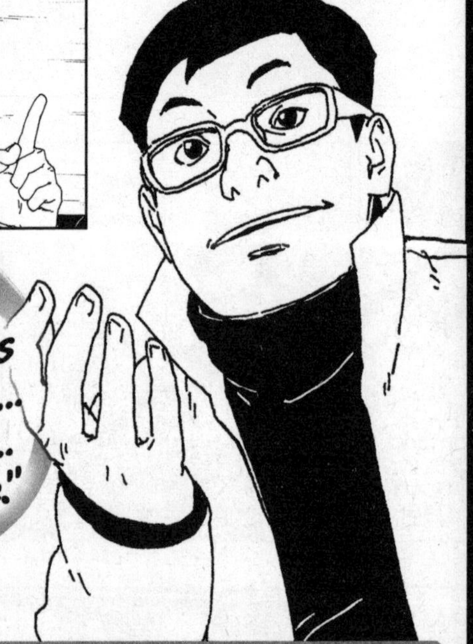
"Well, that's what you... shinobi... are like."

Attributes

Strength	60	Dexterity	100
Intelligence	154	Chakra	55
Perception	122	Negotiation	130

Skills

Science ☆☆☆☆ Verbalizing ☆☆☆☆ Disinformation ☆☆ etc.

Ninja Arts

Basic ninjutsu such as Substitution Jutsu, Doppelganger Jutsu, Transformation Jutsu, etc.

*Average attribute value is 60 for ordinary people and 90 for genin. Skill values range from 1 to 5☆ with 5☆ signifying super top-notch.

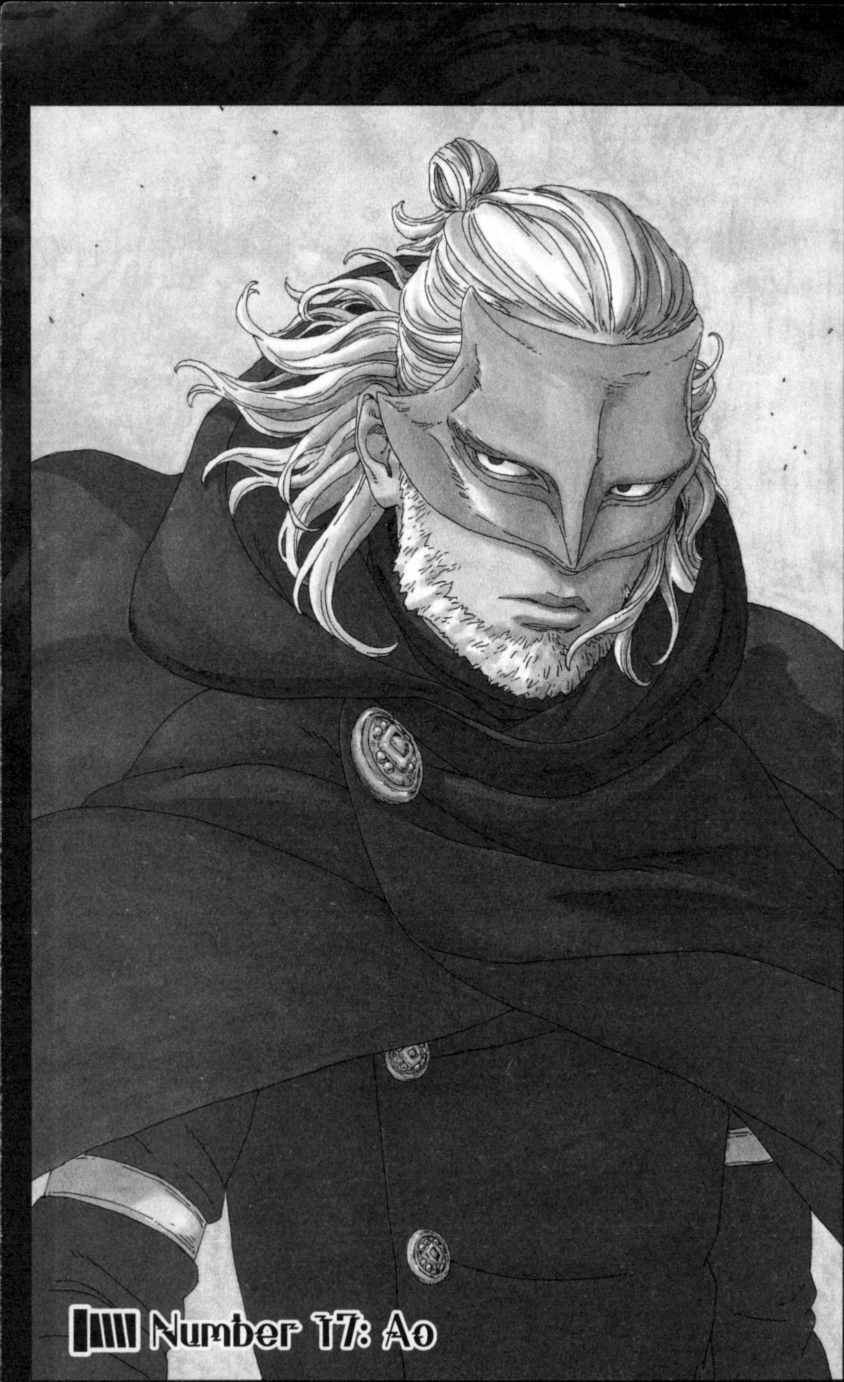
Number 17: Ao

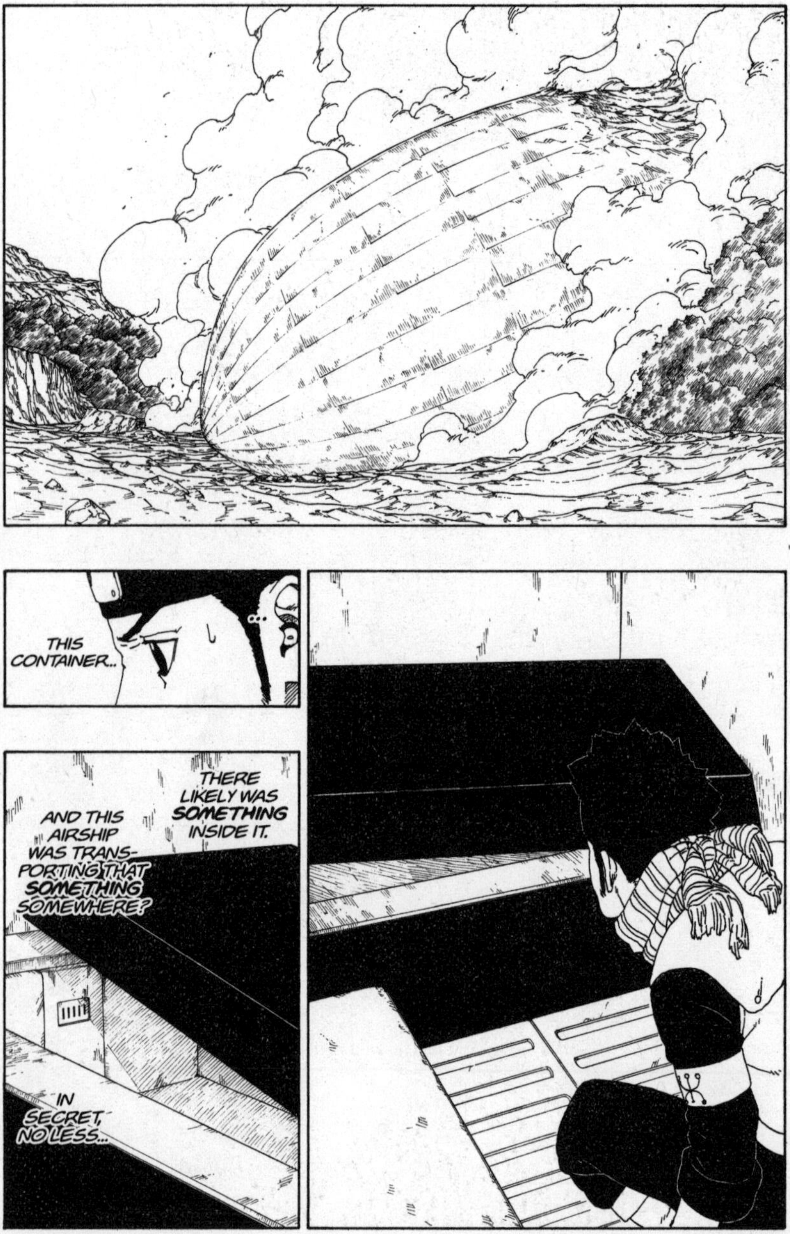
THIS CONTAINER..
THERE LIKELY WAS SOMETHING INSIDE IT.
AND THIS AIRSHIP WAS TRANS-PORTING THAT SOMETHING SOMEWHERE?
IN SECRET, NO LESS...

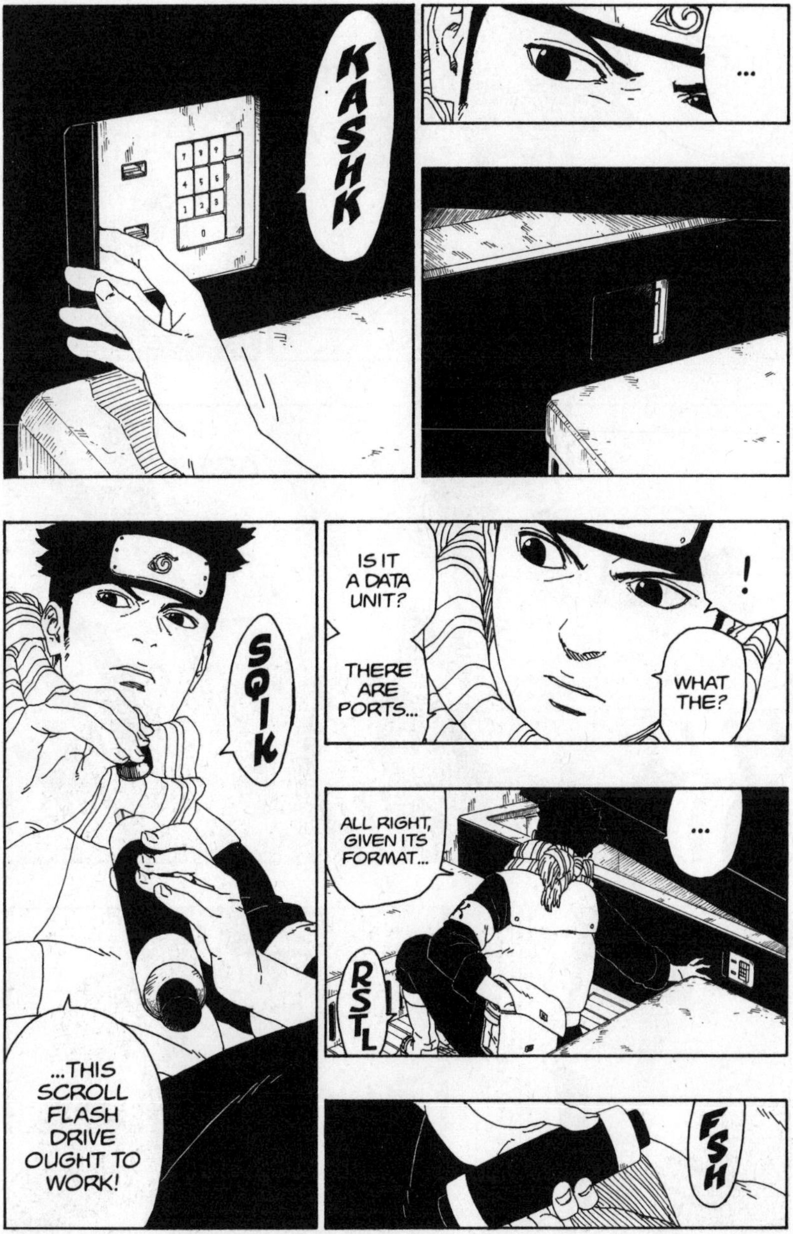
...
KASHK
!
WHAT THE?
IS IT A DATA UNIT?
THERE ARE PORTS...
...
ALL RIGHT, GIVEN ITS FORMAT...
RSTL
FSH
SQIK
...THIS SCROLL FLASH DRIVE OUGHT TO WORK!

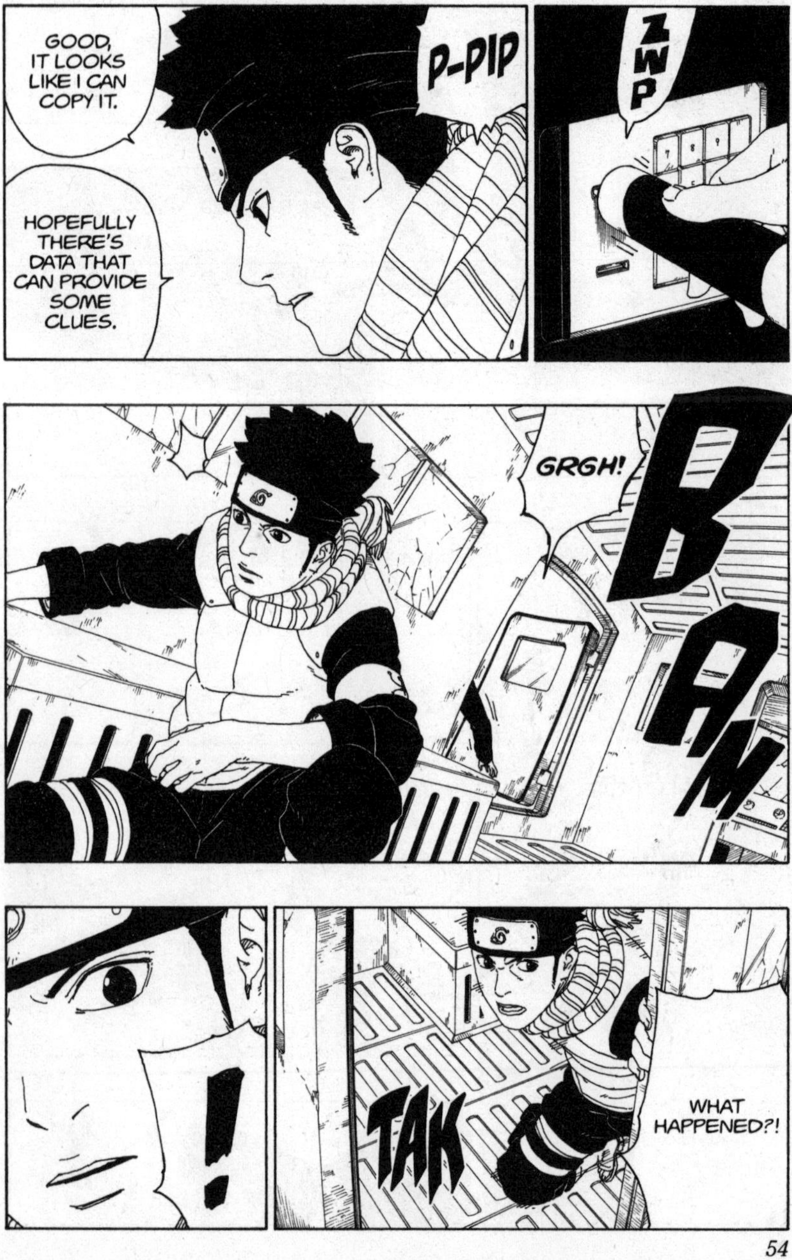
ZWP
P-PIP
GOOD, IT LOOKS LIKE I CAN COPY IT.
HOPEFULLY THERE'S DATA THAT CAN PROVIDE SOME CLUES.
BAM
GRGH!
WHAT HAPPENED?!
TAK
!

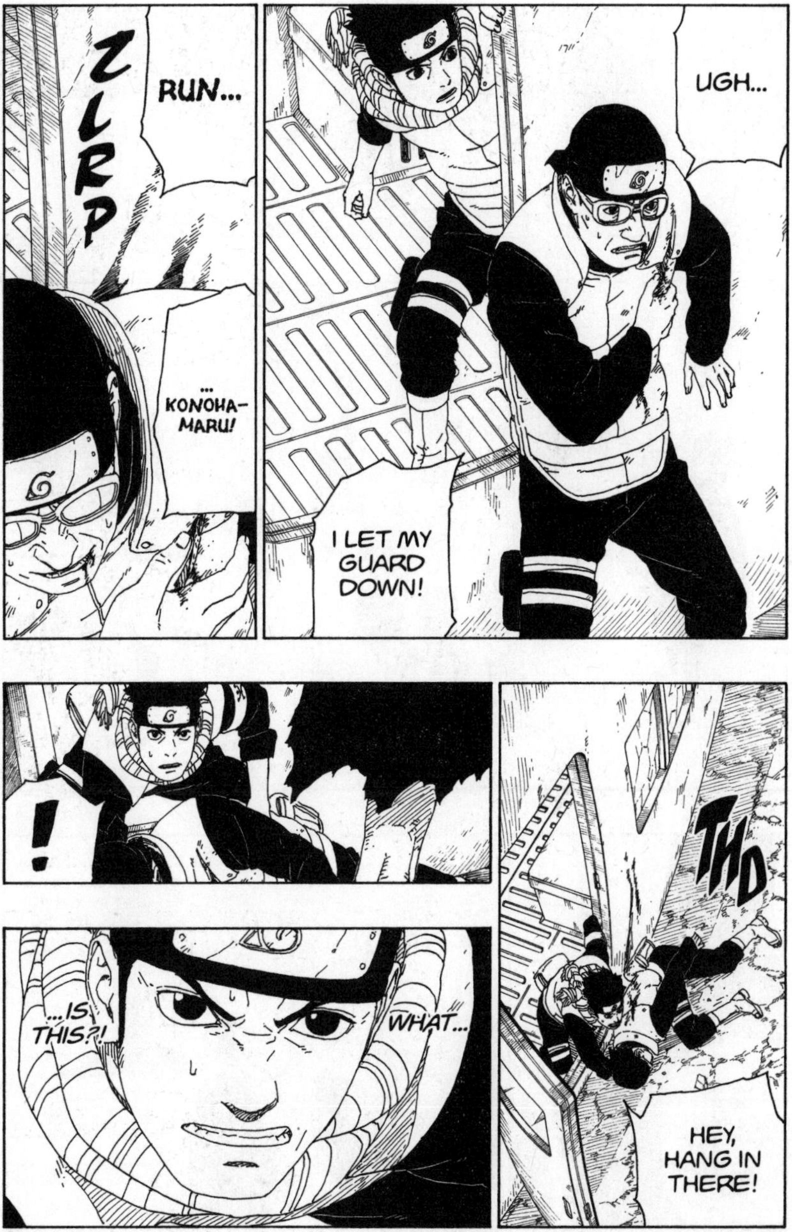
UGH...
I LET MY GUARD DOWN!
RUN...
ZLRP
...KONOHA-MARU!
THD
HEY, HANG IN THERE!
!
WHAT...
...IS THIS?!

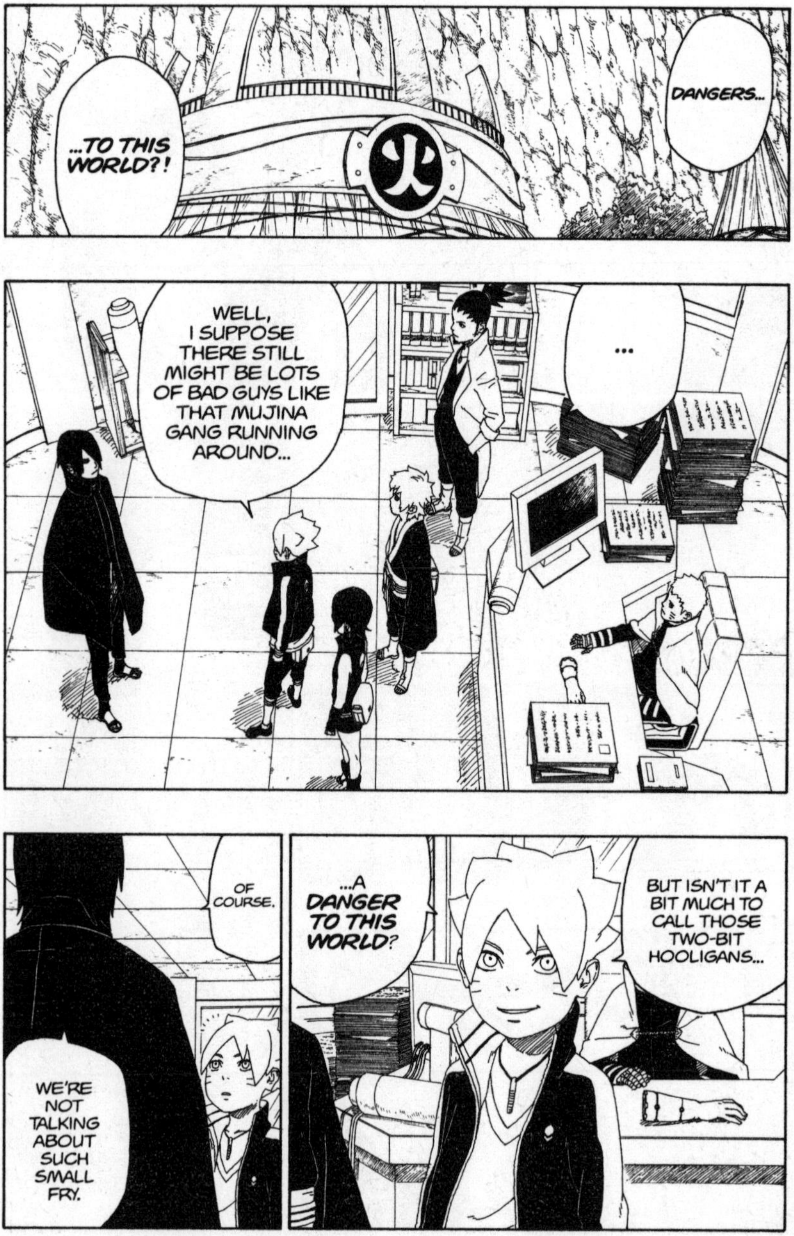
DANGERS...
...TO THIS WORLD?!
...
WELL, I SUPPOSE THERE STILL MIGHT BE LOTS OF BAD GUYS LIKE THAT MUJINA GANG RUNNING AROUND...
BUT ISN'T IT A BIT MUCH TO CALL THOSE TWO-BIT HOOLIGANS...
...A DANGER TO THIS WORLD?
OF COURSE.
WE'RE NOT TALKING ABOUT SUCH SMALL FRY.

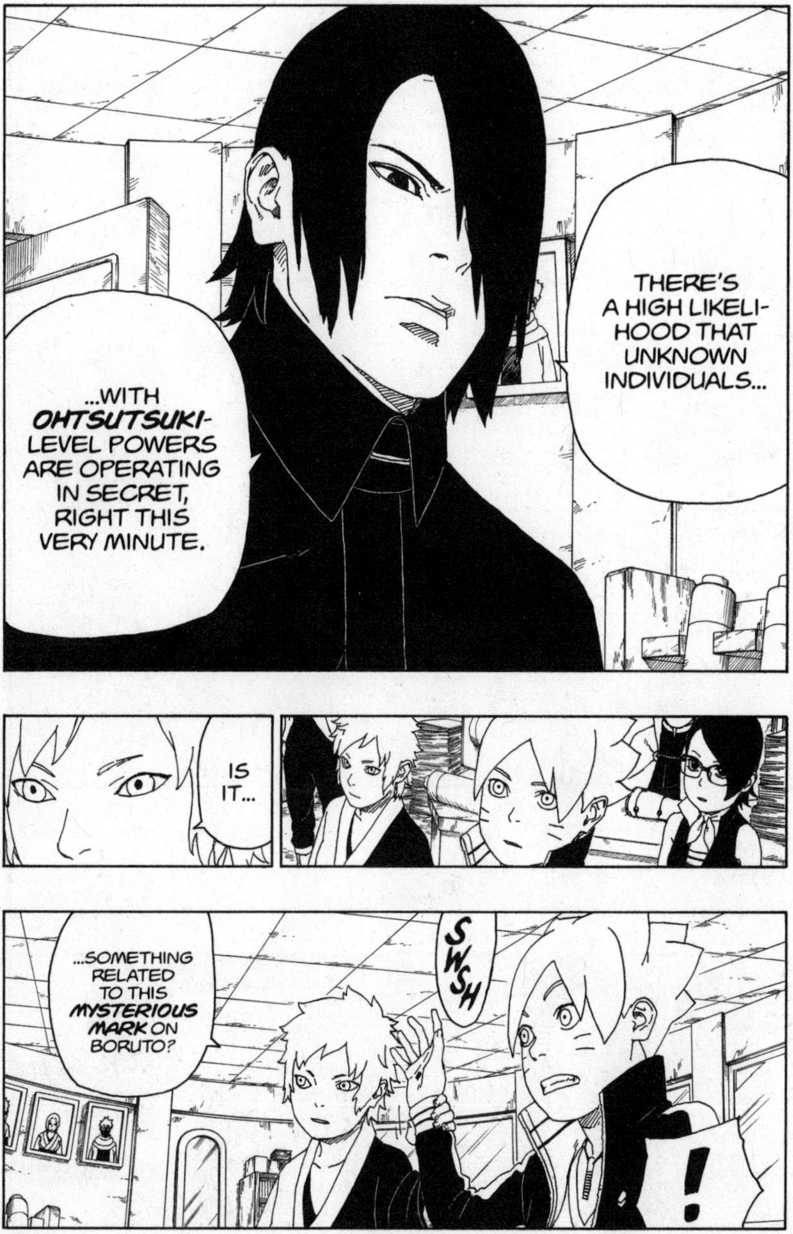
THERE'S A HIGH LIKELIHOOD THAT UNKNOWN INDIVIDUALS...
...WITH **OHTSUTSUKI**-LEVEL POWERS ARE OPERATING IN SECRET, RIGHT THIS VERY MINUTE.
IS IT...
SWSH
...SOMETHING RELATED TO THIS **MYSTERIOUS MARK** ON BORUTO?
!

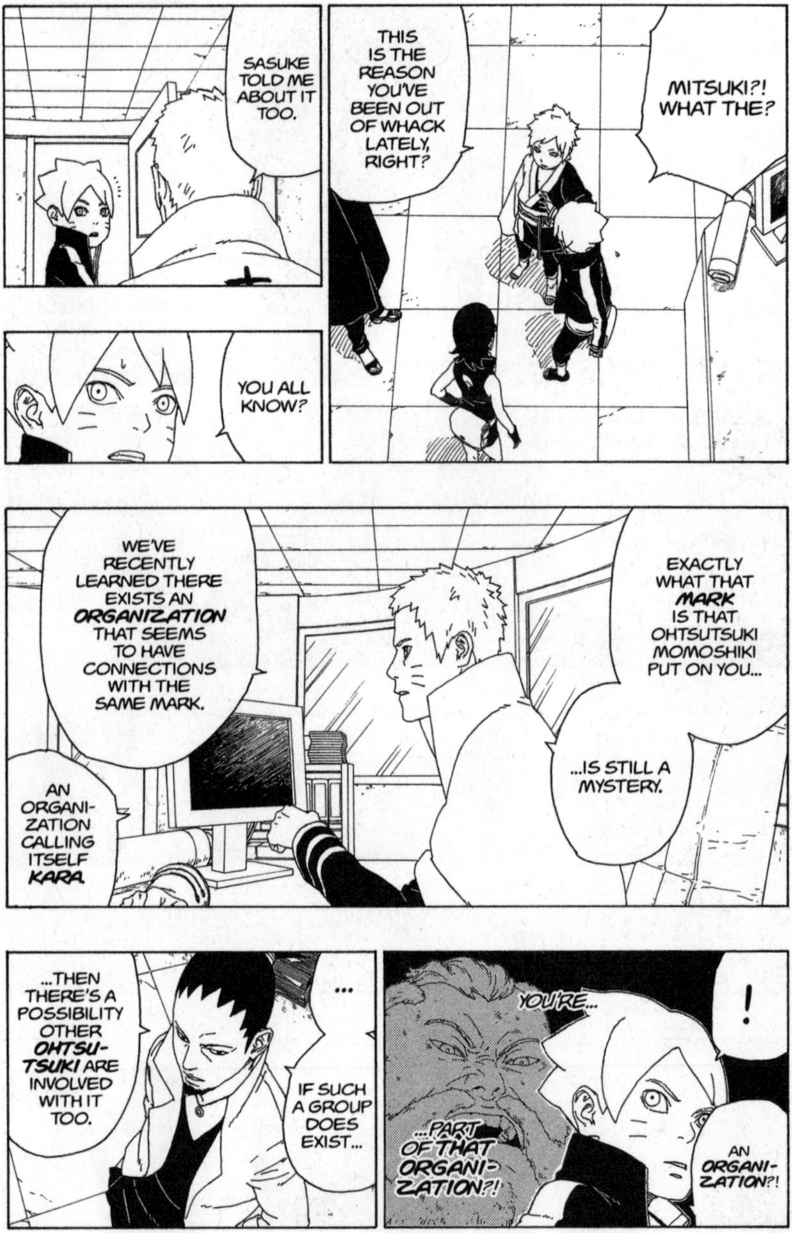

MITSUKI?! WHAT THE?
THIS IS THE REASON YOU'VE BEEN OUT OF WHACK LATELY, RIGHT?
SASUKE TOLD ME ABOUT IT TOO.
YOU ALL KNOW?
EXACTLY WHAT THAT MARK IS THAT OHTSUTSUKI MOMOSHIKI PUT ON YOU...
...IS STILL A MYSTERY.
WE'VE RECENTLY LEARNED THERE EXISTS AN ORGANIZATION THAT SEEMS TO HAVE CONNECTIONS WITH THE SAME MARK.
AN ORGANIZATION CALLING ITSELF KARA.
!
AN ORGANIZATION?!
YOU'RE...
...PART OF THAT ORGANIZATION?!
...
IF SUCH A GROUP DOES EXIST...
...THEN THERE'S A POSSIBILITY OTHER OHTSUTSUKI ARE INVOLVED WITH IT TOO.

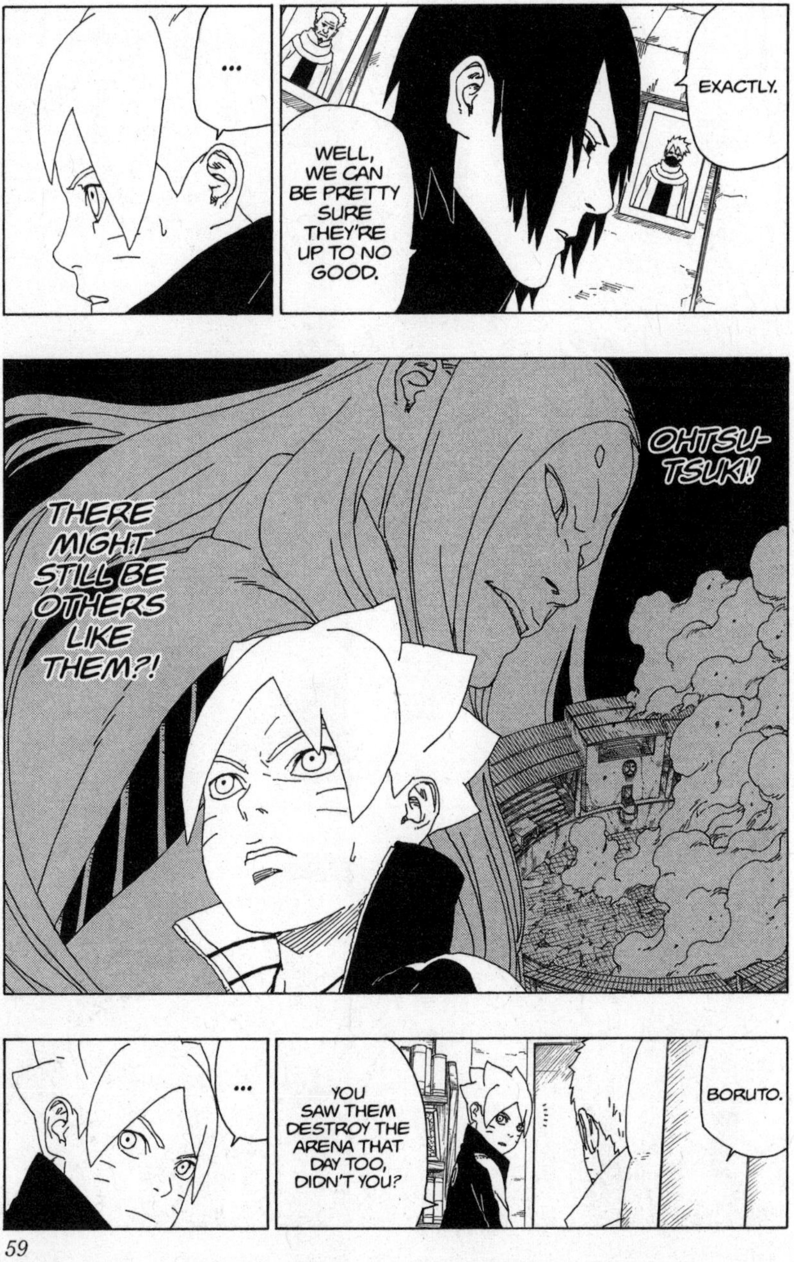
EXACTLY.
WELL, WE CAN BE PRETTY SURE THEY'RE UP TO NO GOOD.
...
OHTSU-TSUKI!
THERE MIGHT STILL BE OTHERS LIKE THEM?!
BORUTO.
YOU SAW THEM DESTROY THE ARENA THAT DAY TOO, DIDN'T YOU?
...

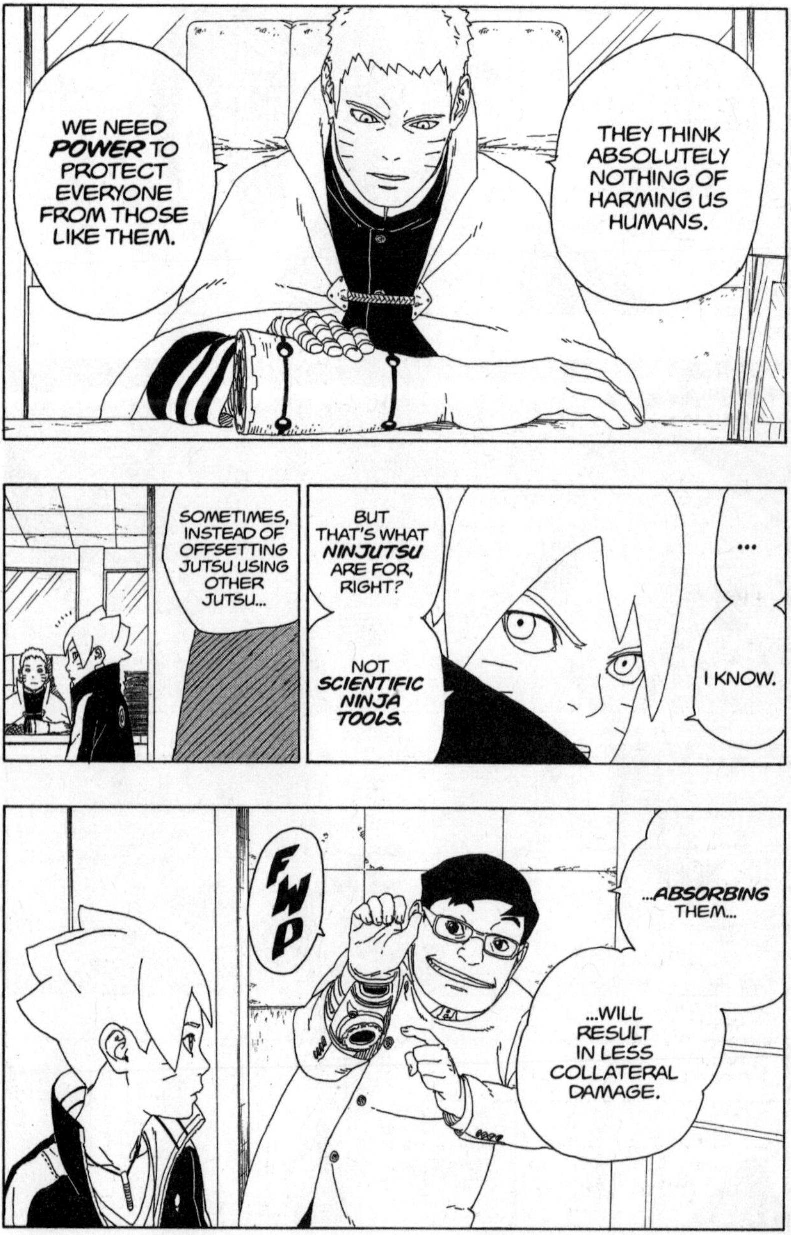

THEY THINK ABSOLUTELY NOTHING OF HARMING US HUMANS.
WE NEED POWER TO PROTECT EVERYONE FROM THOSE LIKE THEM.
...
I KNOW.
BUT THAT'S WHAT NINJUTSU ARE FOR, RIGHT?
NOT SCIENTIFIC NINJA TOOLS.
SOMETIMES, INSTEAD OF OFFSETTING JUTSU USING OTHER JUTSU...
...ABSORBING THEM...
...WILL RESULT IN LESS COLLATERAL DAMAGE.
FWP

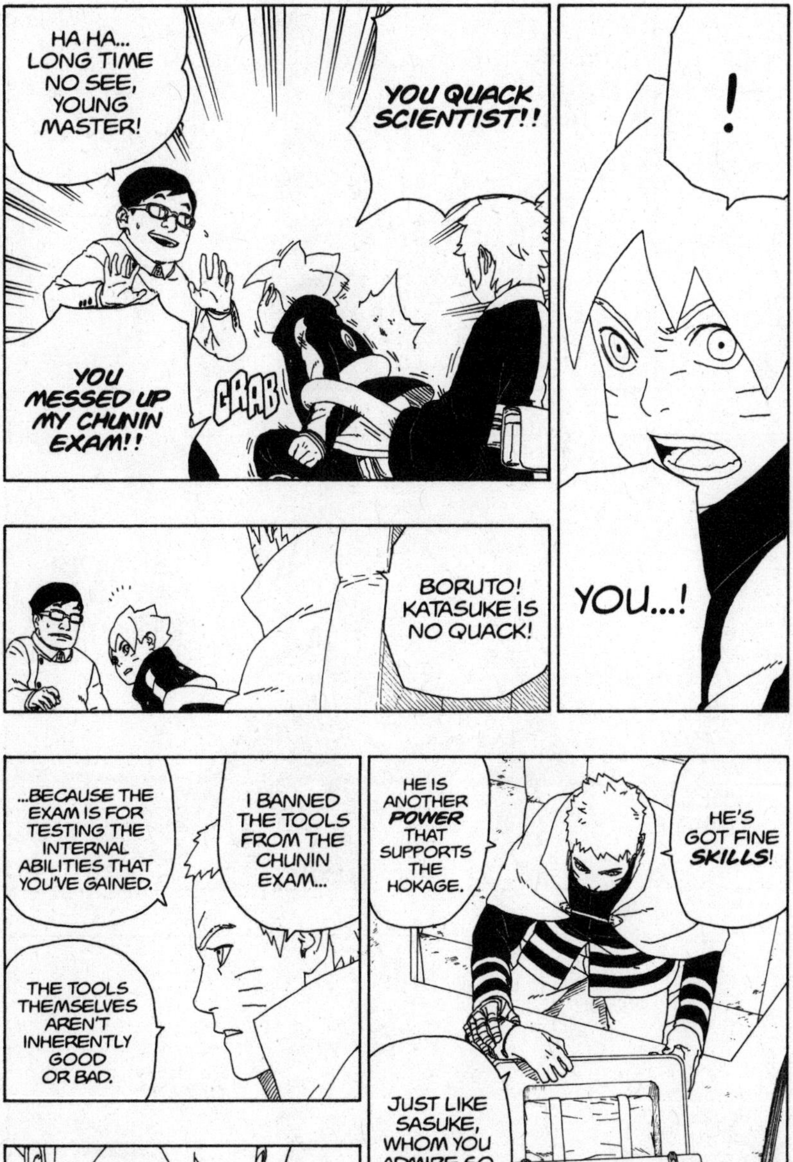

!
YOU...!
YOU QUACK SCIENTIST!!
HA HA... LONG TIME NO SEE, YOUNG MASTER!
GRAB
YOU MESSED UP MY CHUNIN EXAM!!
BORUTO! KATASUKE IS NO QUACK!
HE'S GOT FINE SKILLS!
HE IS ANOTHER POWER THAT SUPPORTS THE HOKAGE.
JUST LIKE SASUKE, WHOM YOU ADMIRE SO MUCH.
I BANNED THE TOOLS FROM THE CHUNIN EXAM...
...BECAUSE THE EXAM IS FOR TESTING THE INTERNAL ABILITIES THAT YOU'VE GAINED.
THE TOOLS THEMSELVES AREN'T INHERENTLY GOOD OR BAD.
...

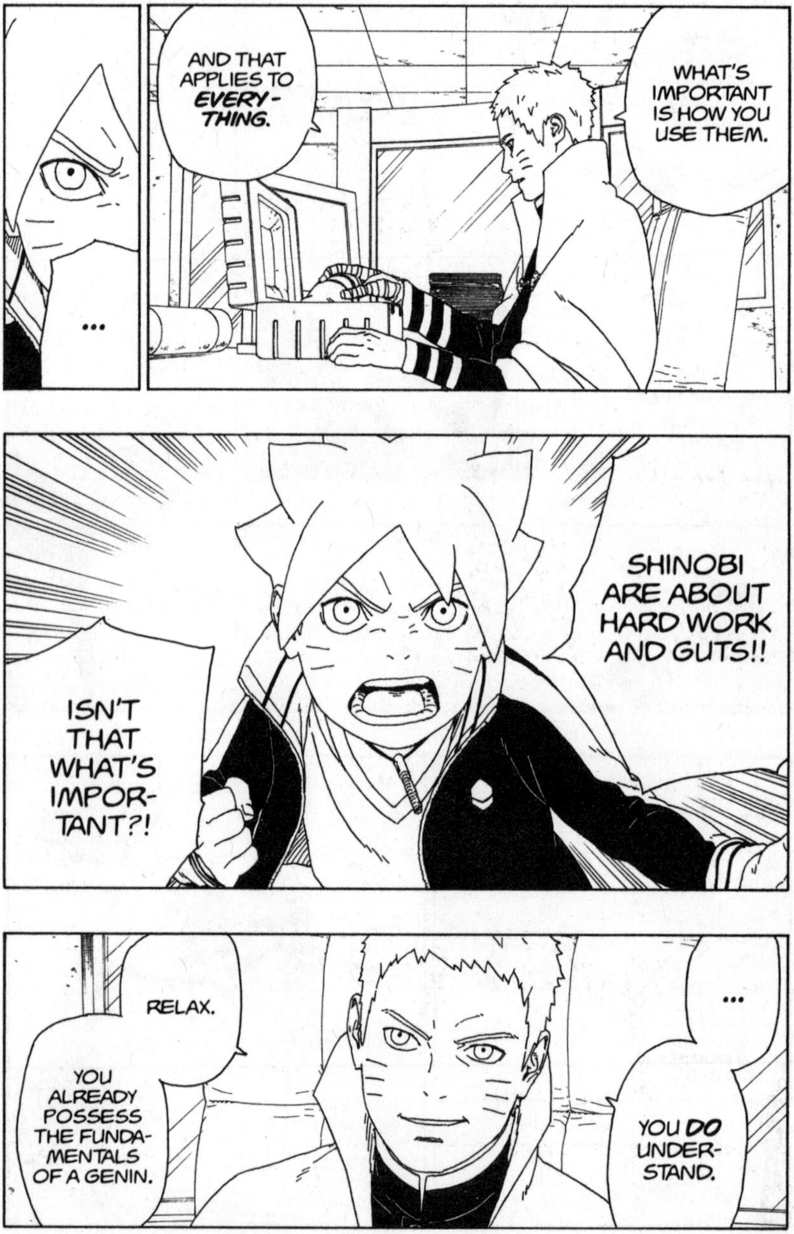
WHAT'S IMPORTANT IS HOW YOU USE THEM.
AND THAT APPLIES TO **EVERY-THING.**
...
SHINOBI ARE ABOUT HARD WORK AND GUTS!!
ISN'T THAT WHAT'S IMPOR-TANT?!
...
YOU **DO** UNDER-STAND.
RELAX.
YOU ALREADY POSSESS THE FUNDA-MENTALS OF A GENIN.

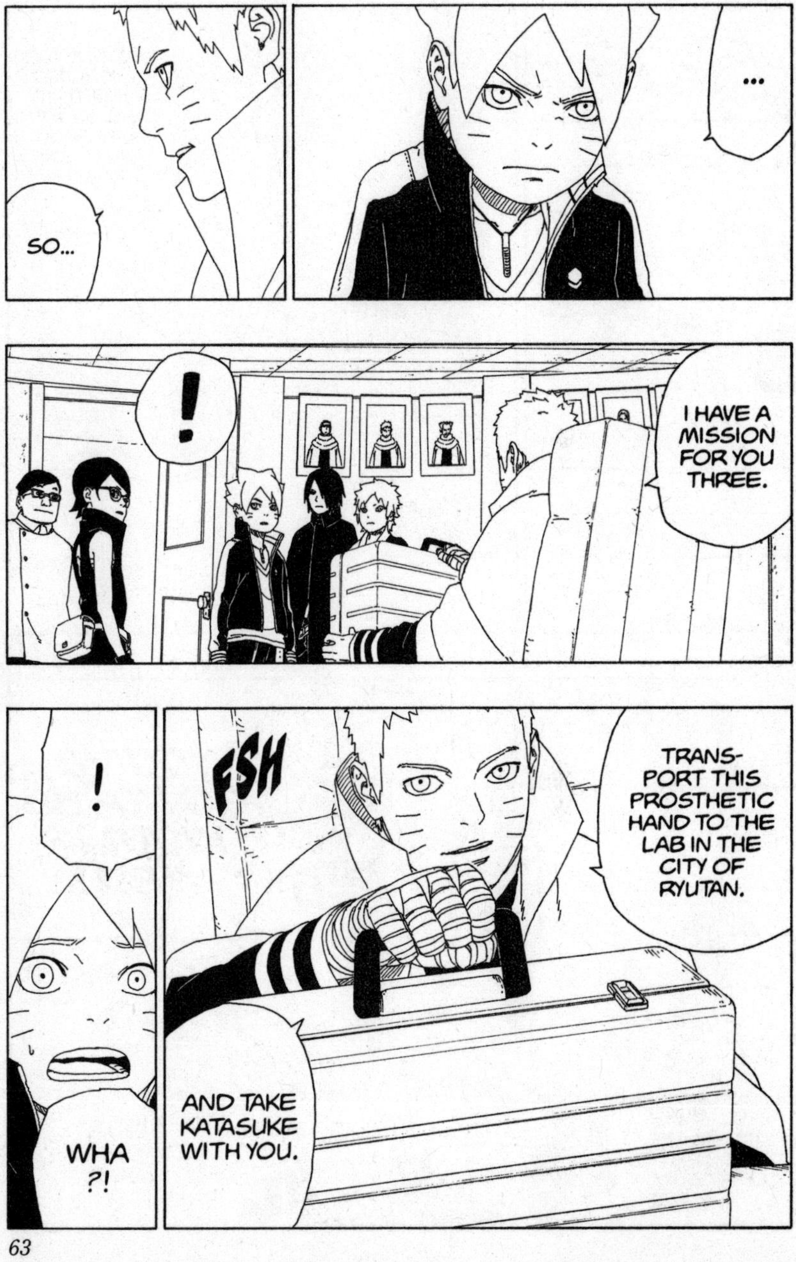
...
SO...
I HAVE A MISSION FOR YOU THREE.
!
TRANS-PORT THIS PROSTHETIC HAND TO THE LAB IN THE CITY OF RYUTAN.
FSH
AND TAKE KATASUKE WITH YOU.
!
WHA ?!

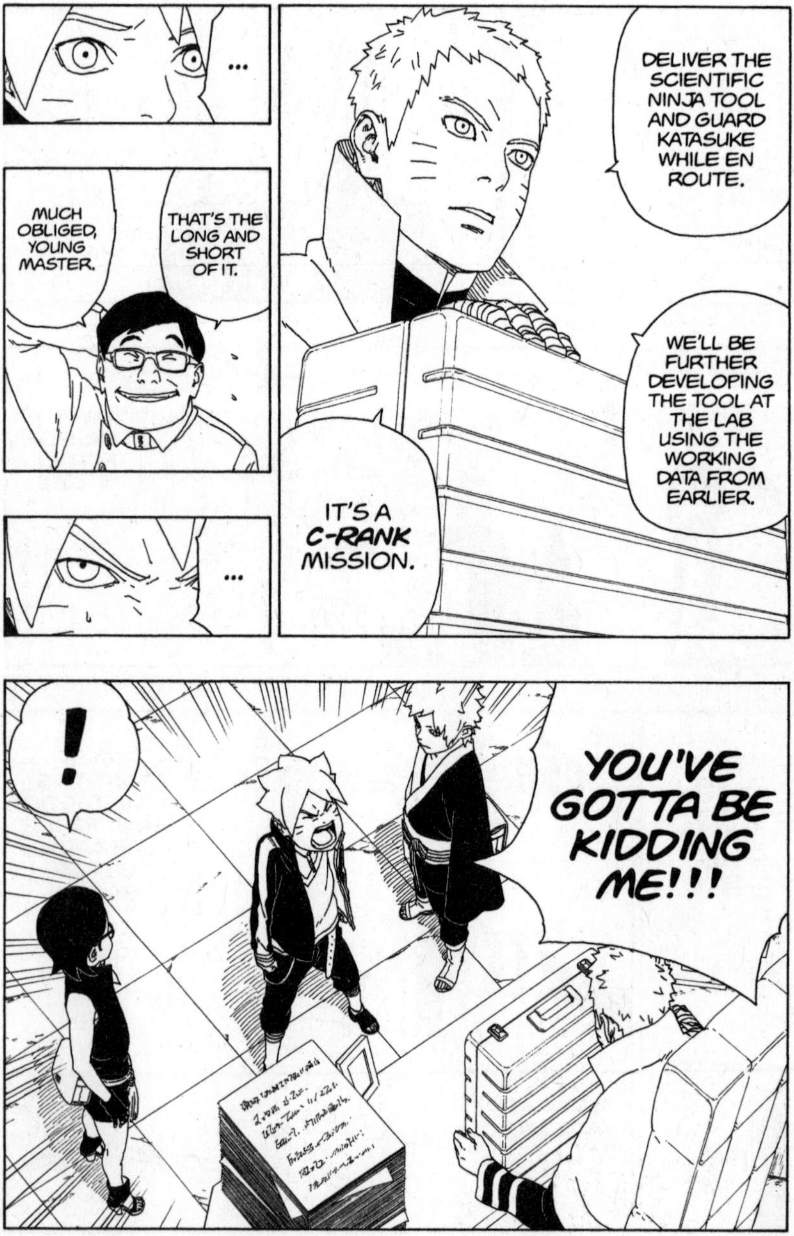
DELIVER THE SCIENTIFIC NINJA TOOL AND GUARD KATASUKE WHILE EN ROUTE.
WE'LL BE FURTHER DEVELOPING THE TOOL AT THE LAB USING THE WORKING DATA FROM EARLIER.
IT'S A C-RANK MISSION.
...
THAT'S THE LONG AND SHORT OF IT.
MUCH OBLIGED, YOUNG MASTER.
...
YOU'VE GOTTA BE KIDDING ME!!!
!

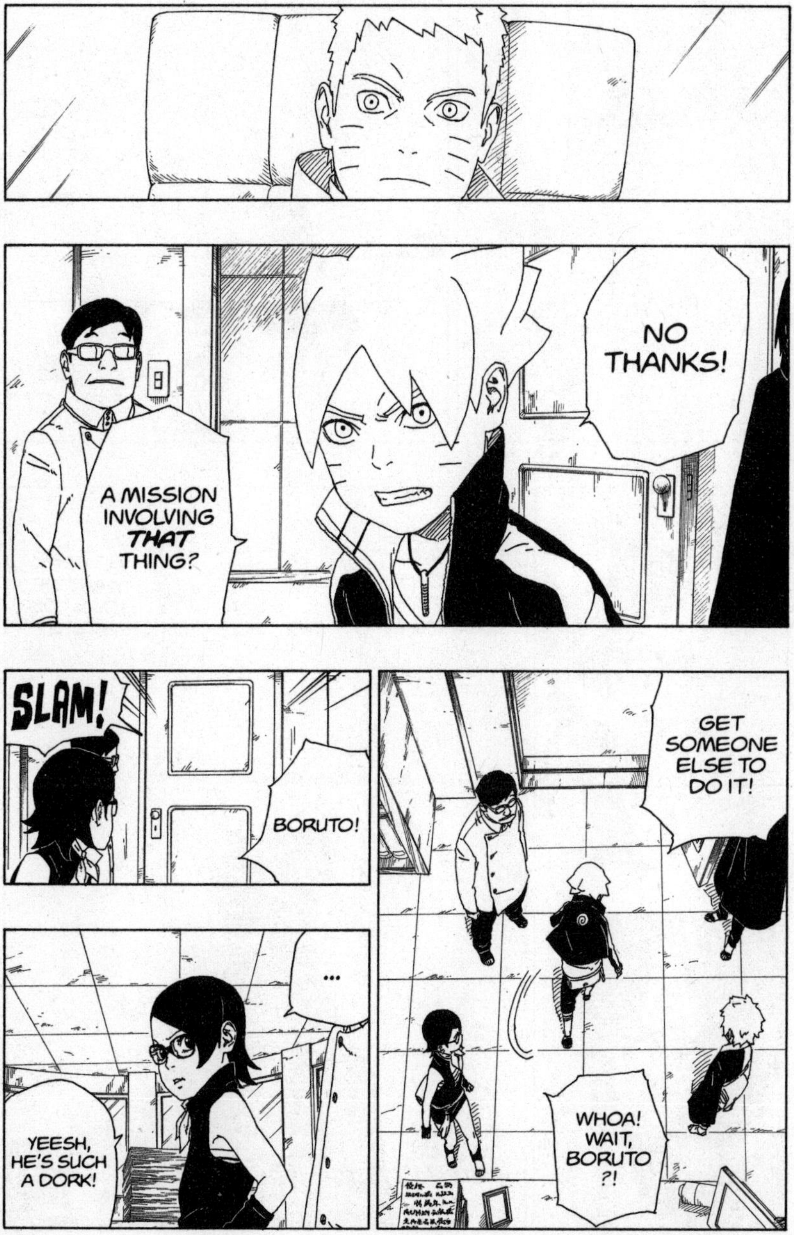

NO THANKS!
A MISSION INVOLVING *THAT* THING?
GET SOMEONE ELSE TO DO IT!
WHOA! WAIT, BORUTO?!
SLAM!
BORUTO!
...
YEESH, HE'S SUCH A DORK!

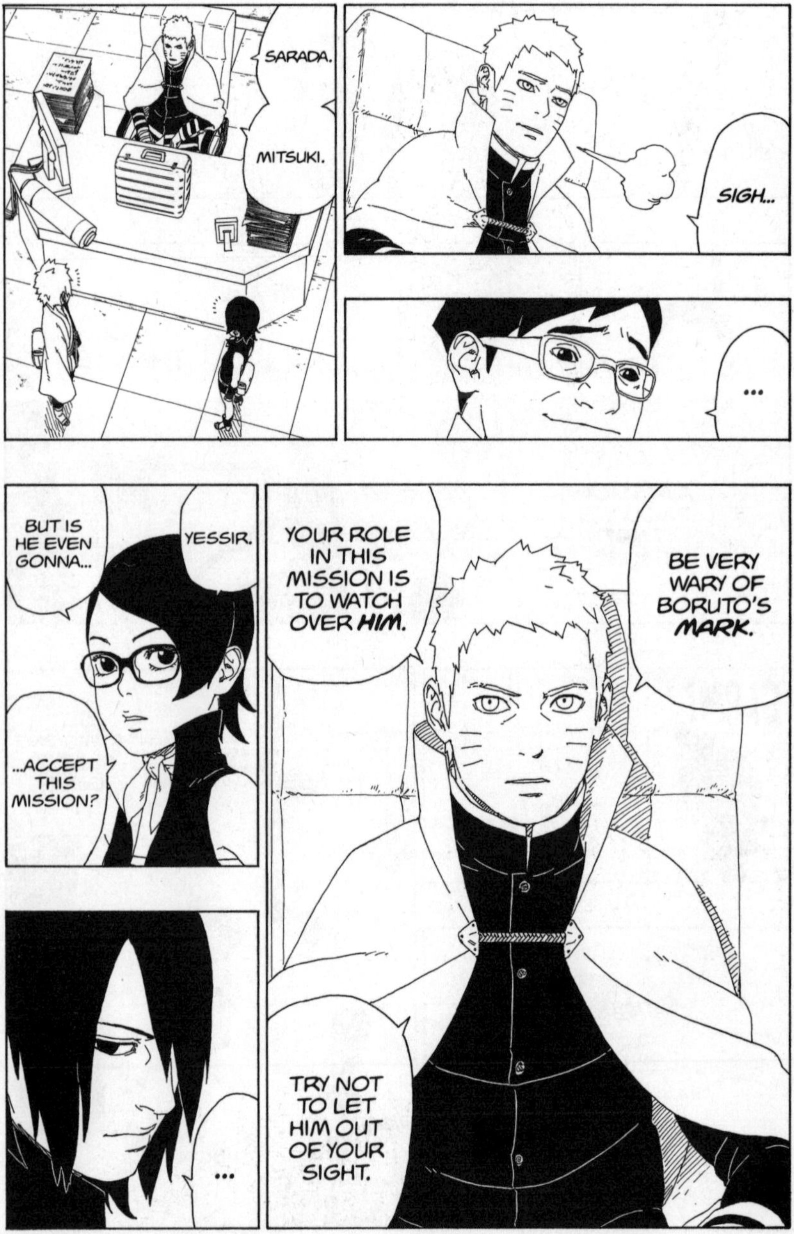
SIGH...
...
SARADA.
MITSUKI.
BE VERY WARY OF BORUTO'S **MARK.**
YOUR ROLE IN THIS MISSION IS TO WATCH OVER **HIM.**
TRY NOT TO LET HIM OUT OF YOUR SIGHT.
YESSIR.
BUT IS HE EVEN GONNA...
...ACCEPT THIS MISSION?
...

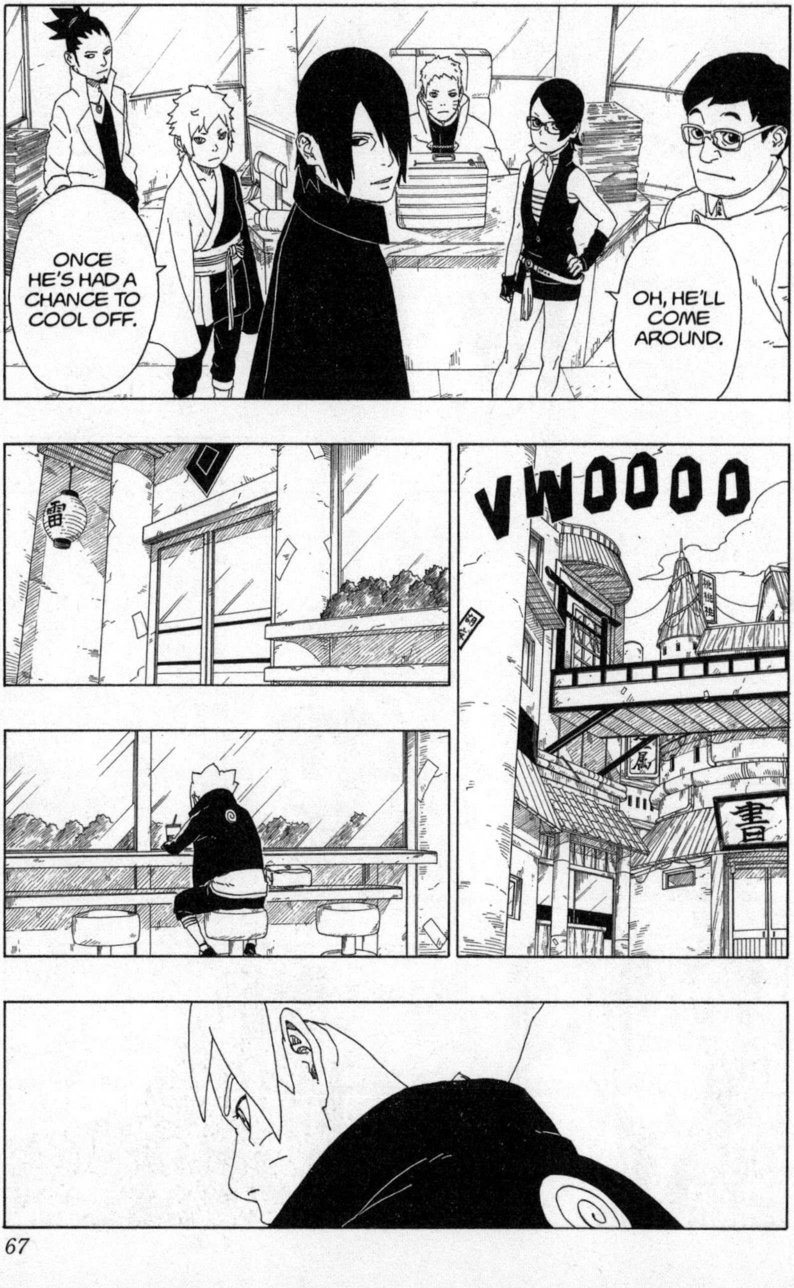
OH, HE'LL COME AROUND.
ONCE HE'S HAD A CHANCE TO COOL OFF.
VWOOOO
書
雷

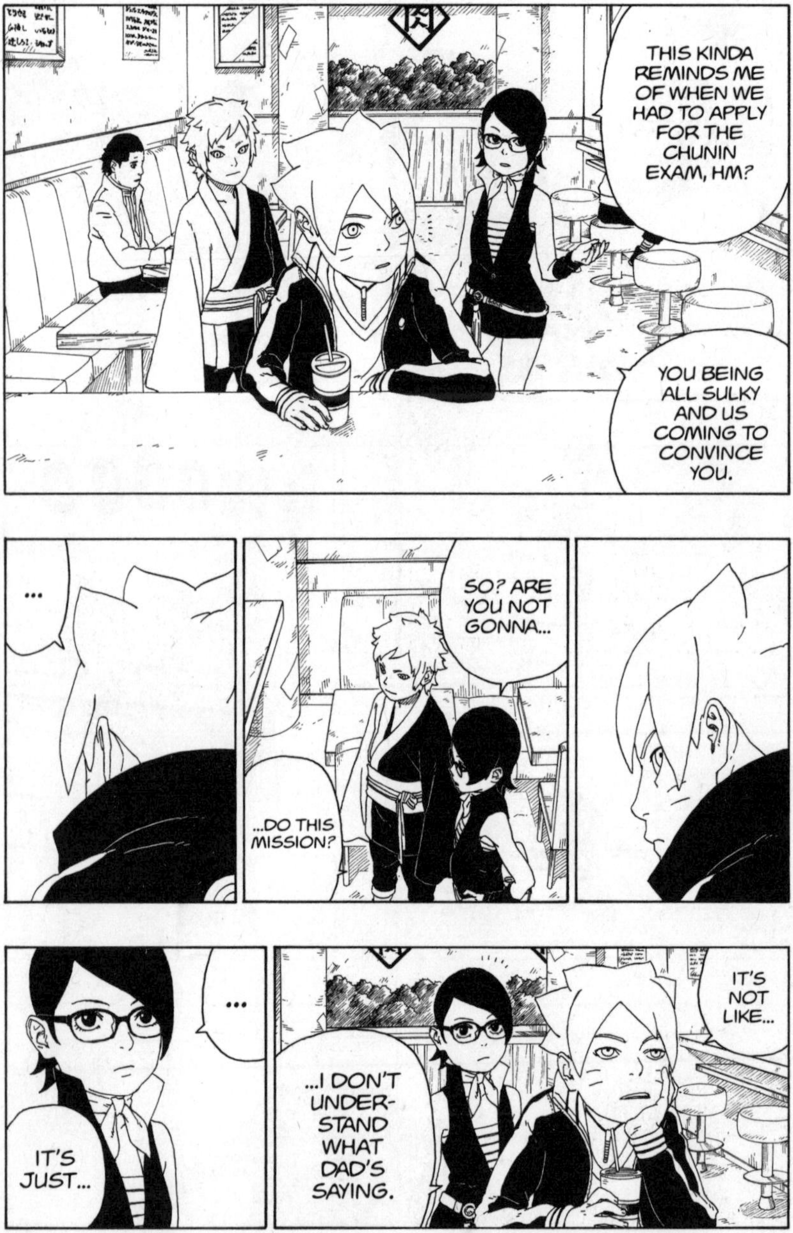
THIS KINDA REMINDS ME OF WHEN WE HAD TO APPLY FOR THE CHUNIN EXAM, HM?
YOU BEING ALL SULKY AND US COMING TO CONVINCE YOU.
SO? ARE YOU NOT GONNA...
...DO THIS MISSION?
...
IT'S NOT LIKE...
...I DON'T UNDER-STAND WHAT DAD'S SAYING.
...
IT'S JUST...

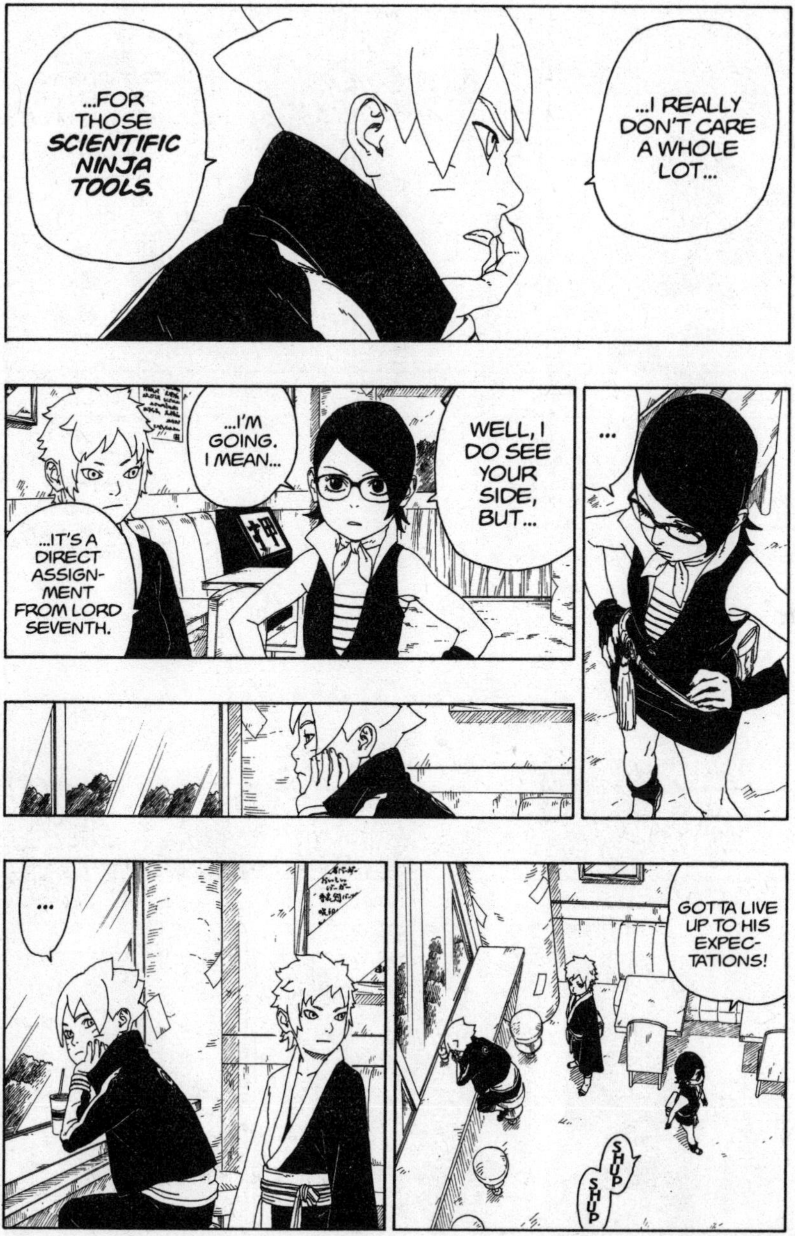
...I REALLY DON'T CARE A WHOLE LOT...
...FOR THOSE SCIENTIFIC NINJA TOOLS.
...
WELL, I DO SEE YOUR SIDE, BUT...
...I'M GOING. I MEAN...
...IT'S A DIRECT ASSIGNMENT FROM LORD SEVENTH.
GOTTA LIVE UP TO HIS EXPECTATIONS!
SHUP SHUP
...

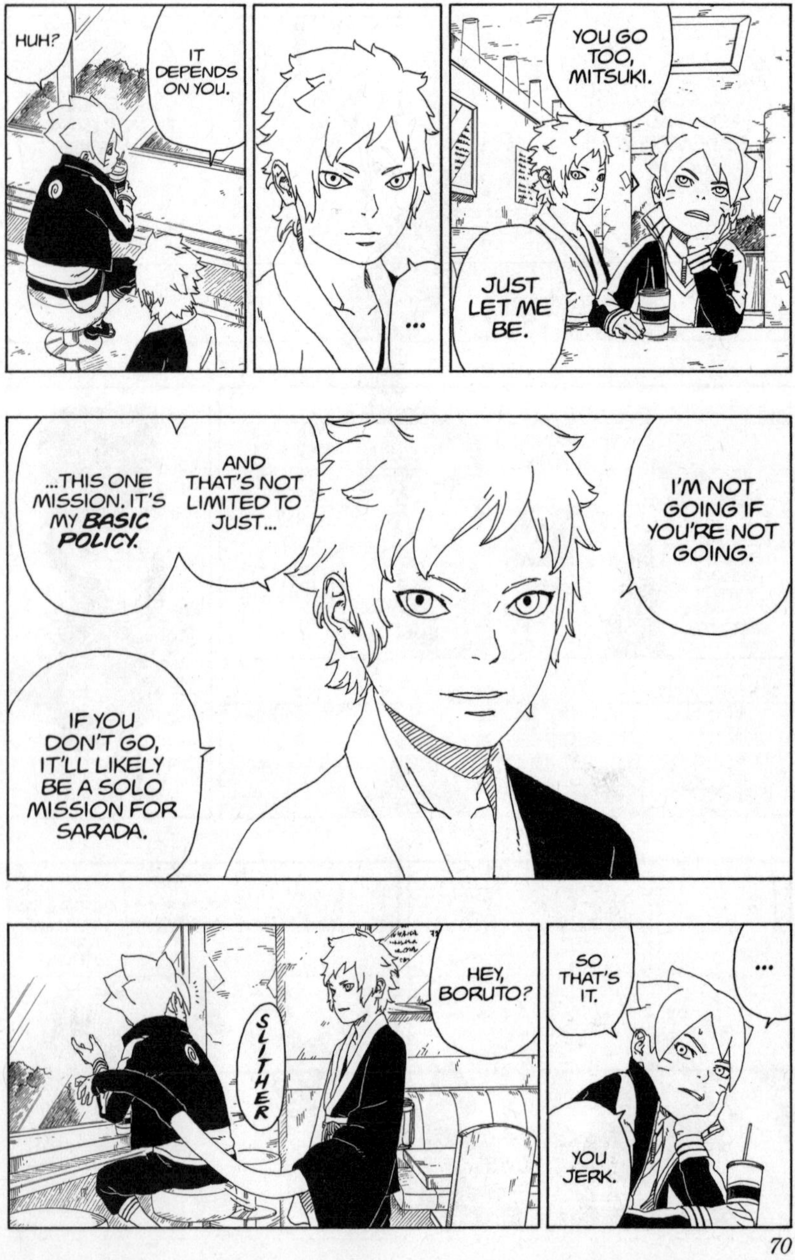
YOU GO TOO, MITSUKI.
JUST LET ME BE.
...
IT DEPENDS ON YOU.
HUH?
I'M NOT GOING IF YOU'RE NOT GOING.
AND THAT'S NOT LIMITED TO JUST...
...THIS ONE MISSION. IT'S MY BASIC POLICY.
IF YOU DON'T GO, IT'LL LIKELY BE A SOLO MISSION FOR SARADA.
...
SO THAT'S IT.
YOU JERK.
HEY, BORUTO?
SLITHER

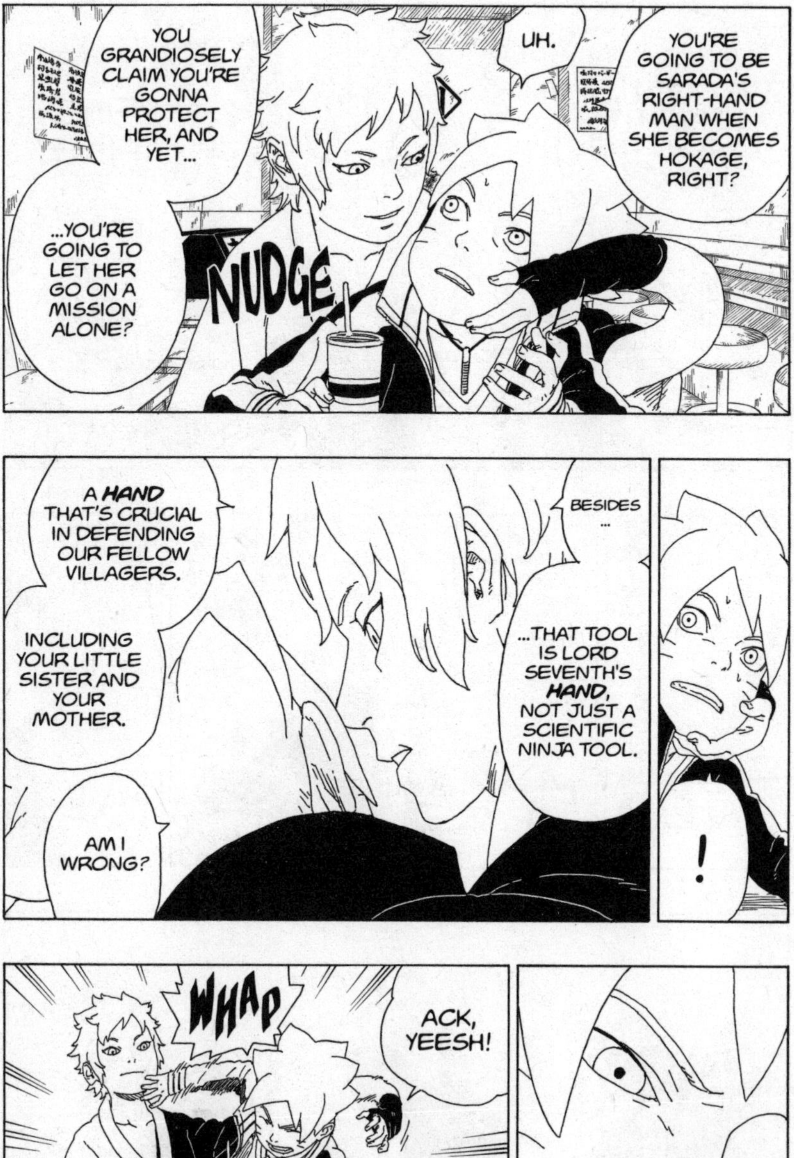
YOU'RE GOING TO BE SARADA'S RIGHT-HAND MAN WHEN SHE BECOMES HOKAGE, RIGHT?
UH.
YOU GRANDIOSELY CLAIM YOU'RE GONNA PROTECT HER, AND YET...
...YOU'RE GOING TO LET HER GO ON A MISSION ALONE?
NUDGE
!
BESIDES ...
...THAT TOOL IS LORD SEVENTH'S HAND, NOT JUST A SCIENTIFIC NINJA TOOL.
A HAND THAT'S CRUCIAL IN DEFENDING OUR FELLOW VILLAGERS.
INCLUDING YOUR LITTLE SISTER AND YOUR MOTHER.
AM I WRONG?
...
ACK, YEESH!
WHAP

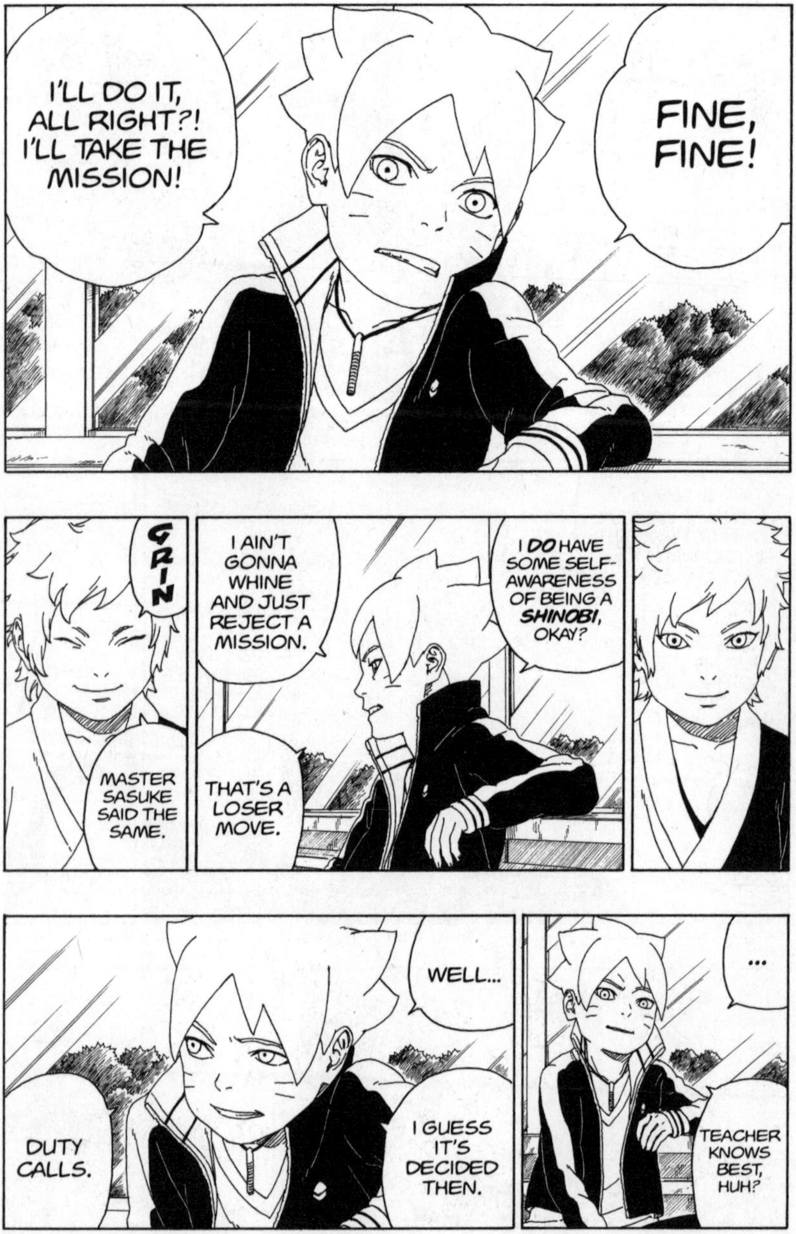
FINE, FINE!
I'LL DO IT, ALL RIGHT?! I'LL TAKE THE MISSION!
I DO HAVE SOME SELF-AWARENESS OF BEING A SHINOBI, OKAY?
I AIN'T GONNA WHINE AND JUST REJECT A MISSION.
THAT'S A LOSER MOVE.
GRIN
MASTER SASUKE SAID THE SAME.
...
TEACHER KNOWS BEST, HUH?
WELL...
I GUESS IT'S DECIDED THEN.
DUTY CALLS.

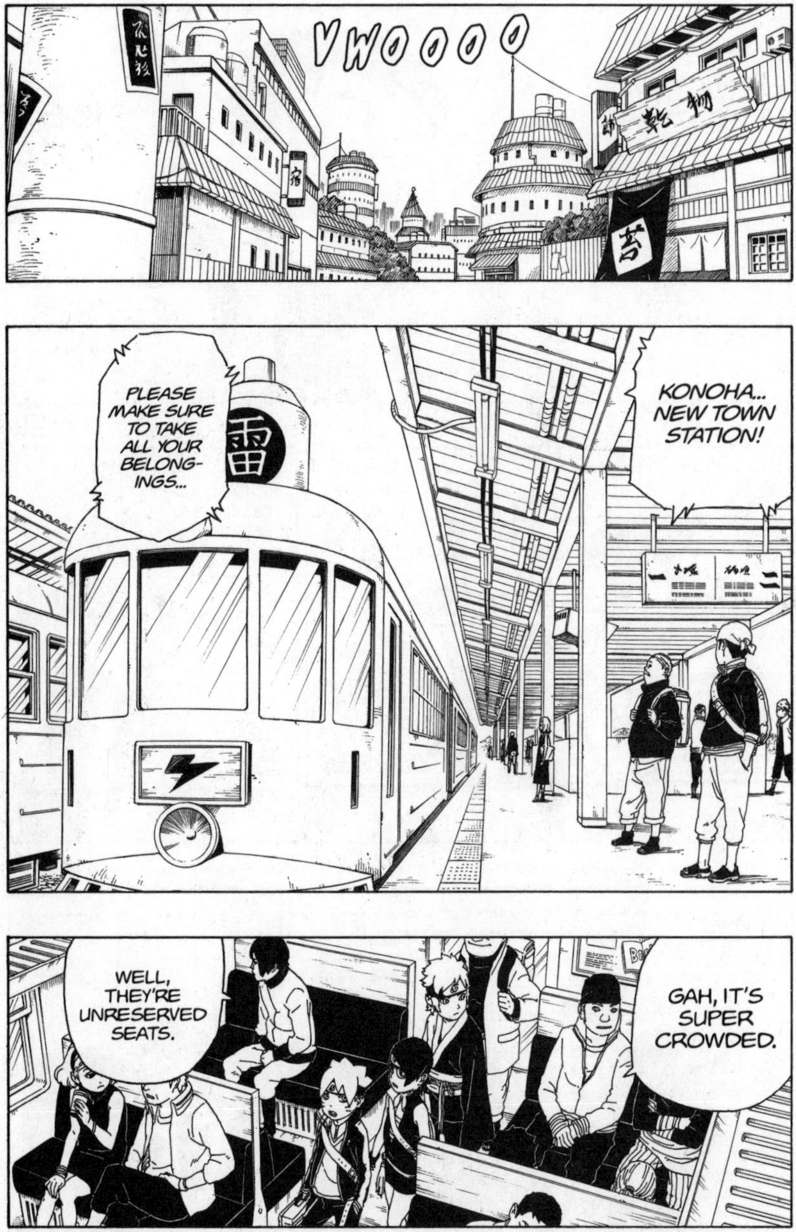
VWOOOO
KONOHA... NEW TOWN STATION!
PLEASE MAKE SURE TO TAKE ALL YOUR BELONGINGS...
GAH, IT'S SUPER CROWDED.
WELL, THEY'RE UNRESERVED SEATS.

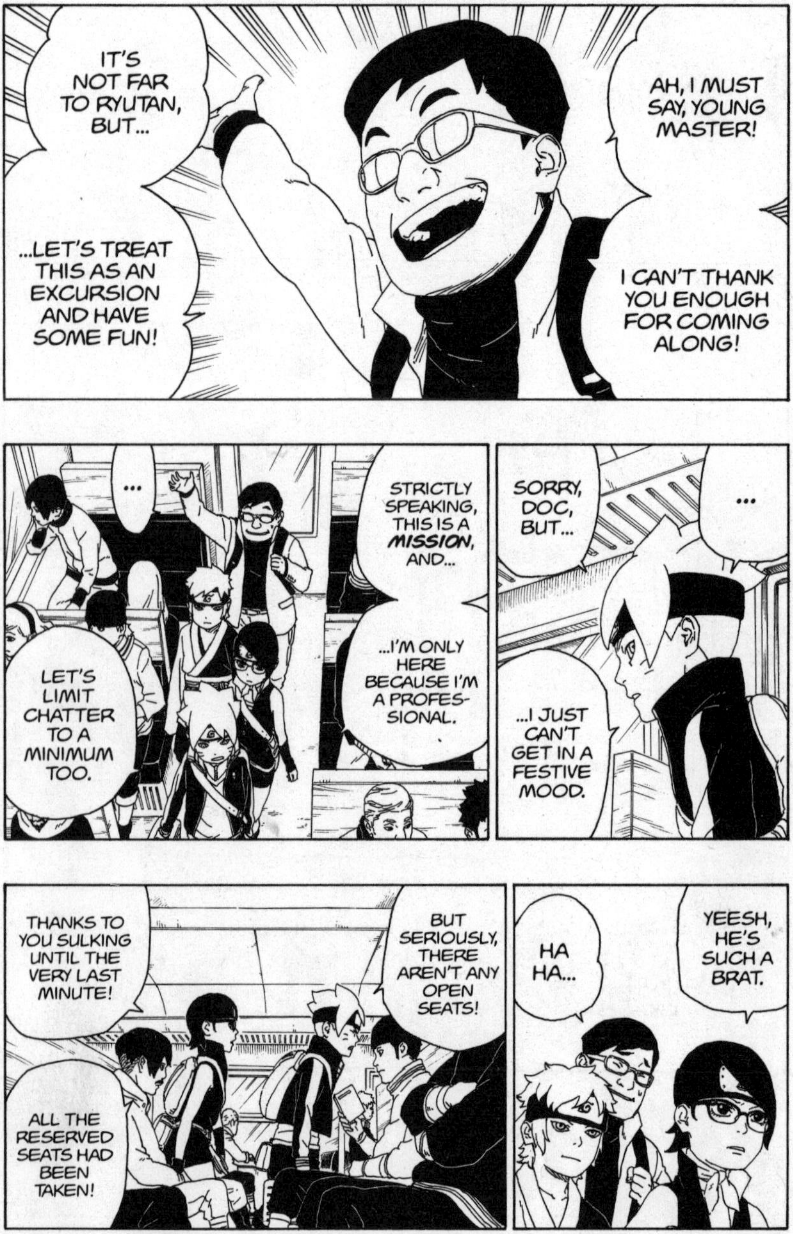
AH, I MUST SAY, YOUNG MASTER!
I CAN'T THANK YOU ENOUGH FOR COMING ALONG!
IT'S NOT FAR TO RYUTAN, BUT...
...LET'S TREAT THIS AS AN EXCURSION AND HAVE SOME FUN!
...
SORRY, DOC, BUT...
...I JUST CAN'T GET IN A FESTIVE MOOD.
STRICTLY SPEAKING, THIS IS A ***MISSION***, AND...
...I'M ONLY HERE BECAUSE I'M A PROFESSIONAL.
...
LET'S LIMIT CHATTER TO A MINIMUM TOO.
YEESH, HE'S SUCH A BRAT.
HA HA...
BUT SERIOUSLY, THERE AREN'T ANY OPEN SEATS!
THANKS TO YOU SULKING UNTIL THE VERY LAST MINUTE!
ALL THE RESERVED SEATS HAD BEEN TAKEN!

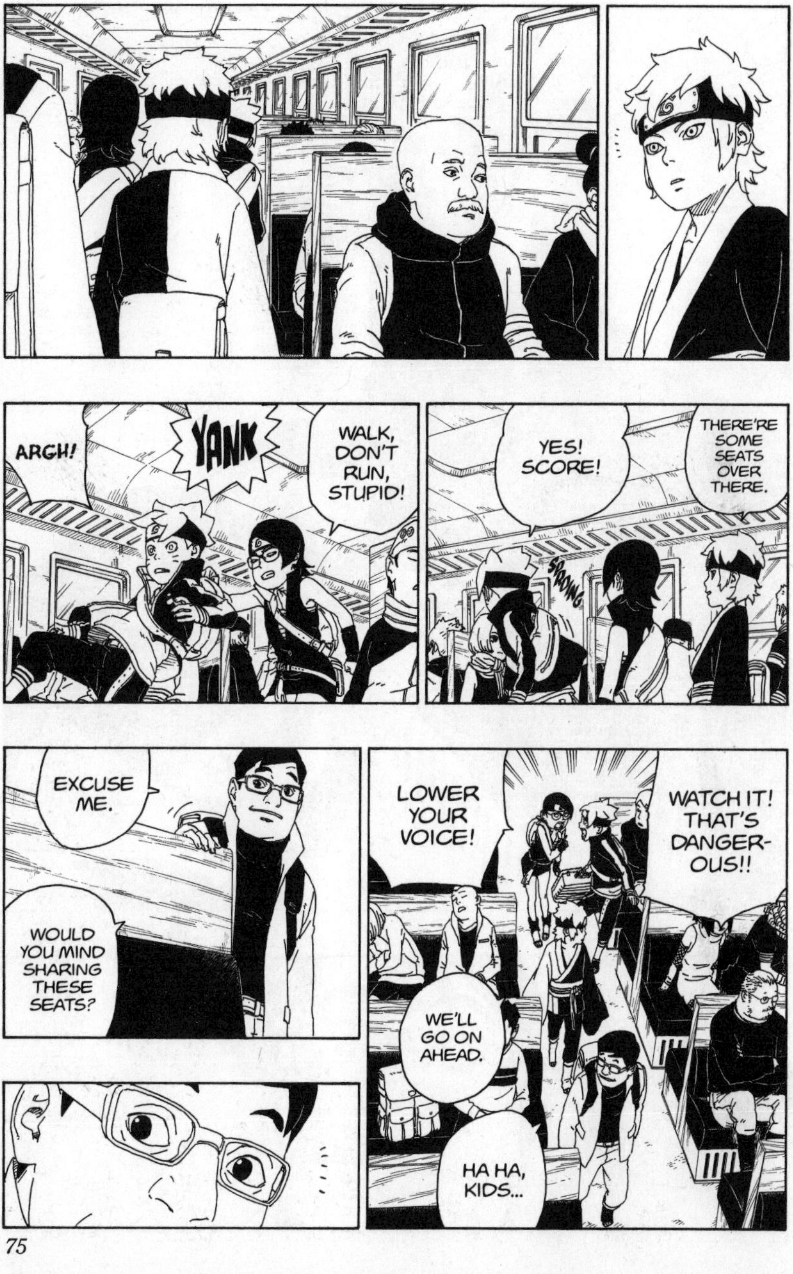
THERE'RE SOME SEATS OVER THERE.
YES! SCORE!
SPROING
WALK, DON'T RUN, STUPID!
YANK
ARGH!
WATCH IT! THAT'S DANGER-OUS!!
LOWER YOUR VOICE!
WE'LL GO ON AHEAD.
HA HA, KIDS...
EXCUSE ME.
WOULD YOU MIND SHARING THESE SEATS?

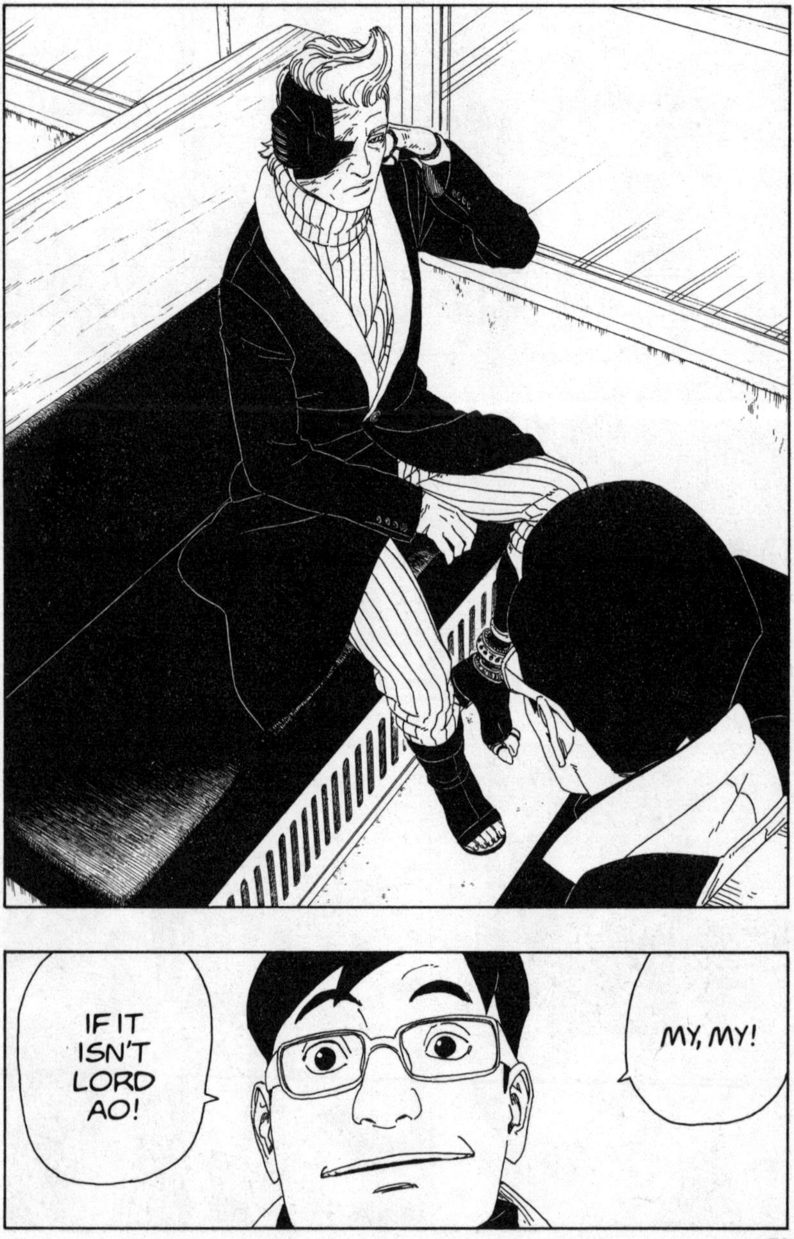
MY, MY!
IF IT ISN'T LORD AO!

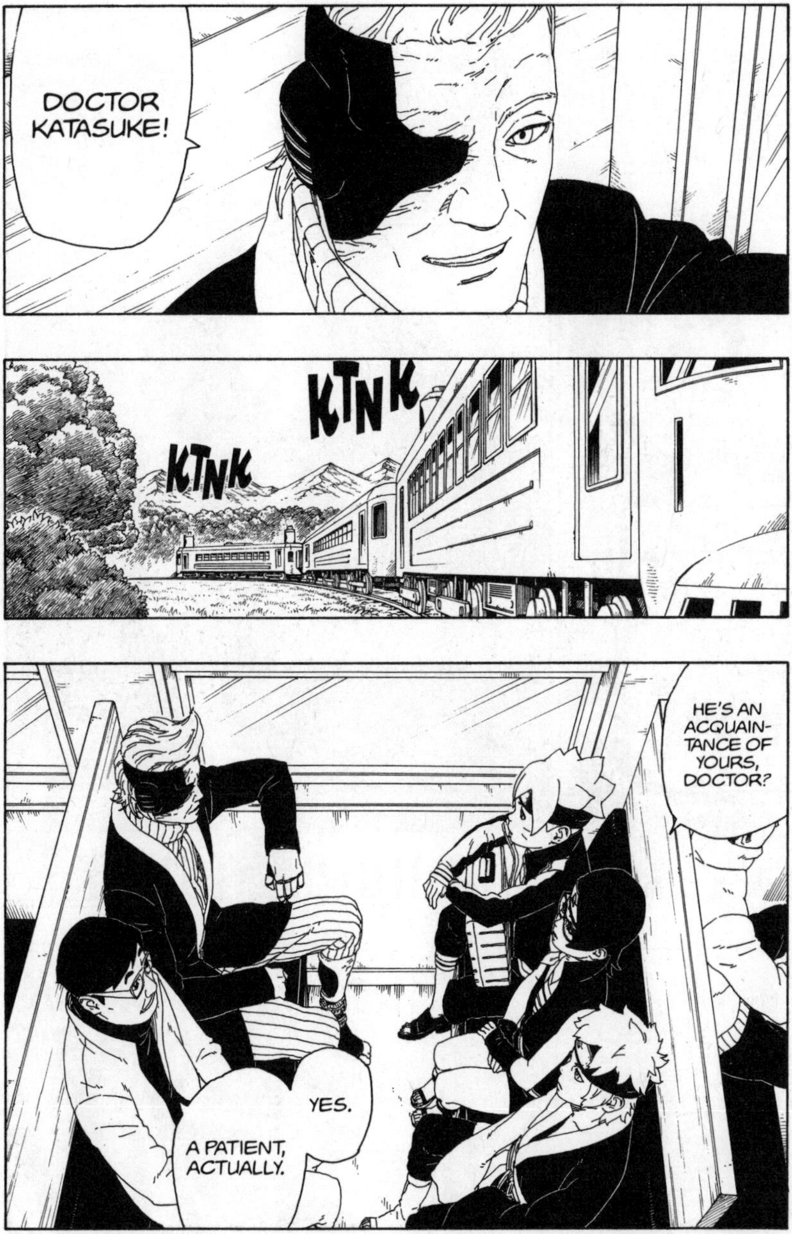
DOCTOR KATASUKE!
KTNK
KTNK
HE'S AN ACQUAINTANCE OF YOURS, DOCTOR?
YES.
A PATIENT, ACTUALLY.

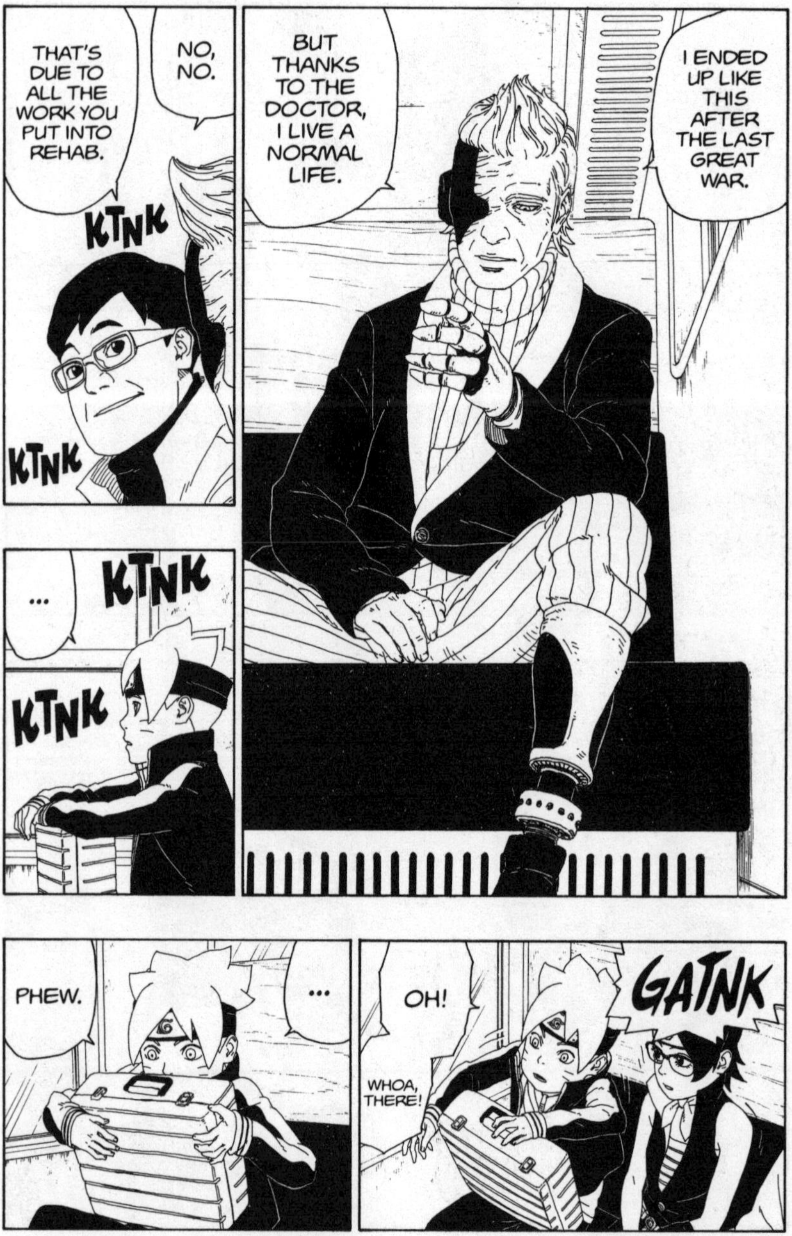
I ENDED UP LIKE THIS AFTER THE LAST GREAT WAR.
BUT THANKS TO THE DOCTOR, I LIVE A NORMAL LIFE.
NO, NO.
THAT'S DUE TO ALL THE WORK YOU PUT INTO REHAB.
KTNK
KTNK
KTNK
...
KTNK
GATNK
OH!
WHOA, THERE!
...
PHEW.

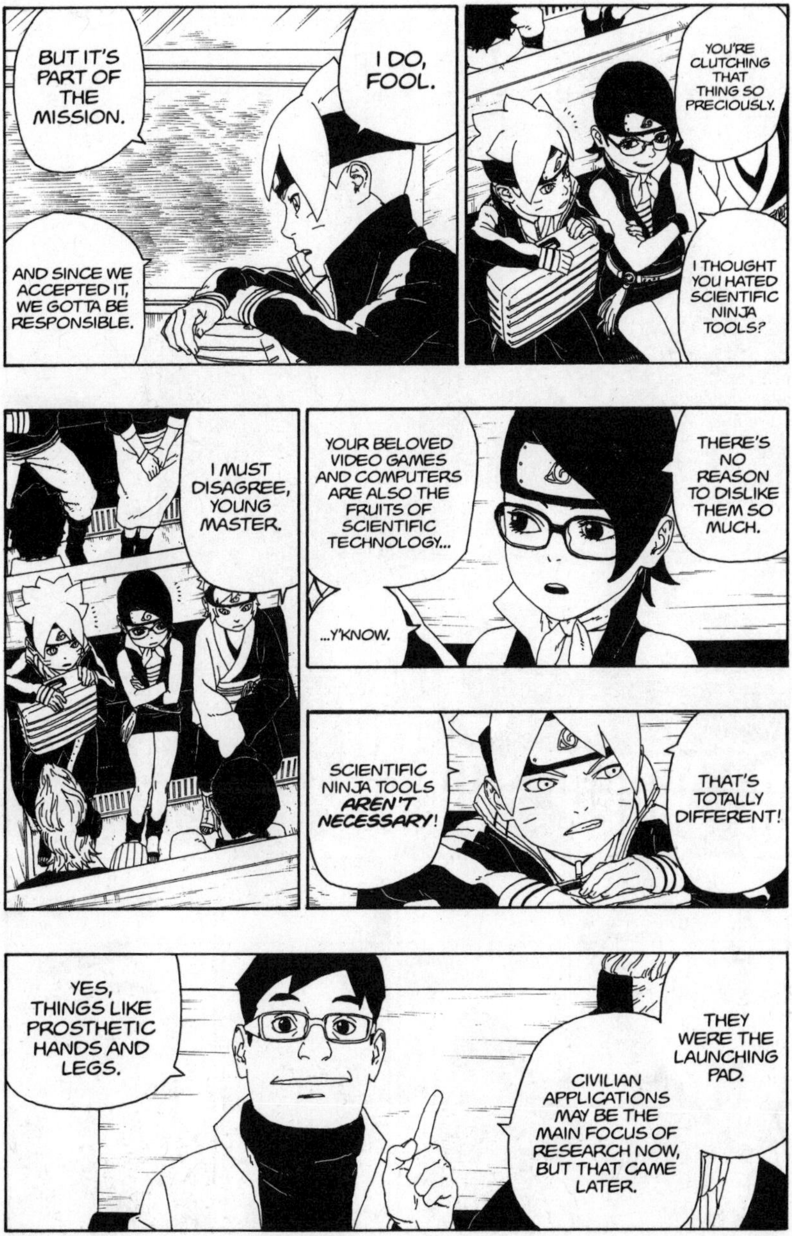
YOU'RE CLUTCHING THAT THING SO PRECIOUSLY.
I THOUGHT YOU HATED SCIENTIFIC NINJA TOOLS?
I DO, FOOL.
BUT IT'S PART OF THE MISSION.
AND SINCE WE ACCEPTED IT, WE GOTTA BE RESPONSIBLE.
THERE'S NO REASON TO DISLIKE THEM SO MUCH.
YOUR BELOVED VIDEO GAMES AND COMPUTERS ARE ALSO THE FRUITS OF SCIENTIFIC TECHNOLOGY...
...Y'KNOW.
THAT'S TOTALLY DIFFERENT!
SCIENTIFIC NINJA TOOLS ***AREN'T NECESSARY***!
I MUST DISAGREE, YOUNG MASTER.
YES, THINGS LIKE PROSTHETIC HANDS AND LEGS.
THEY WERE THE LAUNCHING PAD.
CIVILIAN APPLICATIONS MAY BE THE MAIN FOCUS OF RESEARCH NOW, BUT THAT CAME LATER.

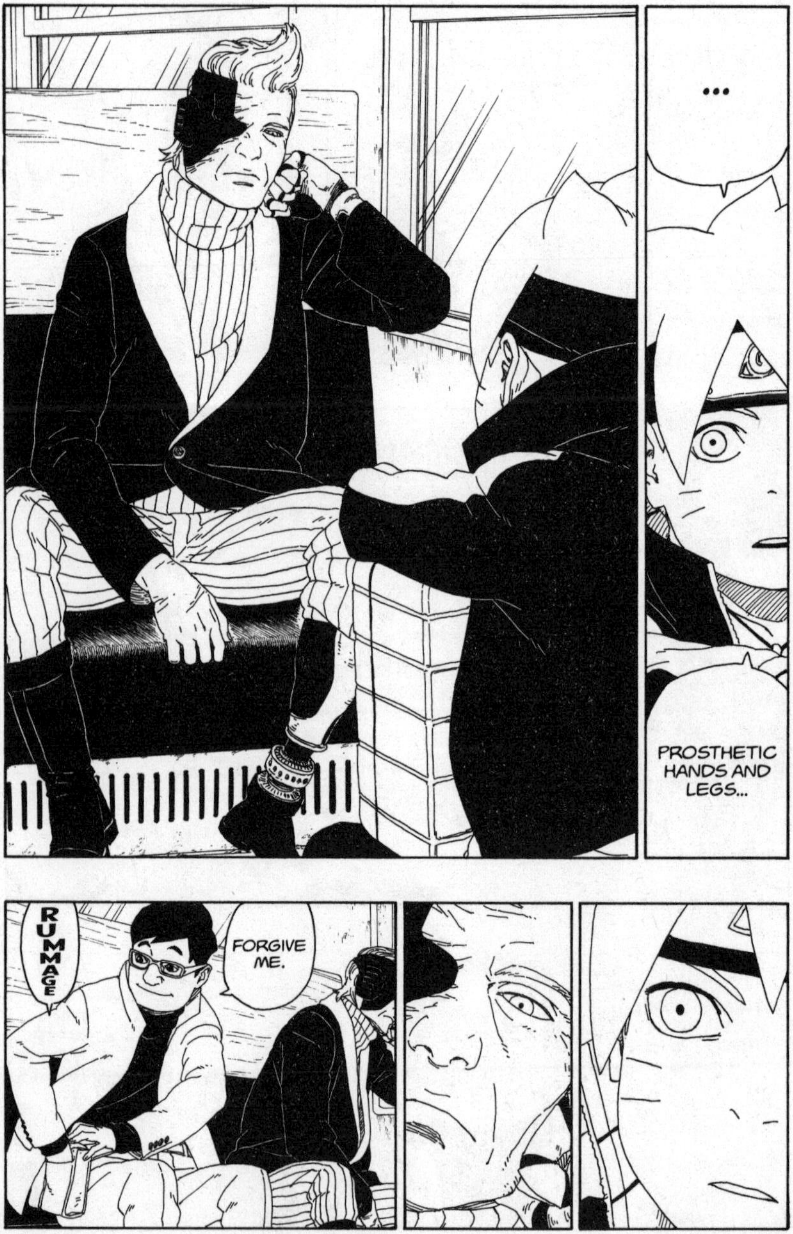
...
PROSTHETIC HANDS AND LEGS...
FORGIVE ME.
RUMMAGE

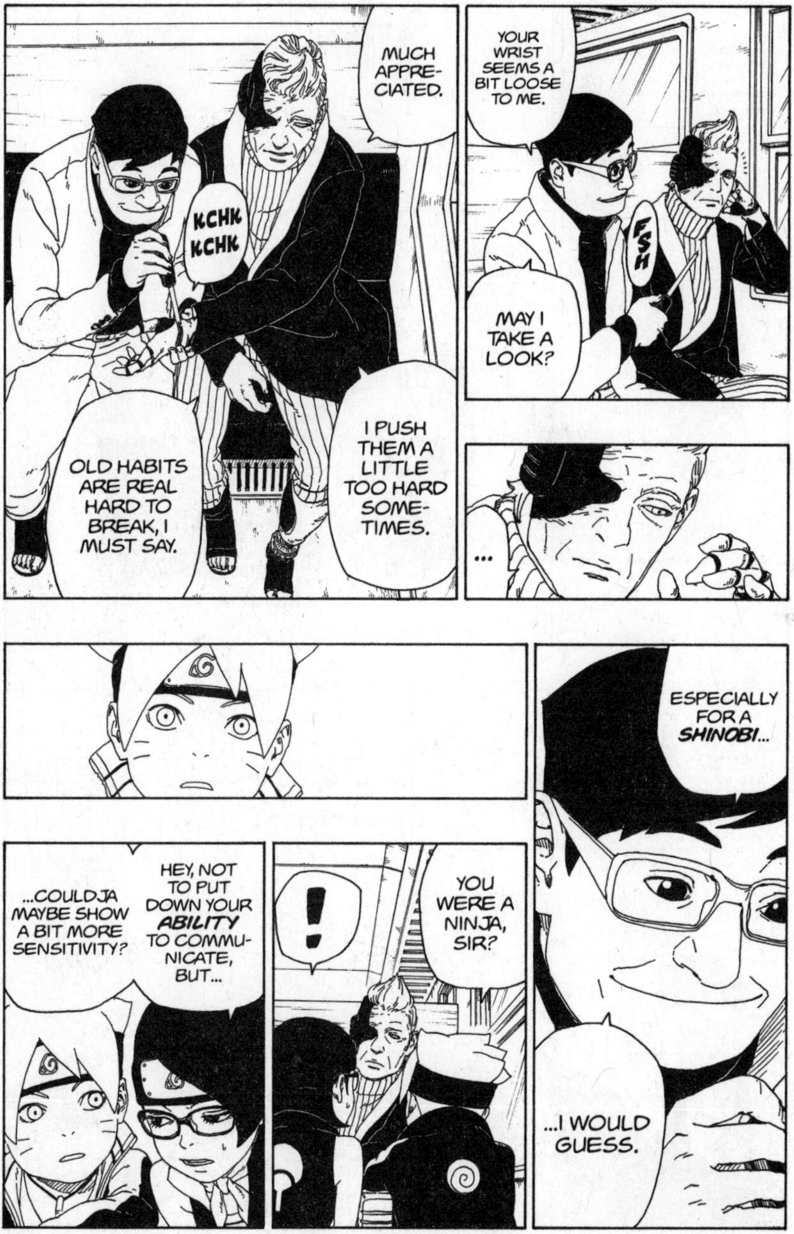
YOUR WRIST SEEMS A BIT LOOSE TO ME.
FSH
MAY I TAKE A LOOK?
...
MUCH APPRECIATED.
KCHK KCHK
I PUSH THEM A LITTLE TOO HARD SOMETIMES.
OLD HABITS ARE REAL HARD TO BREAK, I MUST SAY.
ESPECIALLY FOR A *SHINOBI*...
...I WOULD GUESS.
YOU WERE A NINJA, SIR?
!
HEY, NOT TO PUT DOWN YOUR *ABILITY* TO COMMUNICATE, BUT...
...COULDJA MAYBE SHOW A BIT MORE SENSITIVITY?

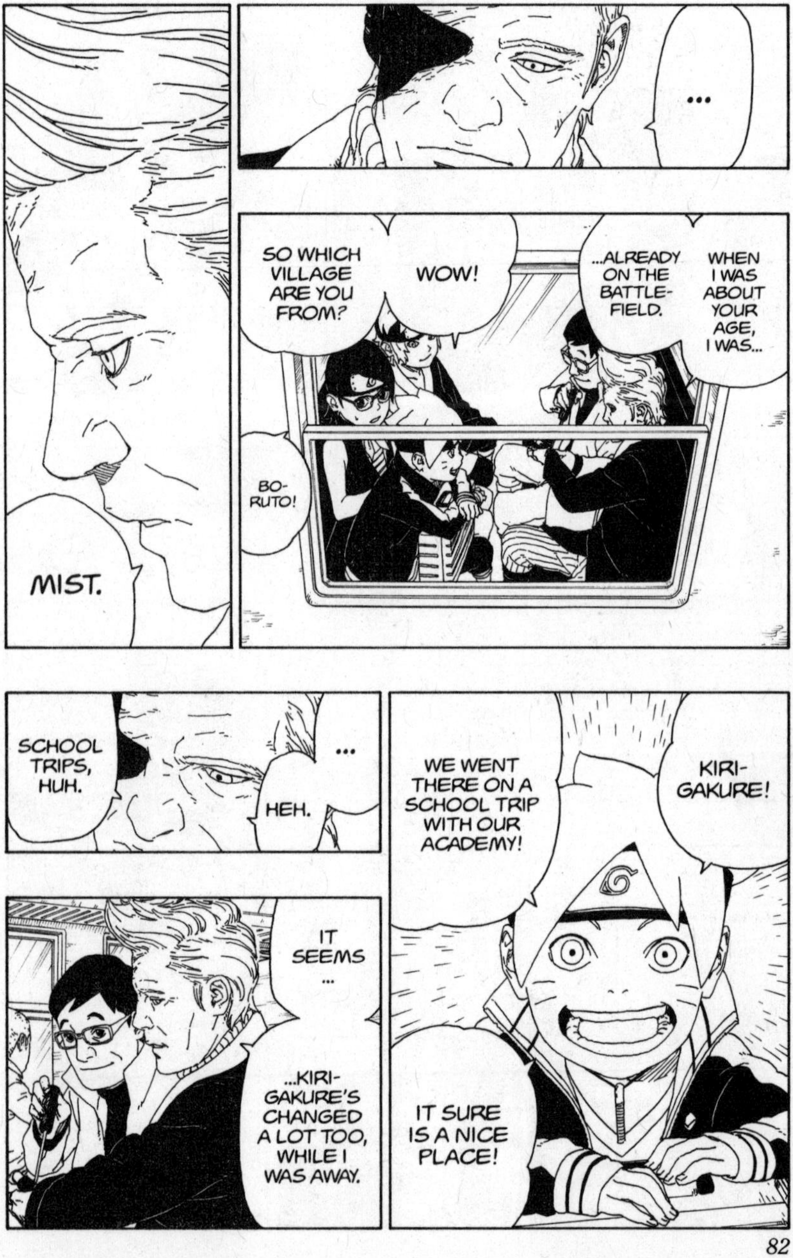
...
WHEN I WAS ABOUT YOUR AGE, I WAS...
...ALREADY ON THE BATTLE-FIELD.
WOW!
SO WHICH VILLAGE ARE YOU FROM?
BO-RUTO!
MIST.
KIRI-GAKURE!
WE WENT THERE ON A SCHOOL TRIP WITH OUR ACADEMY!
IT SURE IS A NICE PLACE!
...
HEH.
SCHOOL TRIPS, HUH.
IT SEEMS ...
...KIRI-GAKURE'S CHANGED A LOT TOO, WHILE I WAS AWAY.

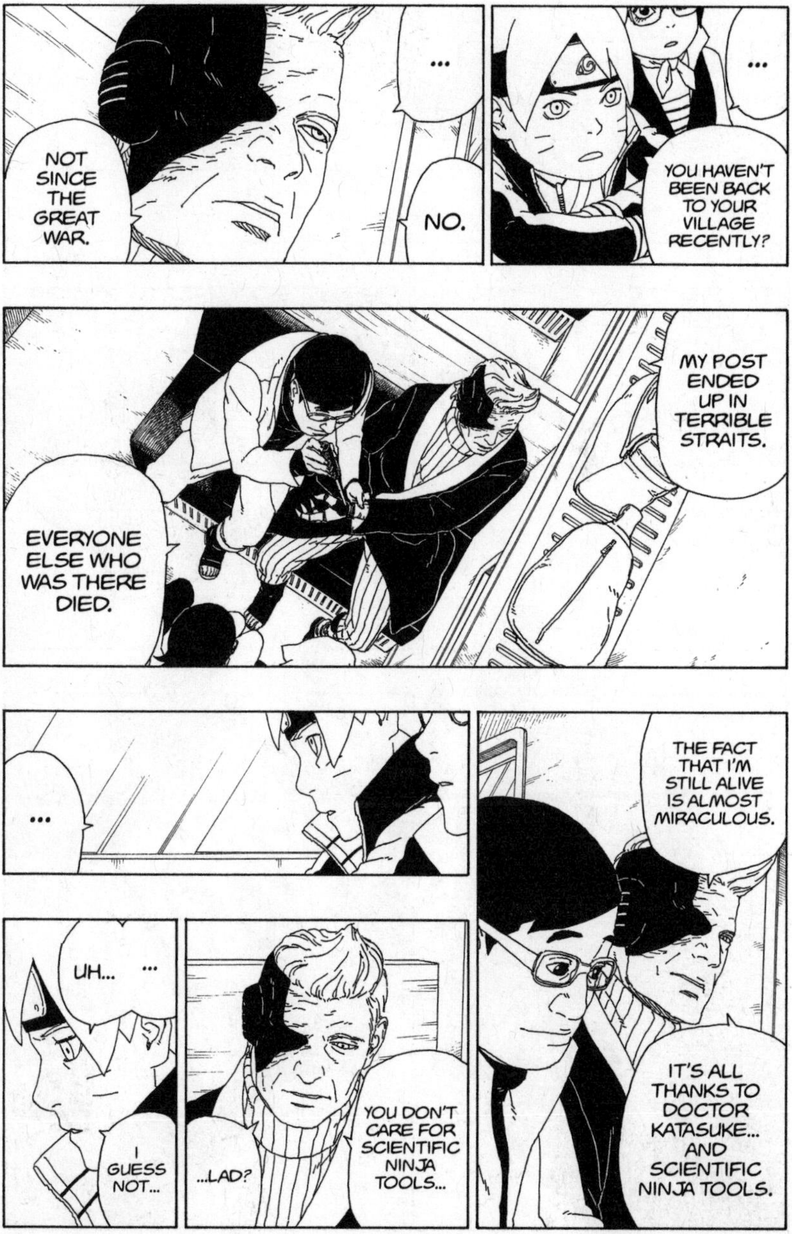
...
YOU HAVEN'T BEEN BACK TO YOUR VILLAGE RECENTLY?
...
NO.
NOT SINCE THE GREAT WAR.
MY POST ENDED UP IN TERRIBLE STRAITS.
EVERYONE ELSE WHO WAS THERE DIED.
THE FACT THAT I'M STILL ALIVE IS ALMOST MIRACULOUS.
IT'S ALL THANKS TO DOCTOR KATASUKE... AND SCIENTIFIC NINJA TOOLS.
...
YOU DON'T CARE FOR SCIENTIFIC NINJA TOOLS...
...LAD?
UH... ...
I GUESS NOT...

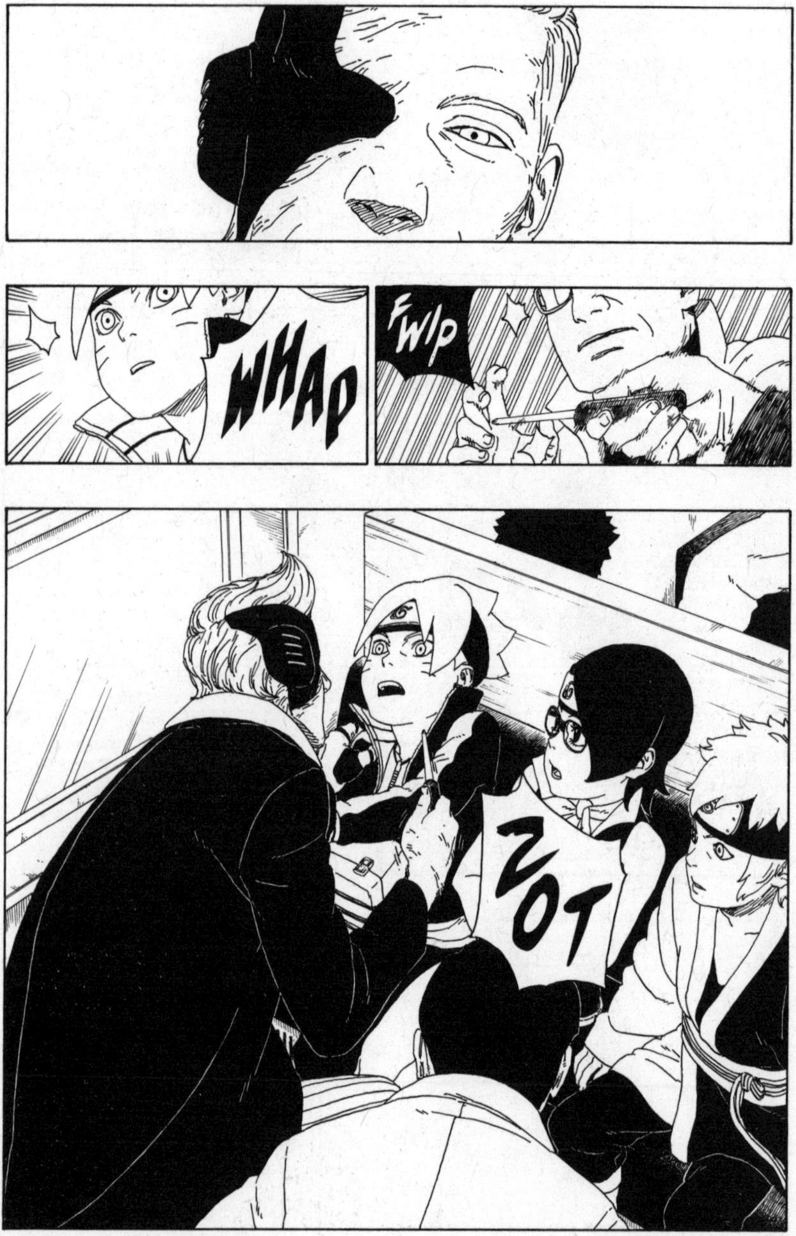
FWIP
WHAP
ZOT

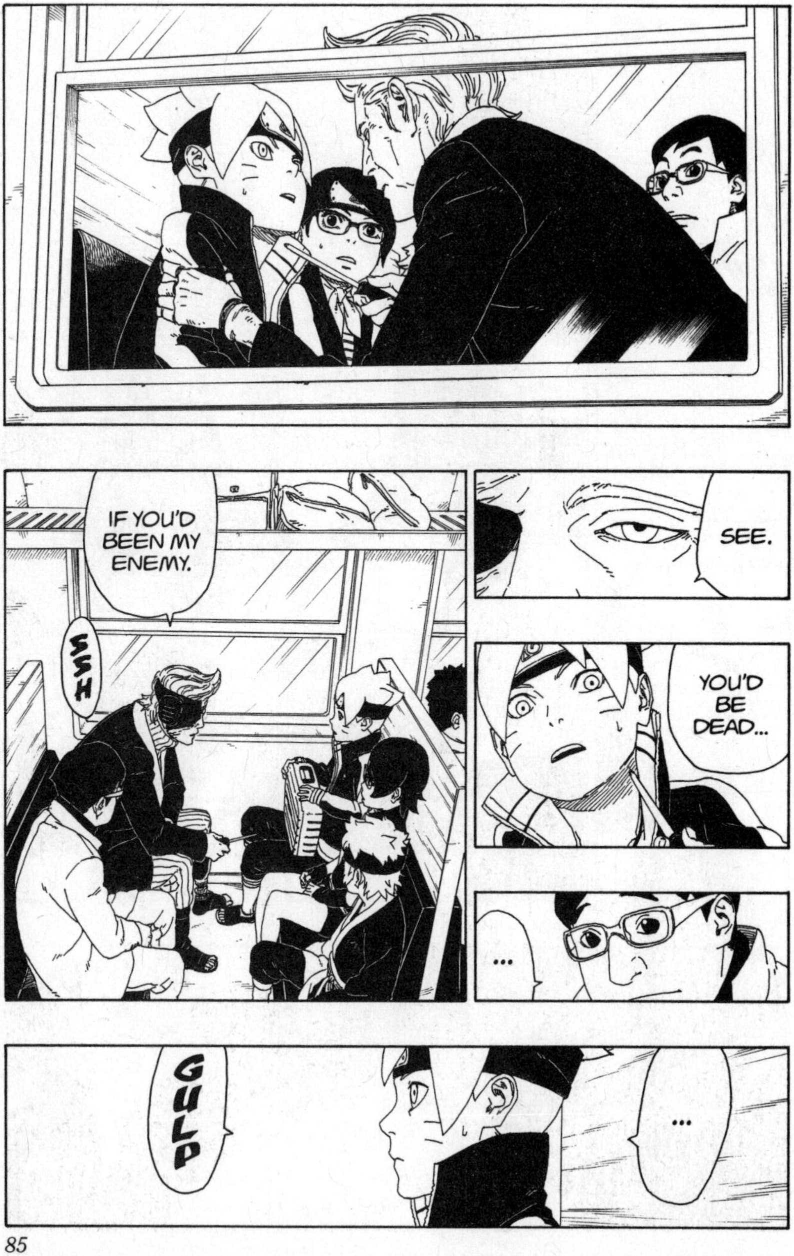
SEE.
YOU'D BE DEAD...
...
SSH
IF YOU'D BEEN MY ENEMY.
...
GULP

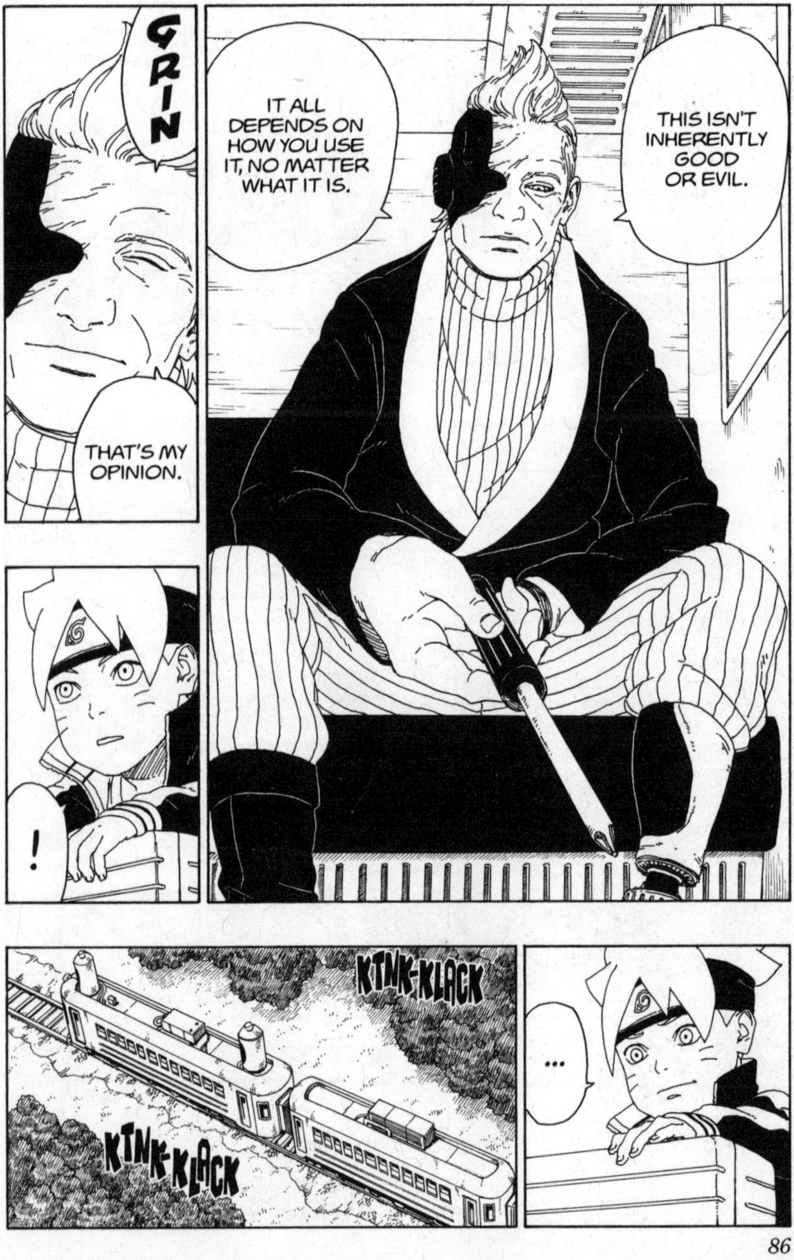
THIS ISN'T INHERENTLY GOOD OR EVIL.
IT ALL DEPENDS ON HOW YOU USE IT, NO MATTER WHAT IT IS.
GRIN
THAT'S MY OPINION.
!
...
KTNK-KLACK
KTNK-KLACK

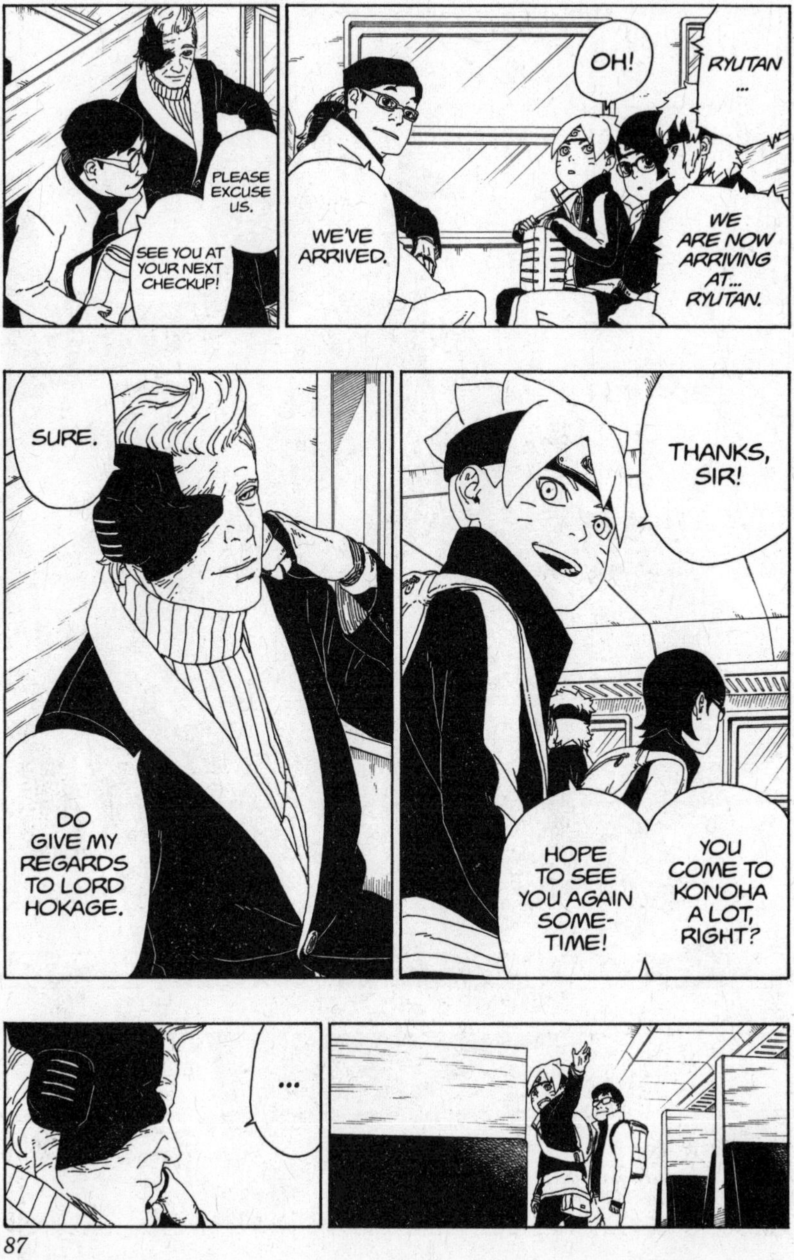
RYUTAN ...
OH!
WE ARE NOW ARRIVING AT... RYUTAN.
WE'VE ARRIVED.
PLEASE EXCUSE US.
SEE YOU AT YOUR NEXT CHECKUP!
THANKS, SIR!
YOU COME TO KONOHA A LOT, RIGHT?
HOPE TO SEE YOU AGAIN SOME-TIME!
SURE.
DO GIVE MY REGARDS TO LORD HOKAGE.
...

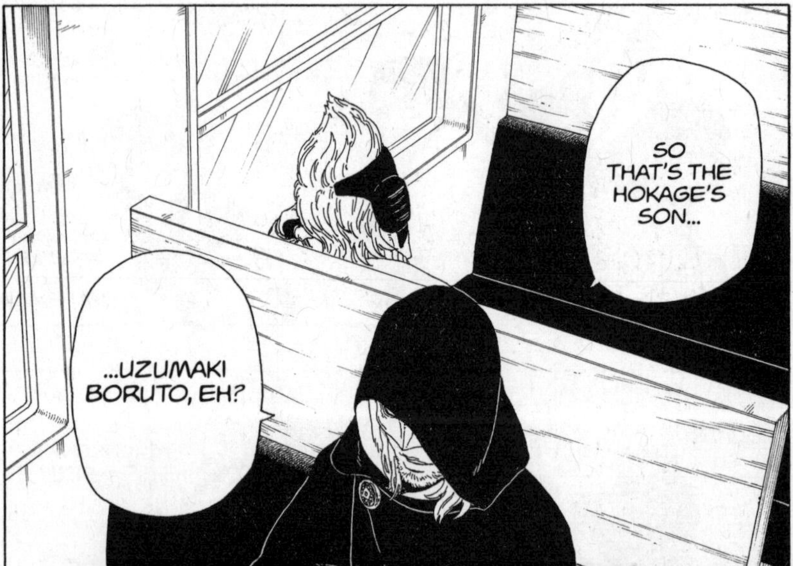
SO THAT'S THE HOKAGE'S SON...
...UZUMAKI BORUTO, EH?

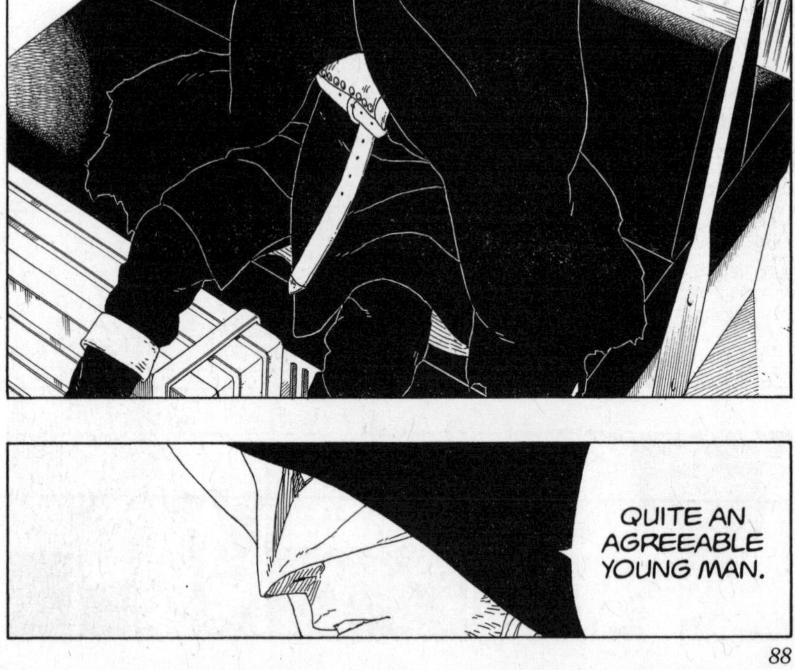
QUITE AN AGREEABLE YOUNG MAN.

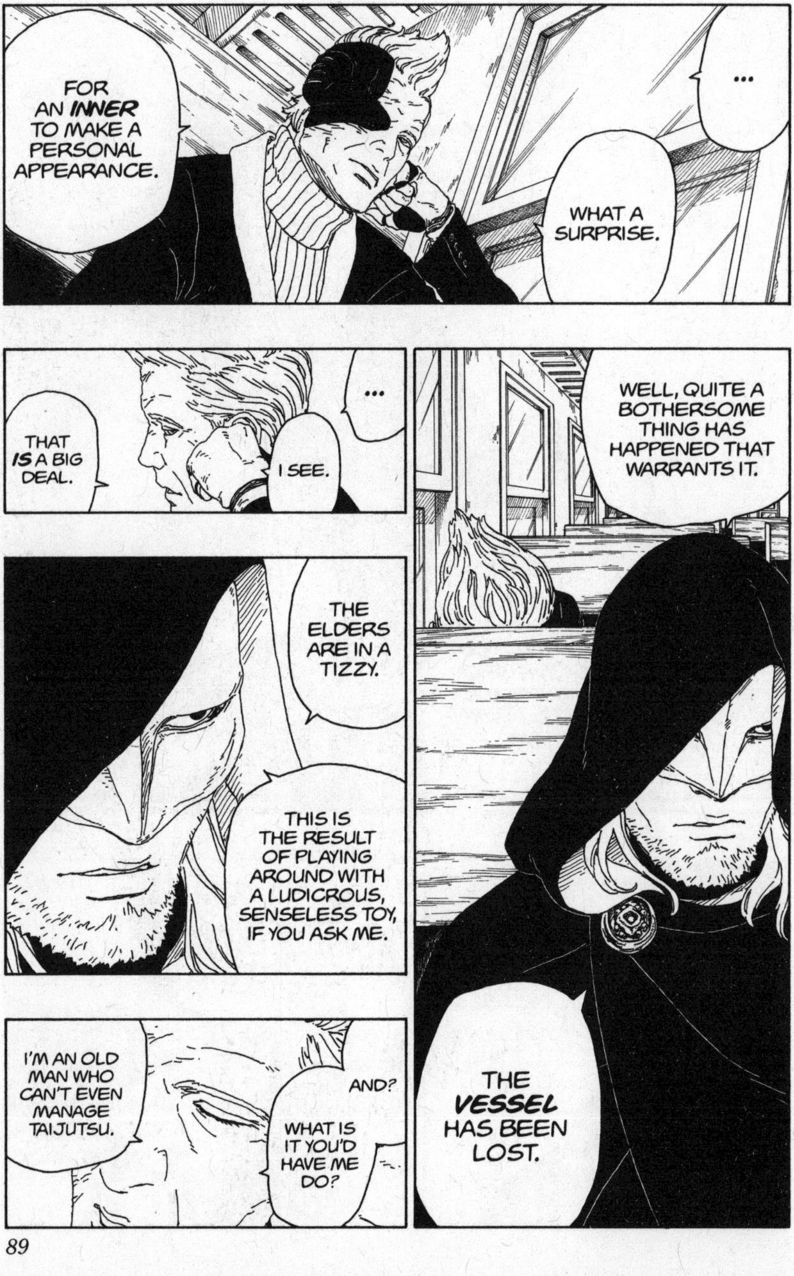
...
WHAT A SURPRISE.
FOR AN **INNER** TO MAKE A PERSONAL APPEARANCE.
WELL, QUITE A BOTHERSOME THING HAS HAPPENED THAT WARRANTS IT.
THE **VESSEL** HAS BEEN LOST.
...
I SEE.
THAT **IS** A BIG DEAL.
THE ELDERS ARE IN A TIZZY.
THIS IS THE RESULT OF PLAYING AROUND WITH A LUDICROUS, SENSELESS TOY, IF YOU ASK ME.
AND?
WHAT IS IT YOU'D HAVE ME DO?
I'M AN OLD MAN WHO CAN'T EVEN MANAGE TAIJUTSU.

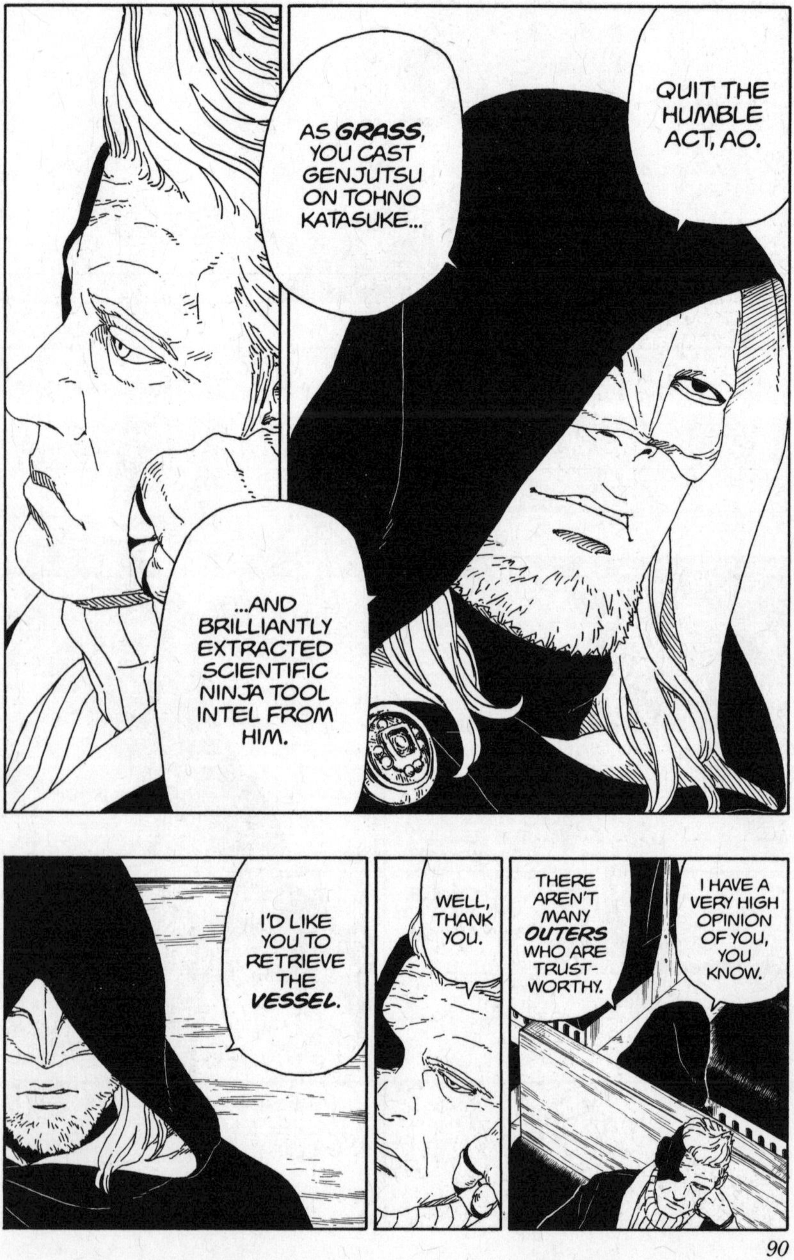
QUIT THE HUMBLE ACT, AO.
AS **GRASS**, YOU CAST GENJUTSU ON TOHNO KATASUKE...
...AND BRILLIANTLY EXTRACTED SCIENTIFIC NINJA TOOL INTEL FROM HIM.
I HAVE A VERY HIGH OPINION OF YOU, YOU KNOW.
THERE AREN'T MANY **OUTERS** WHO ARE TRUST-WORTHY.
WELL, THANK YOU.
I'D LIKE YOU TO RETRIEVE THE **VESSEL**.

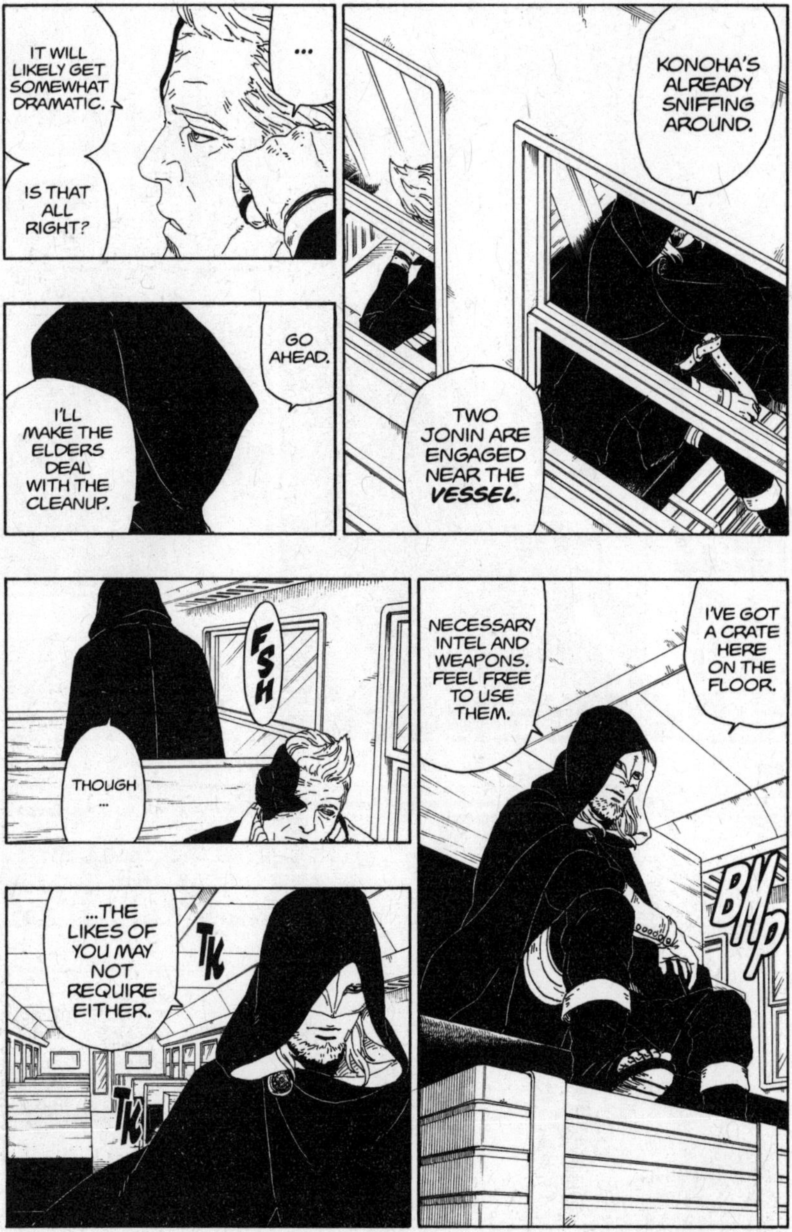
KONOHA'S ALREADY SNIFFING AROUND.
TWO JONIN ARE ENGAGED NEAR THE *VESSEL*.
...
IT WILL LIKELY GET SOMEWHAT DRAMATIC.
IS THAT ALL RIGHT?
GO AHEAD.
I'LL MAKE THE ELDERS DEAL WITH THE CLEANUP.
I'VE GOT A CRATE HERE ON THE FLOOR.
NECESSARY INTEL AND WEAPONS. FEEL FREE TO USE THEM.
BMP
FSH
THOUGH ...
TK
...THE LIKES OF YOU MAY NOT REQUIRE EITHER.
TK

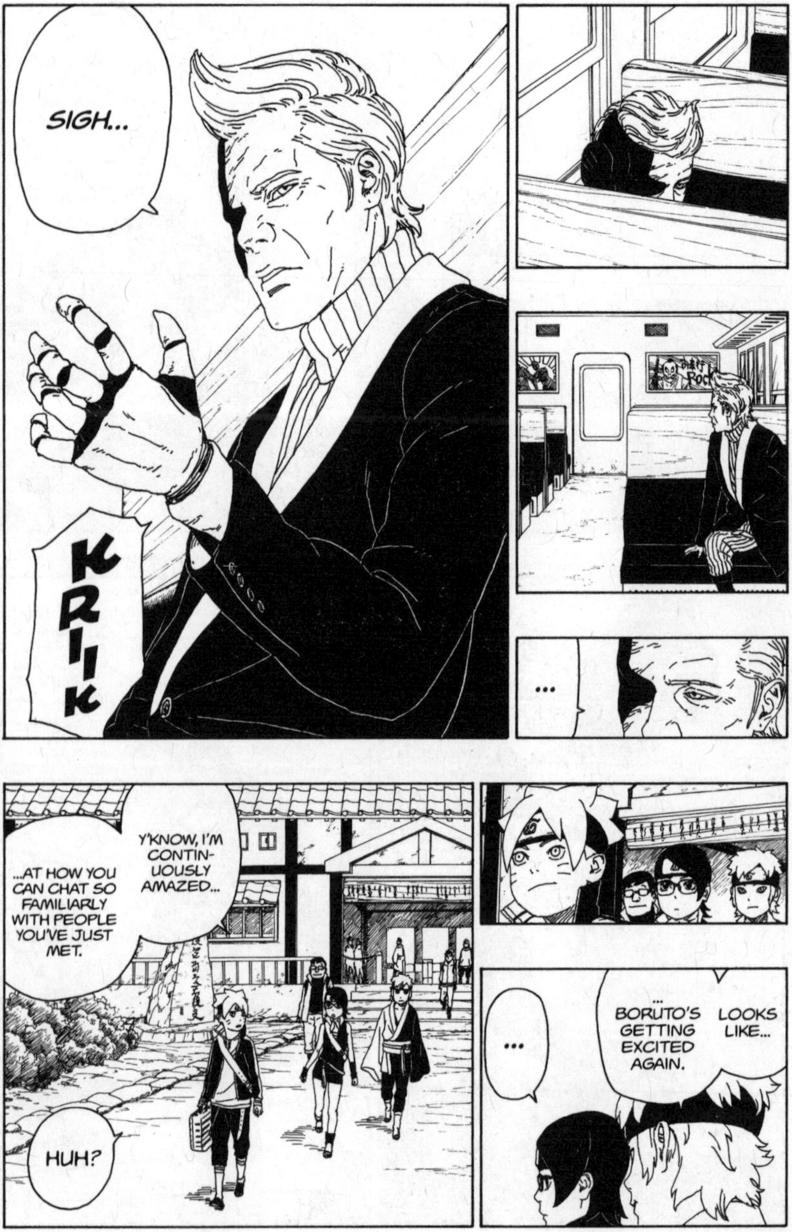
...
SIGH...
KRIIK
LOOKS LIKE... ...BORUTO'S GETTING EXCITED AGAIN.
...
Y'KNOW, I'M CONTIN-UOUSLY AMAZED...
...AT HOW YOU CAN CHAT SO FAMILIARLY WITH PEOPLE YOU'VE JUST MET.
HUH?

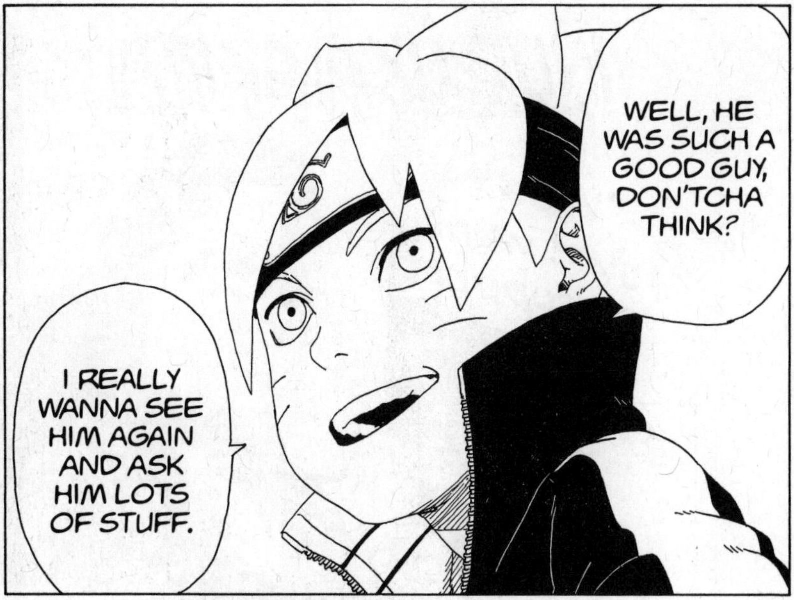
WELL, HE WAS SUCH A GOOD GUY, DON'TCHA THINK?
I REALLY WANNA SEE HIM AGAIN AND ASK HIM LOTS OF STUFF.
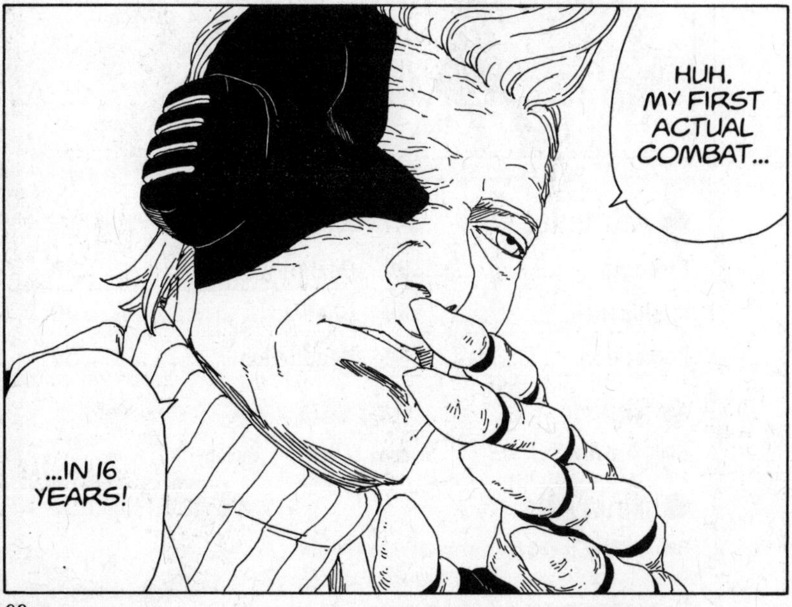
HUH. MY FIRST ACTUAL COMBAT...
...IN 16 YEARS!

NINJA ENCYCLOPEDIA · ENTRY 14

INUZUKA AKITA

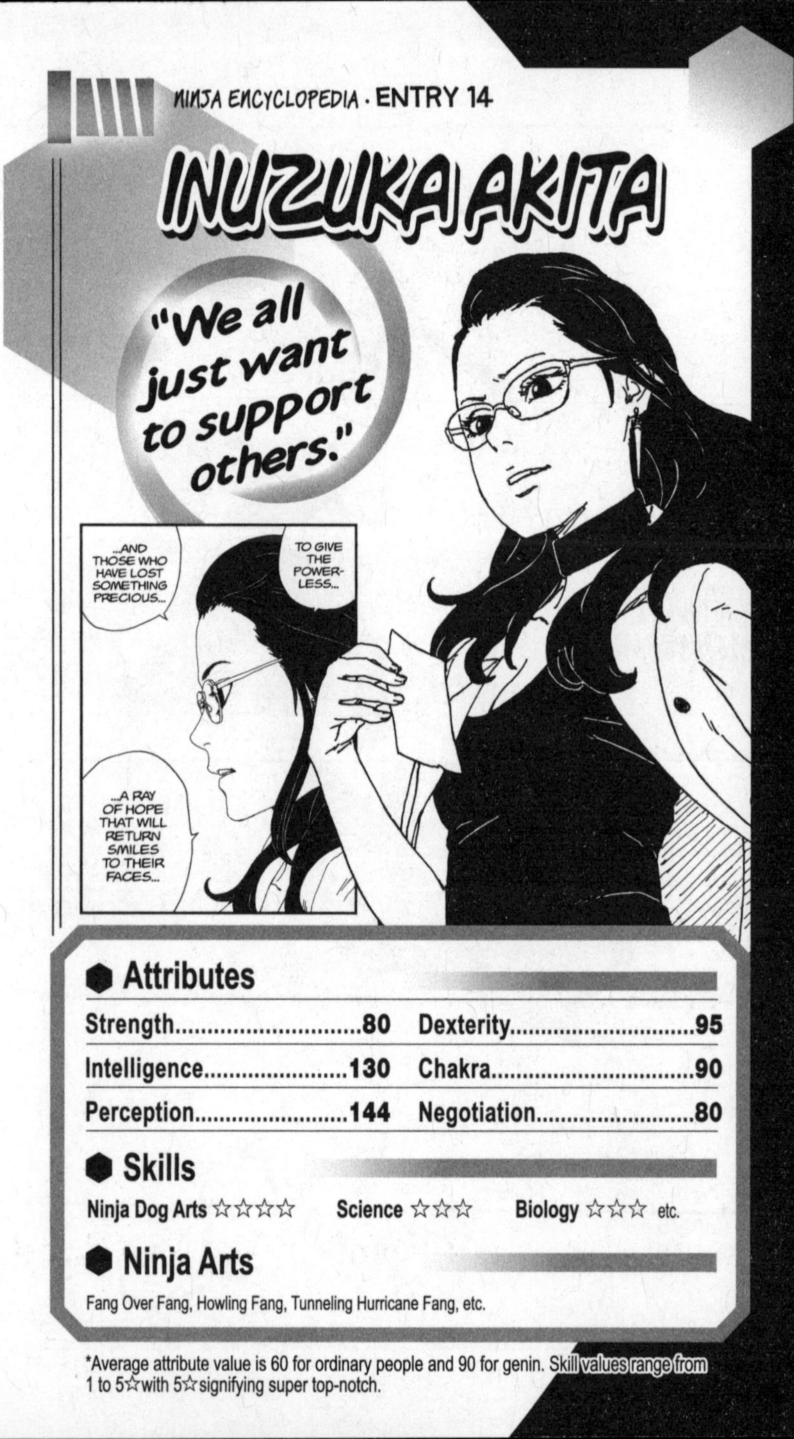
"We all just want to support others."
TO GIVE THE POWERLESS...
...AND THOSE WHO HAVE LOST SOMETHING PRECIOUS...
...A RAY OF HOPE THAT WILL RETURN SMILES TO THEIR FACES...

Attributes

Strength	80	Dexterity	95
Intelligence	130	Chakra	90
Perception	144	Negotiation	80

Skills

Ninja Dog Arts ☆☆☆☆ Science ☆☆☆ Biology ☆☆☆ etc.

Ninja Arts

Fang Over Fang, Howling Fang, Tunneling Hurricane Fang, etc.

*Average attribute value is 60 for ordinary people and 90 for genin. Skill values range from 1 to 5☆ with 5☆ signifying super top-notch.

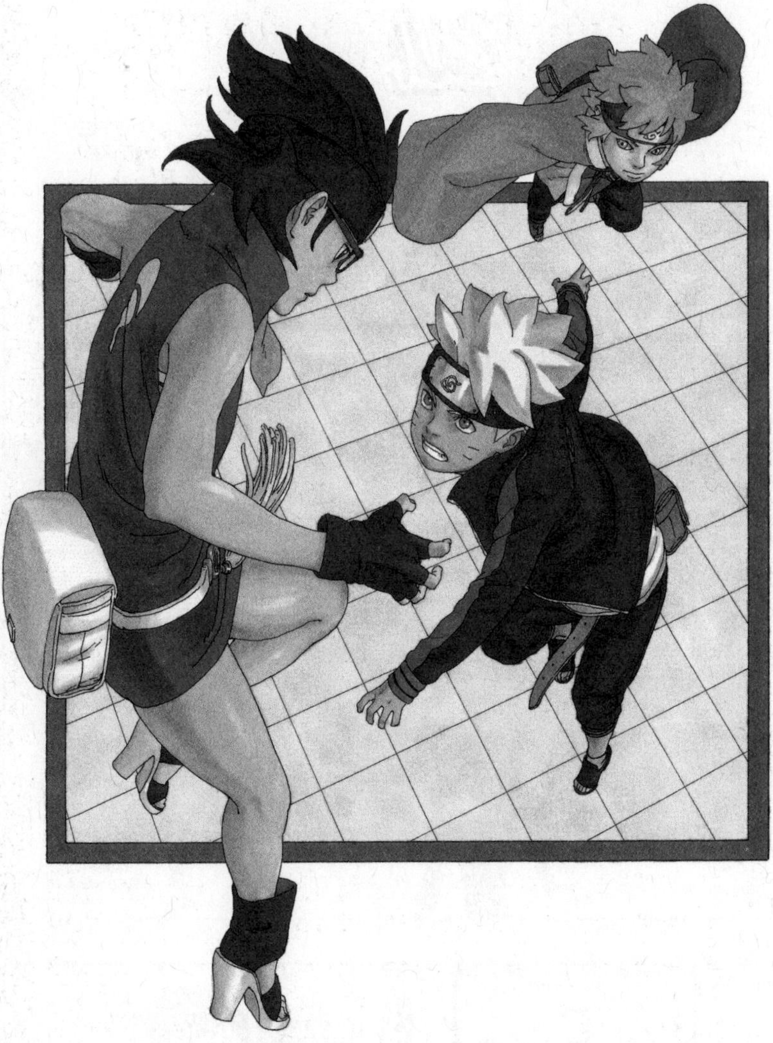

Number 18: The Hand

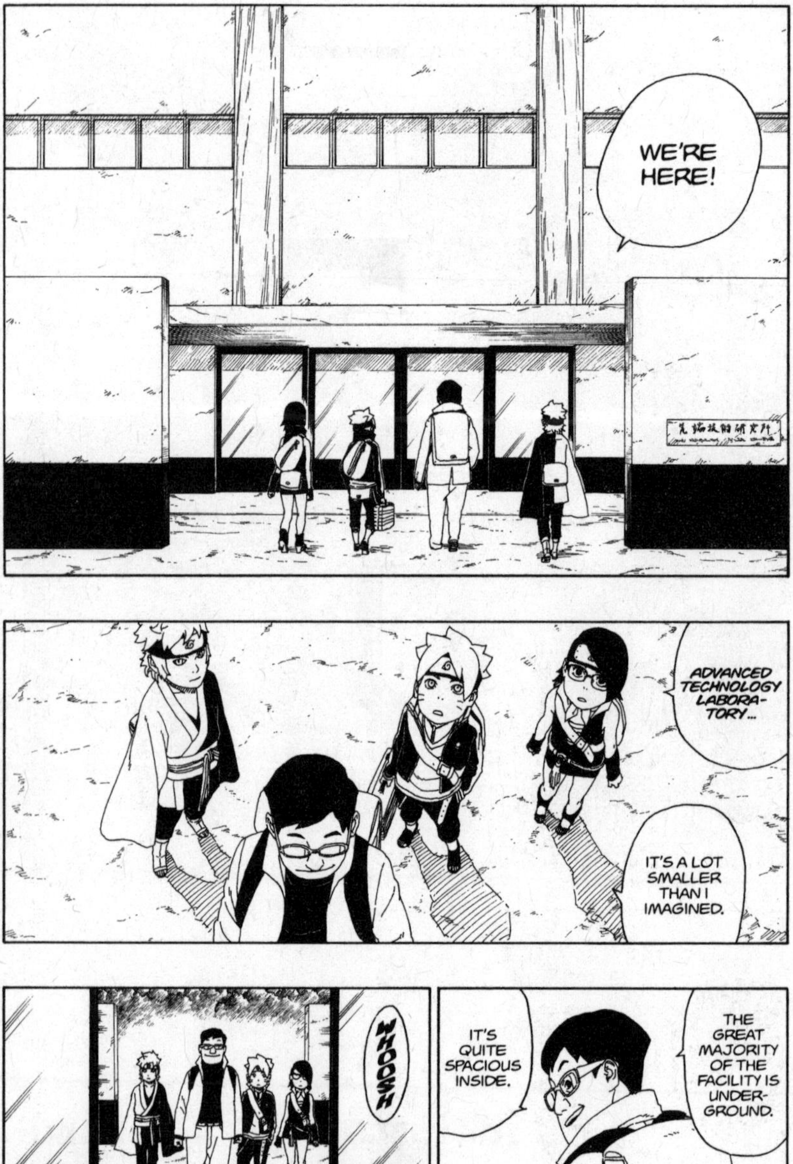
WE'RE HERE!
ADVANCED TECHNOLOGY LABORA-TORY...
IT'S A LOT SMALLER THAN I IMAGINED.
THE GREAT MAJORITY OF THE FACILITY IS UNDER-GROUND.
IT'S QUITE SPACIOUS INSIDE.
WHOOSH

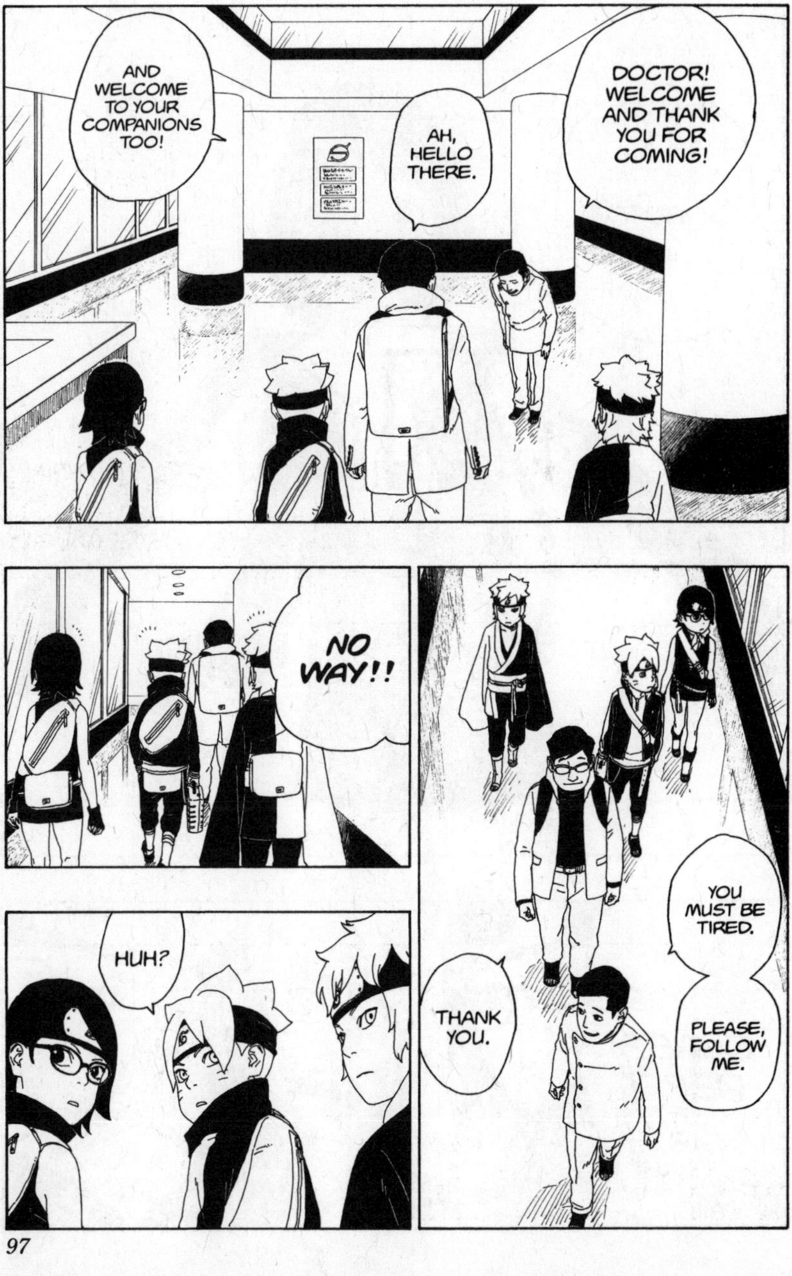
DOCTOR! WELCOME AND THANK YOU FOR COMING!
AH, HELLO THERE.
AND WELCOME TO YOUR COMPANIONS TOO!
YOU MUST BE TIRED.
PLEASE, FOLLOW ME.
THANK YOU.
NO WAY!!
HUH?

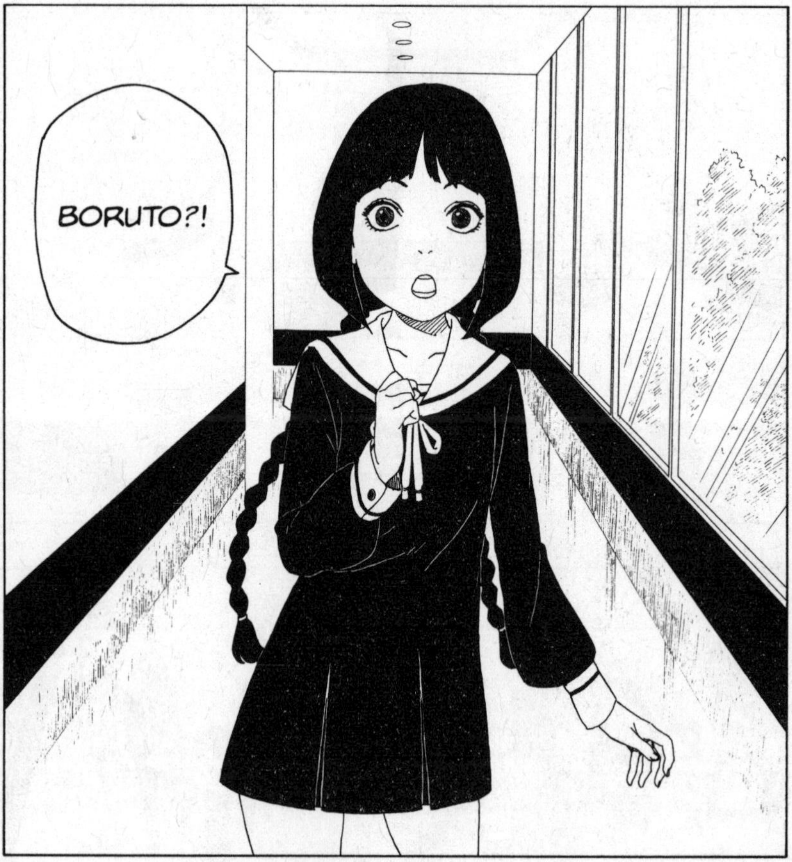
BORUTO?!
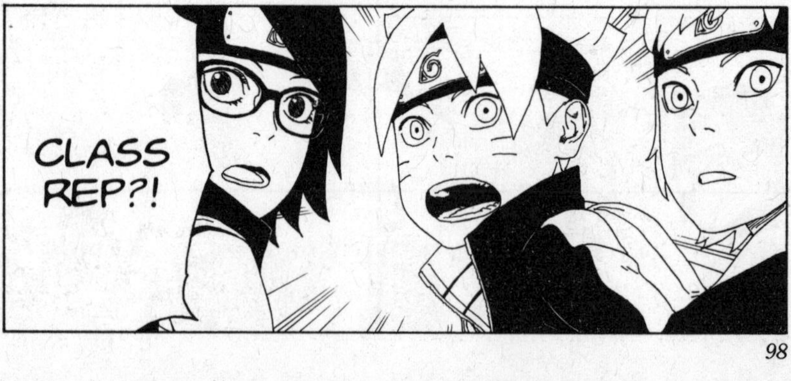
CLASS REP?!

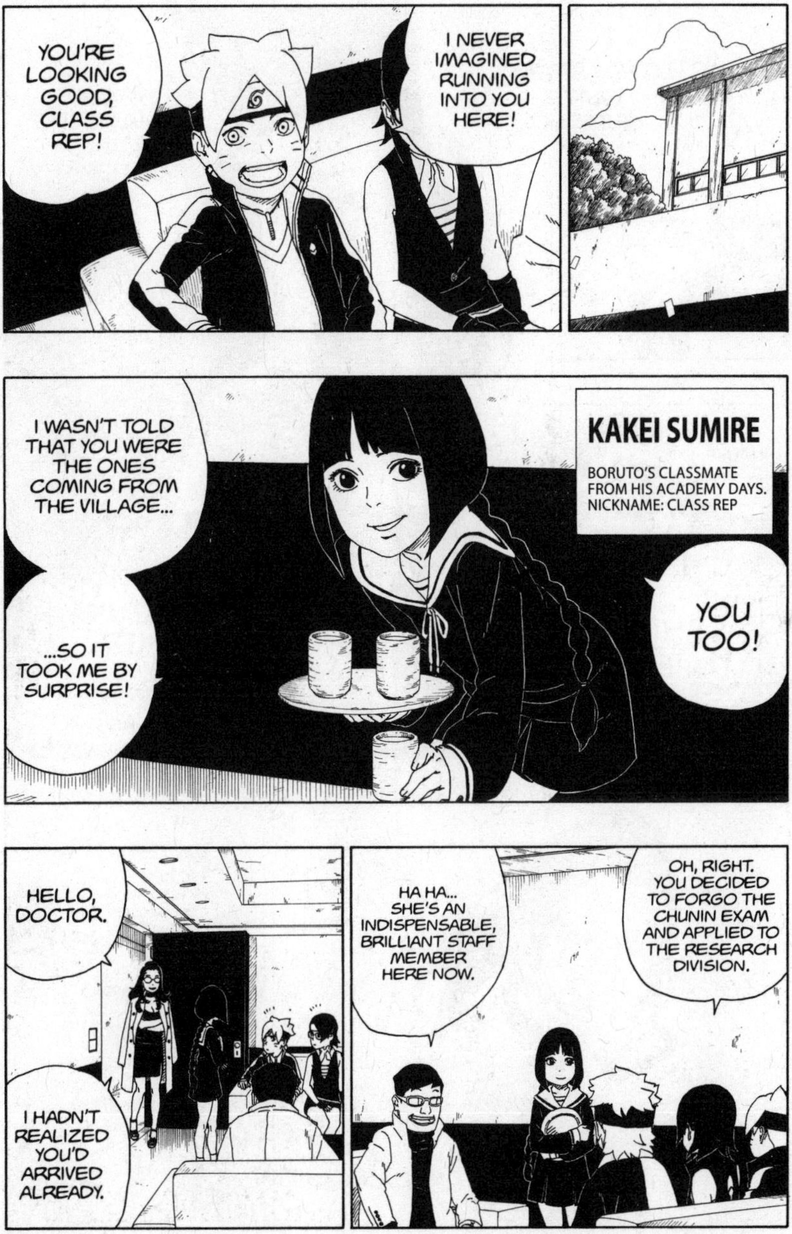
I NEVER IMAGINED RUNNING INTO YOU HERE!
YOU'RE LOOKING GOOD, CLASS REP!
KAKEI SUMIRE
BORUTO'S CLASSMATE FROM HIS ACADEMY DAYS. NICKNAME: CLASS REP
YOU TOO!
I WASN'T TOLD THAT YOU WERE THE ONES COMING FROM THE VILLAGE...
...SO IT TOOK ME BY SURPRISE!
OH, RIGHT. YOU DECIDED TO FORGO THE CHUNIN EXAM AND APPLIED TO THE RESEARCH DIVISION.
HA HA... SHE'S AN INDISPENSABLE, BRILLIANT STAFF MEMBER HERE NOW.
HELLO, DOCTOR.
I HADN'T REALIZED YOU'D ARRIVED ALREADY.

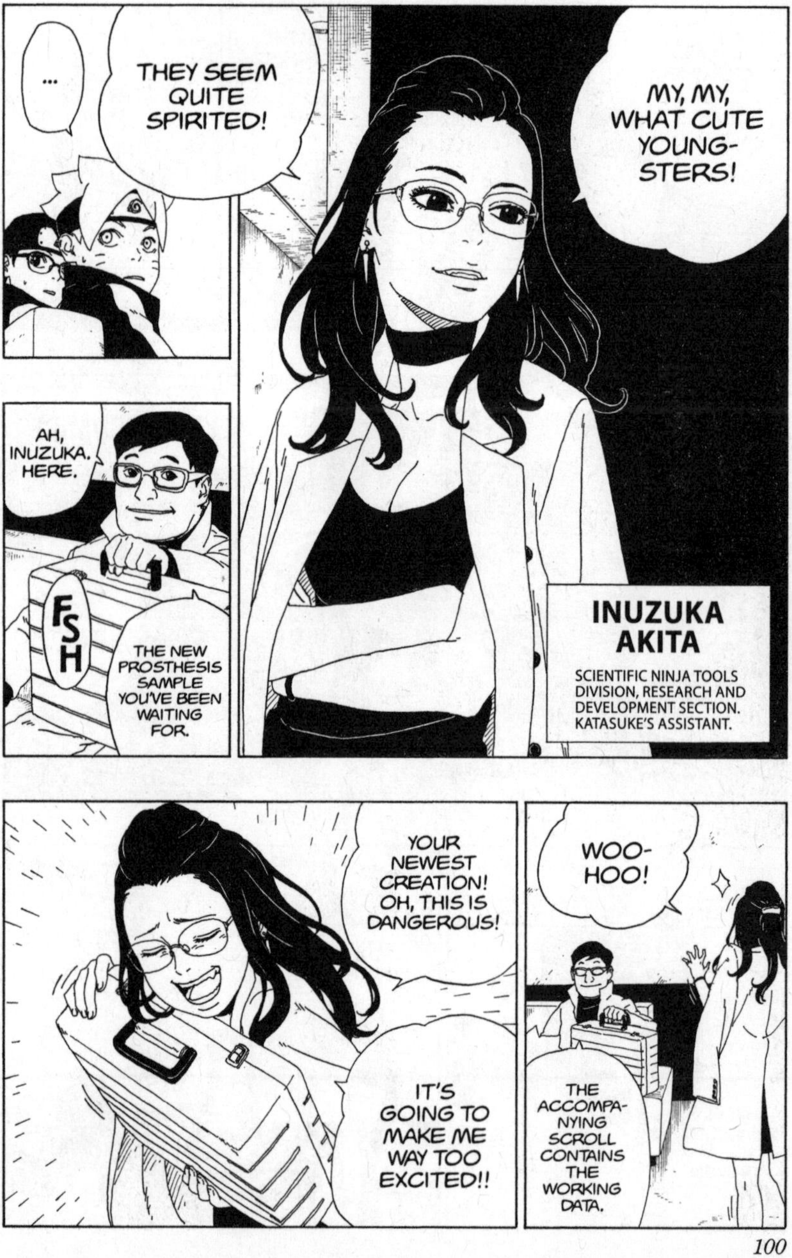
MY, MY, WHAT CUTE YOUNGSTERS!
INUZUKA AKITA
SCIENTIFIC NINJA TOOLS DIVISION, RESEARCH AND DEVELOPMENT SECTION. KATASUKE'S ASSISTANT.
THEY SEEM QUITE SPIRITED!
...
AH, INUZUKA. HERE.
FSH
THE NEW PROSTHESIS SAMPLE YOU'VE BEEN WAITING FOR.
WOO-HOO!
THE ACCOMPANYING SCROLL CONTAINS THE WORKING DATA.
YOUR NEWEST CREATION! OH, THIS IS DANGEROUS!
IT'S GOING TO MAKE ME WAY TOO EXCITED!!

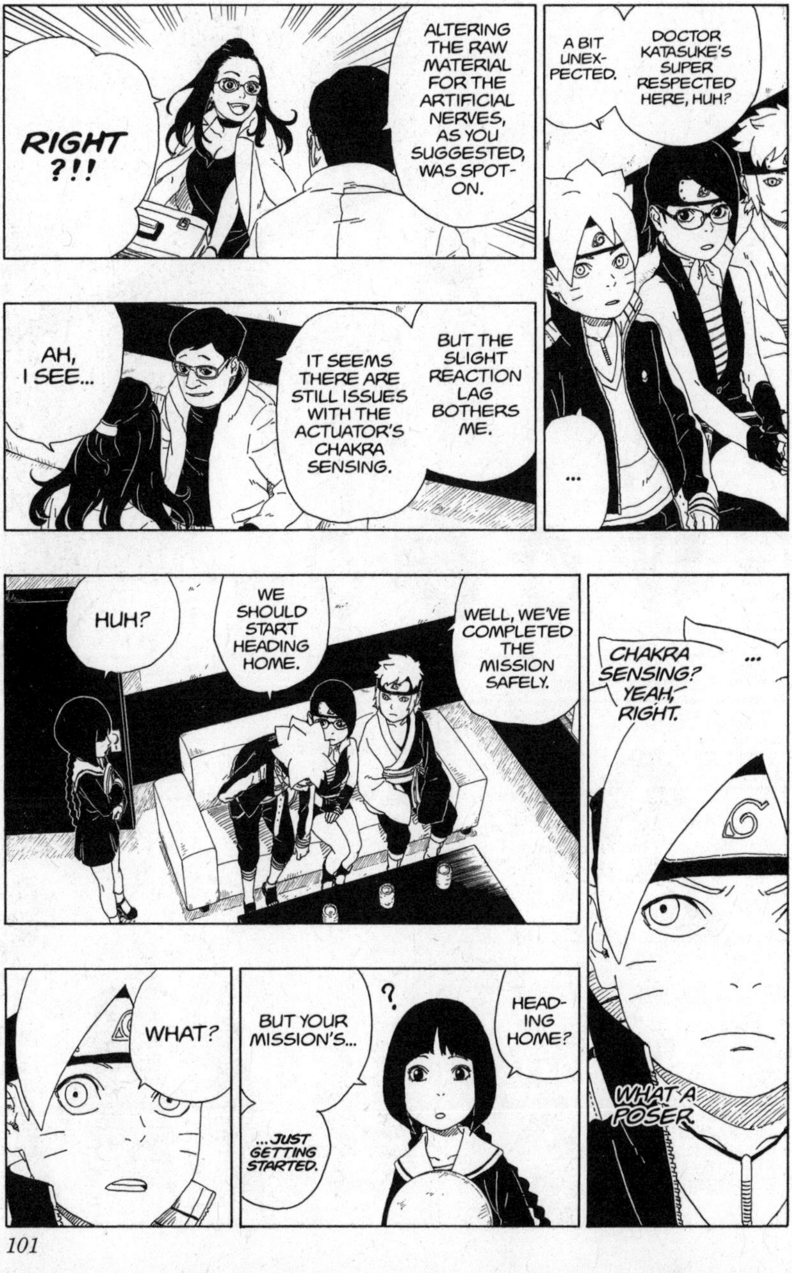
DOCTOR KATASUKE'S SUPER RESPECTED HERE, HUH?
A BIT UNEX-PECTED.
...
ALTERING THE RAW MATERIAL FOR THE ARTIFICIAL NERVES, AS YOU SUGGESTED, WAS SPOT-ON.
RIGHT?!!
BUT THE SLIGHT REACTION LAG BOTHERS ME.
IT SEEMS THERE ARE STILL ISSUES WITH THE ACTUATOR'S CHAKRA SENSING.
AH, I SEE...
...
CHAKRA SENSING? YEAH, RIGHT.
WHAT A POSER.
WELL, WE'VE COMPLETED THE MISSION SAFELY.
WE SHOULD START HEADING HOME.
HUH?
HEAD-ING HOME?
?
BUT YOUR MISSION'S...
...JUST GETTING STARTED.
WHAT?

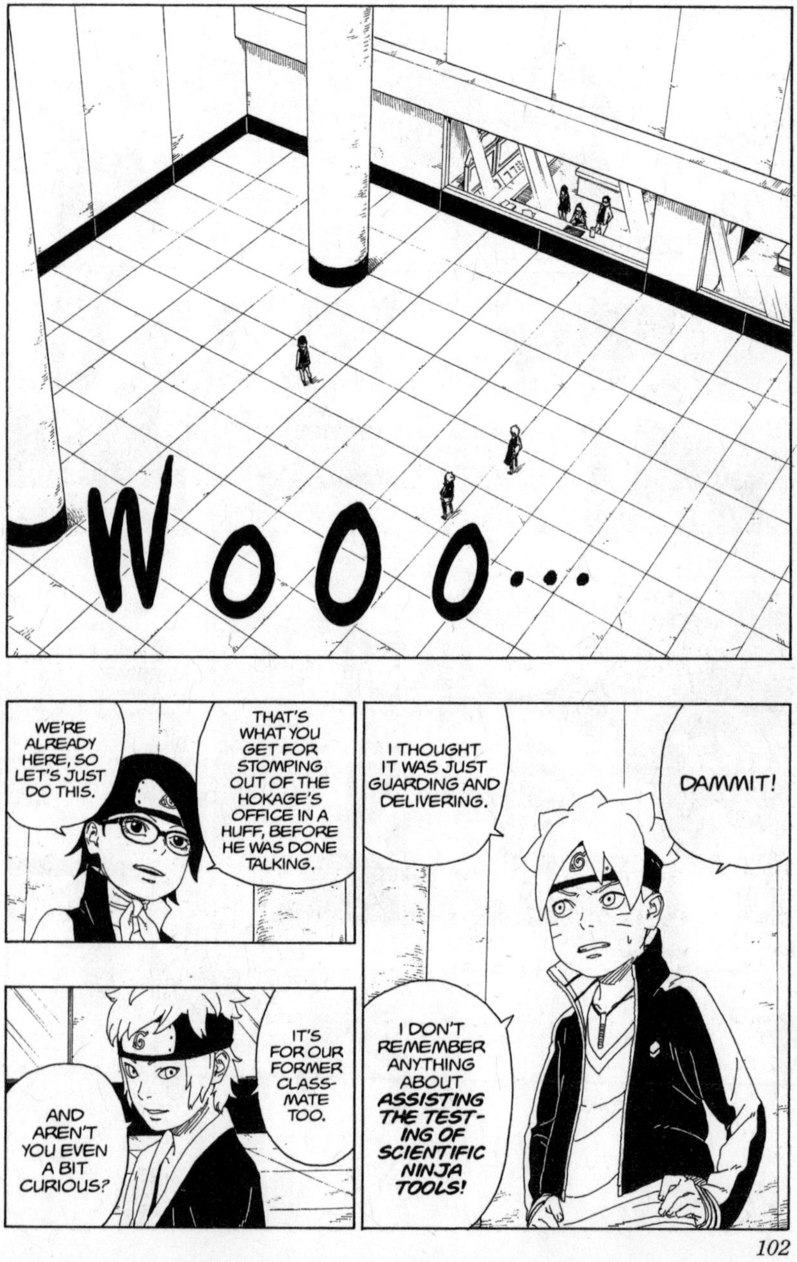
WOOO...
DAMMIT!
I THOUGHT IT WAS JUST GUARDING AND DELIVERING.
I DON'T REMEMBER ANYTHING ABOUT *ASSISTING THE TESTING OF SCIENTIFIC NINJA TOOLS!*
THAT'S WHAT YOU GET FOR STOMPING OUT OF THE HOKAGE'S OFFICE IN A HUFF, BEFORE HE WAS DONE TALKING.
WE'RE ALREADY HERE, SO LET'S JUST DO THIS.
IT'S FOR OUR FORMER CLASSMATE TOO.
AND AREN'T YOU EVEN A BIT CURIOUS?

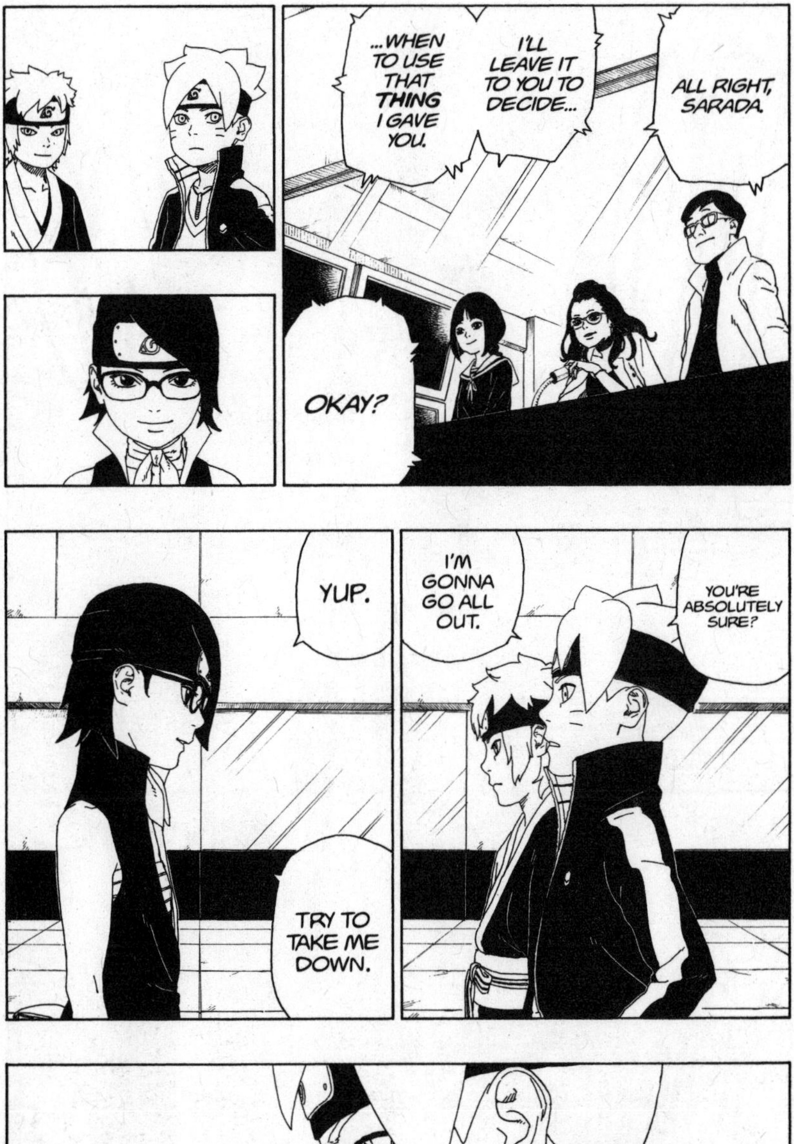
ALL RIGHT, SARADA.
I'LL LEAVE IT TO YOU TO DECIDE...
...WHEN TO USE THAT THING I GAVE YOU.
OKAY?
YOU'RE ABSOLUTELY SURE?
I'M GONNA GO ALL OUT.
YUP.
TRY TO TAKE ME DOWN.

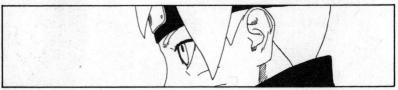

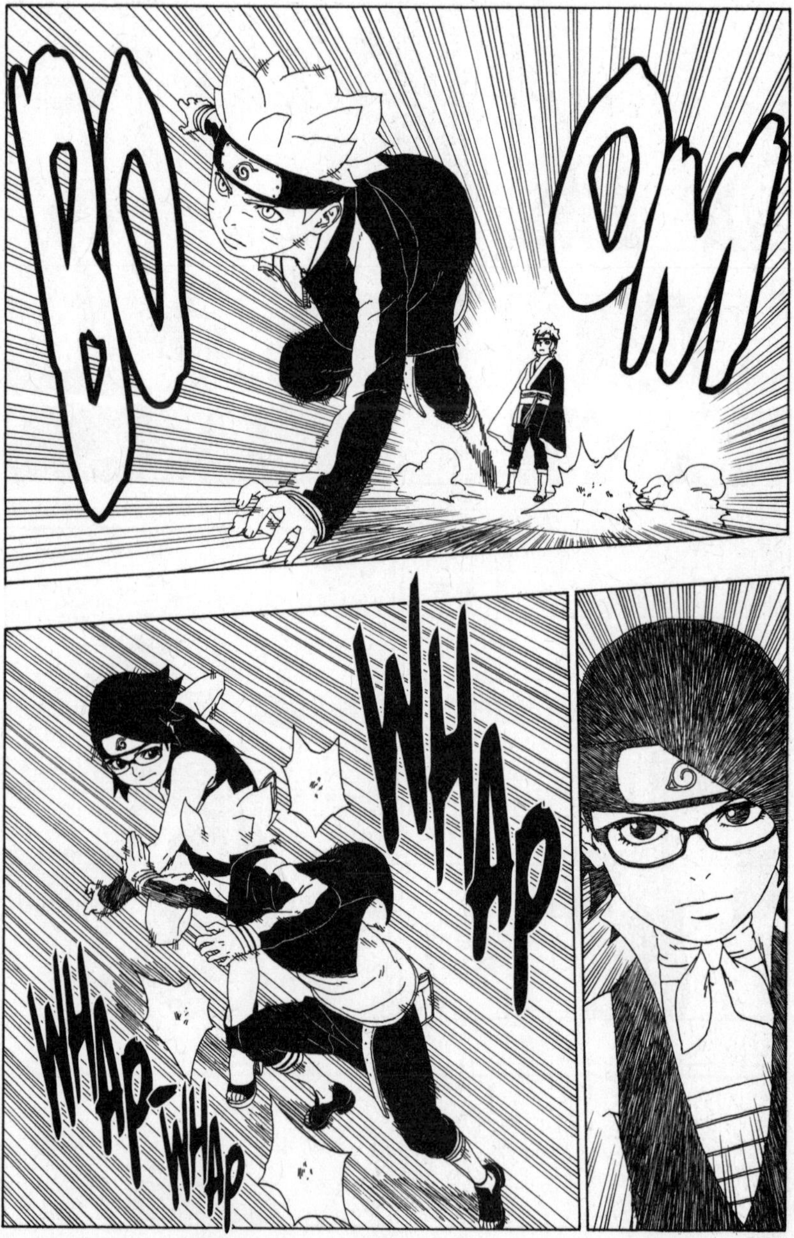
BOOM
WHAP
WHAP-WHAP

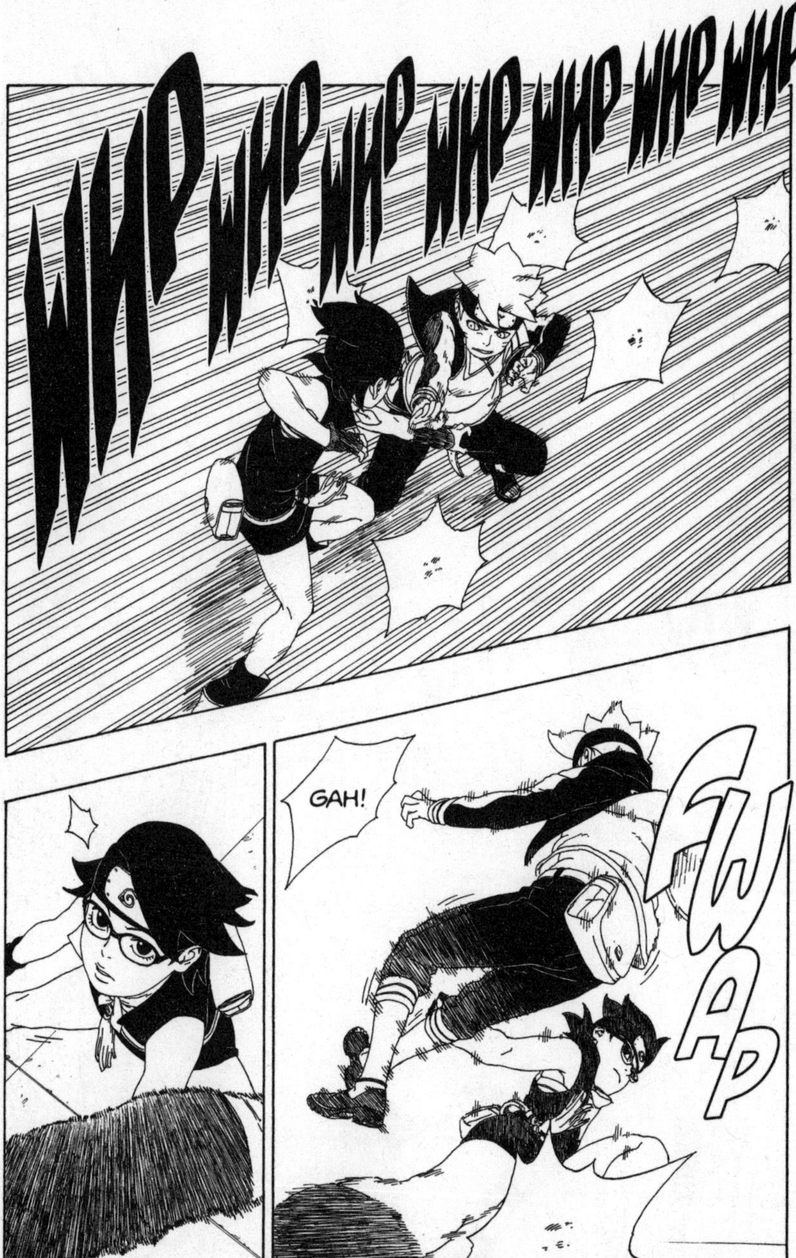
WHIP WHIP WHIP WHIP WHIP WHIP WHIP WHIP
FWAP
GAH!

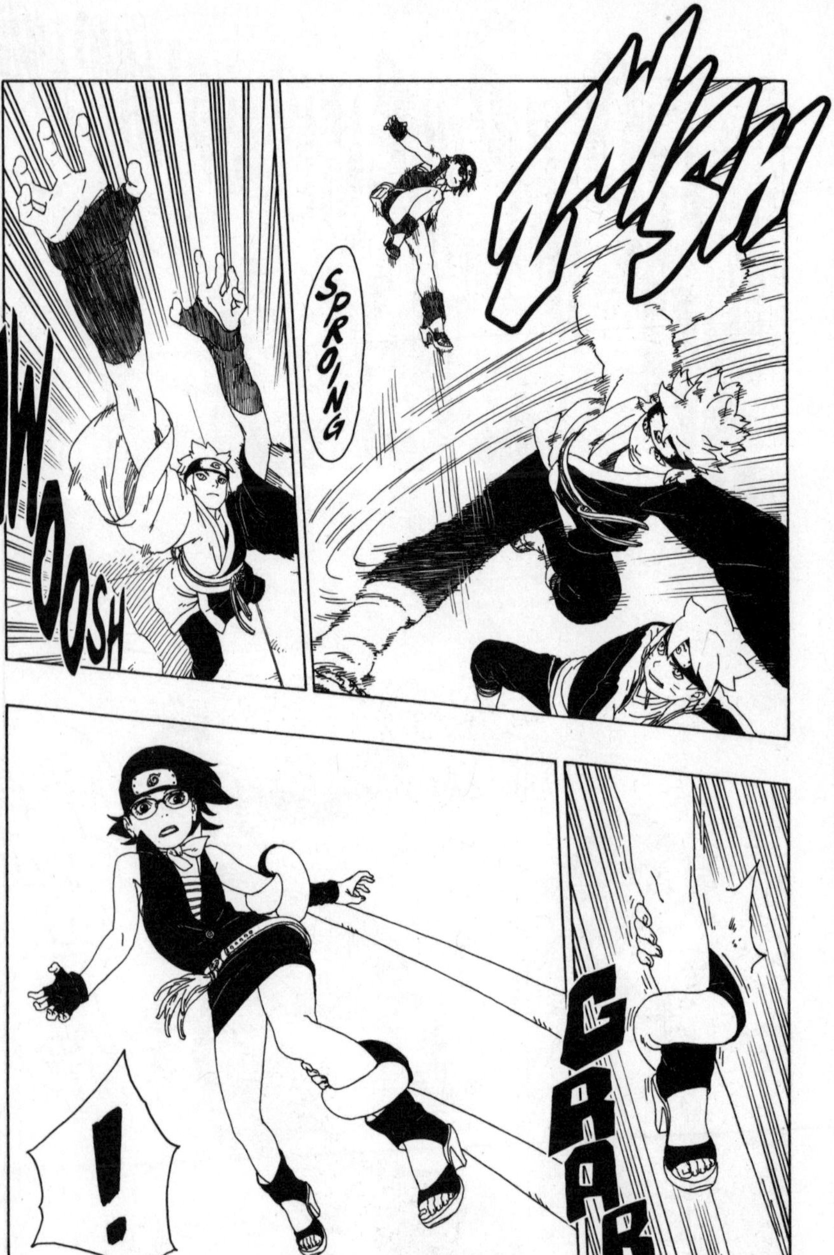
SPROING
WOOSH
GRAB
!

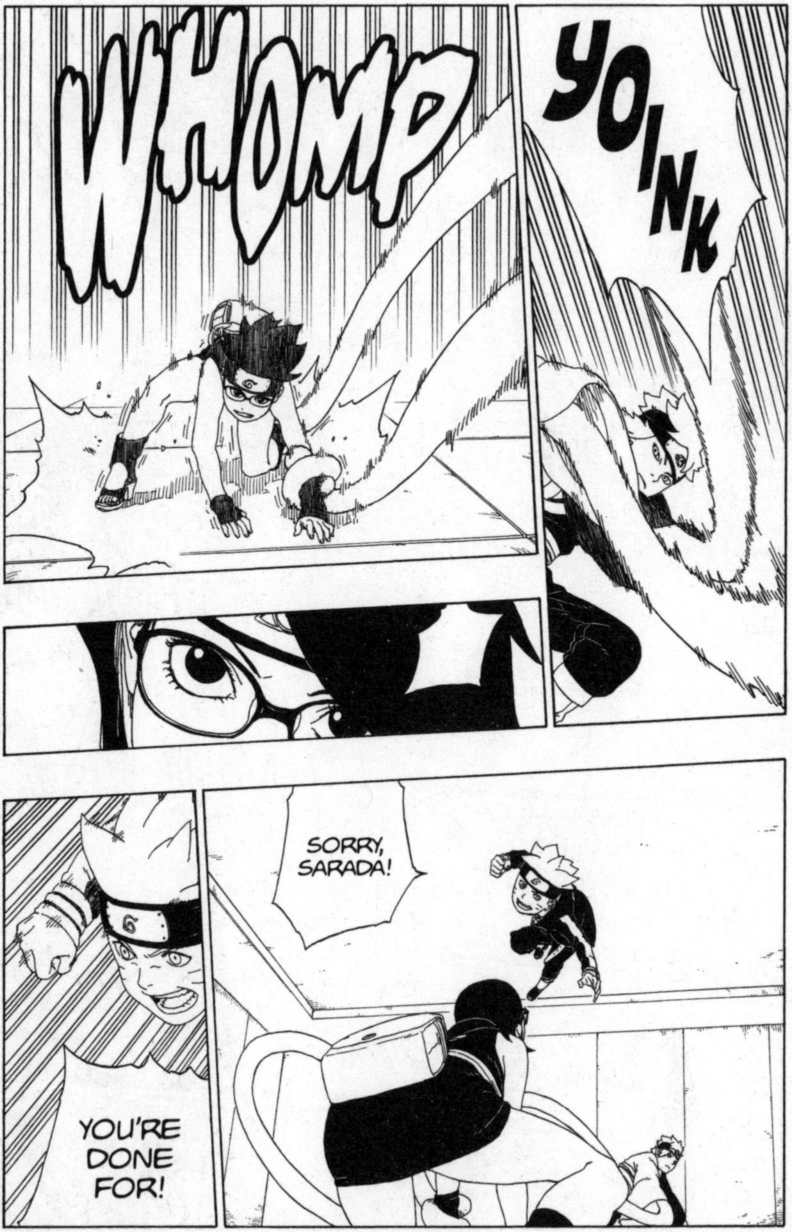
YOINK
WHOMP
SORRY, SARADA!
YOU'RE DONE FOR!

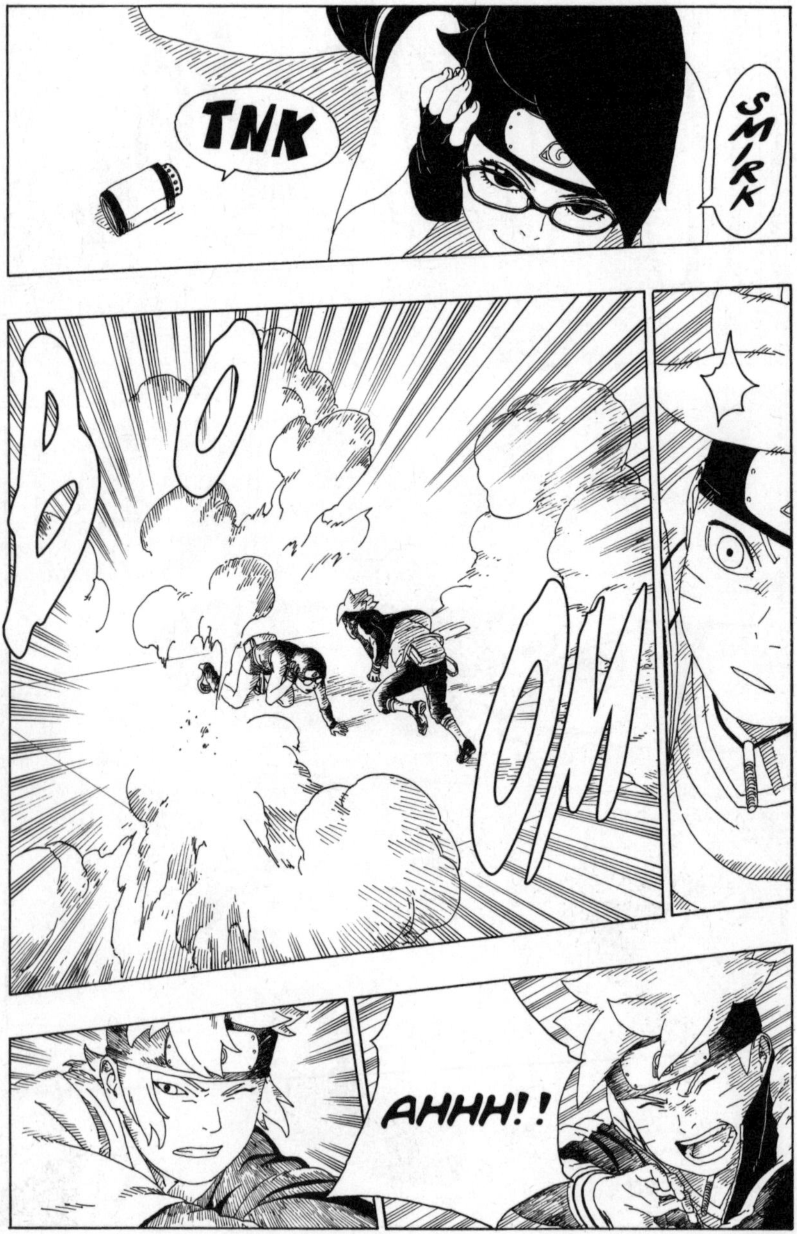
SMIRK
TNK
BOOM
AHHH!!

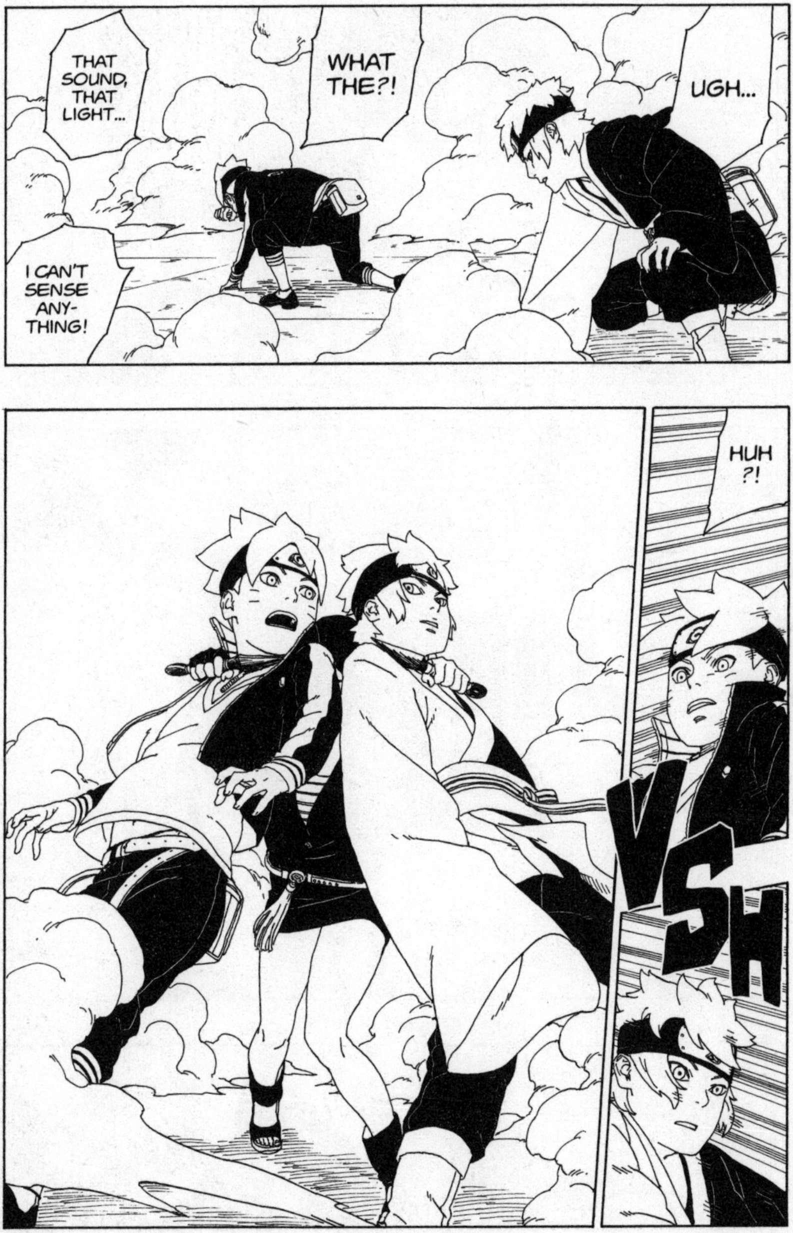
UGH...
WHAT THE?!
THAT SOUND, THAT LIGHT...
I CAN'T SENSE ANY-THING!
HUH ?!
VSH

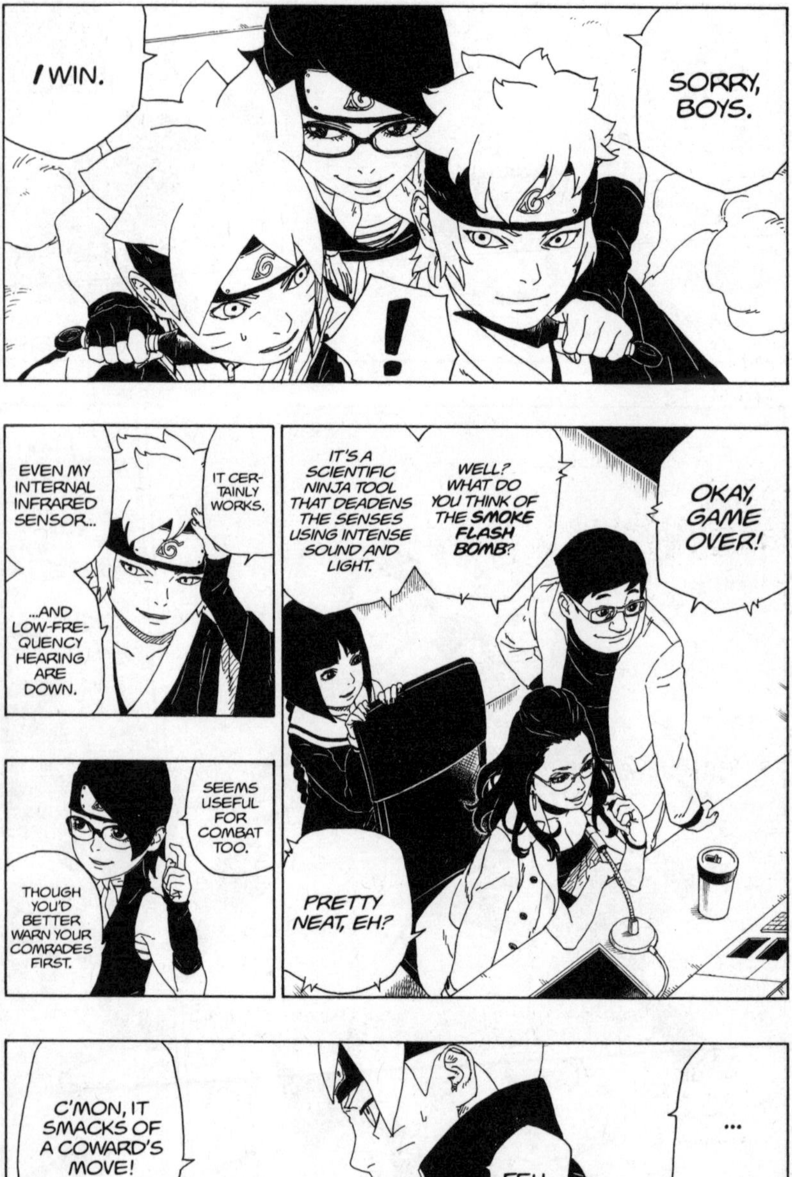
SORRY, BOYS.
I WIN.
!
OKAY, GAME OVER!
WELL? WHAT DO YOU THINK OF THE **SMOKE FLASH BOMB**?
IT'S A SCIENTIFIC NINJA TOOL THAT DEADENS THE SENSES USING INTENSE SOUND AND LIGHT.
PRETTY NEAT, EH?
IT CER-TAINLY WORKS.
EVEN MY INTERNAL INFRARED SENSOR...
...AND LOW-FRE-QUENCY HEARING ARE DOWN.
SEEMS USEFUL FOR COMBAT TOO.
THOUGH YOU'D BETTER WARN YOUR COMRADES FIRST.
...
FEH.
C'MON, IT SMACKS OF A COWARD'S MOVE!

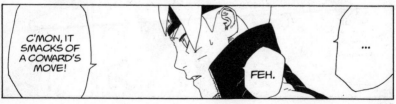

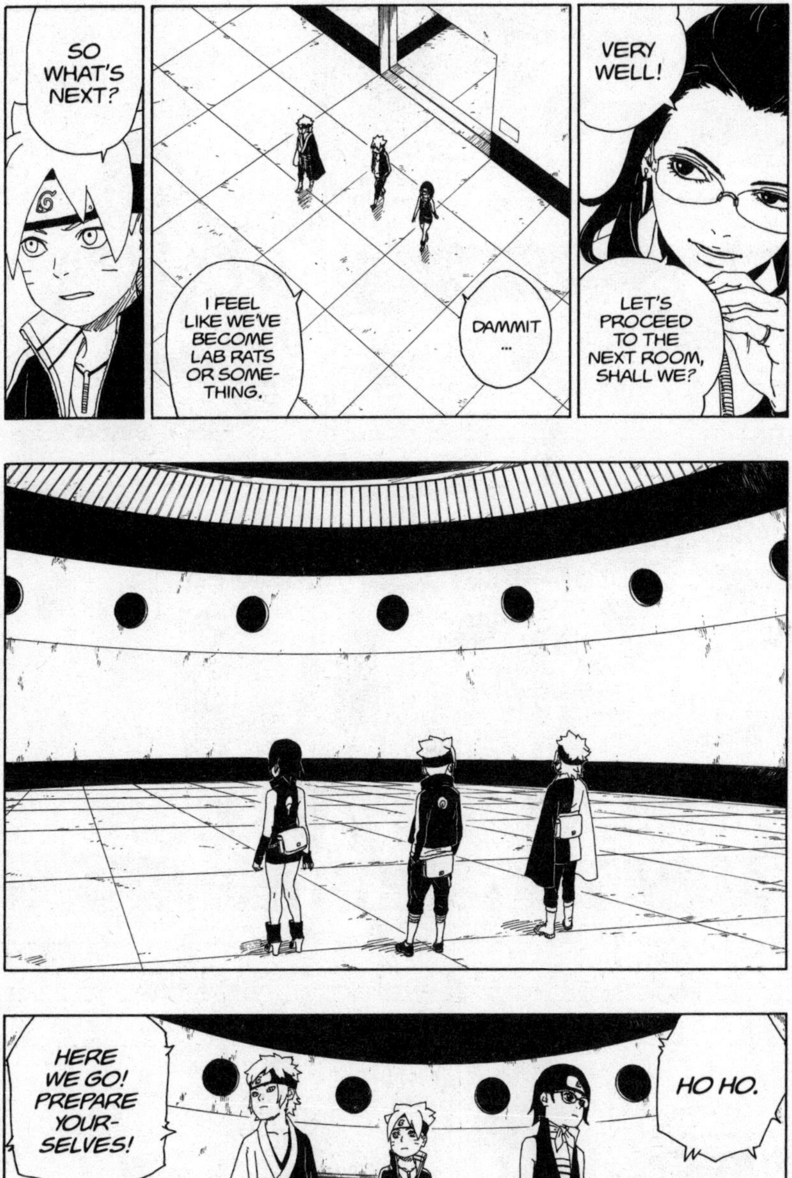
VERY WELL!
LET'S PROCEED TO THE NEXT ROOM, SHALL WE?
DAMMIT ...
I FEEL LIKE WE'VE BECOME LAB RATS OR SOME- THING.
SO WHAT'S NEXT?
HO HO.
HERE WE GO! PREPARE YOUR- SELVES!

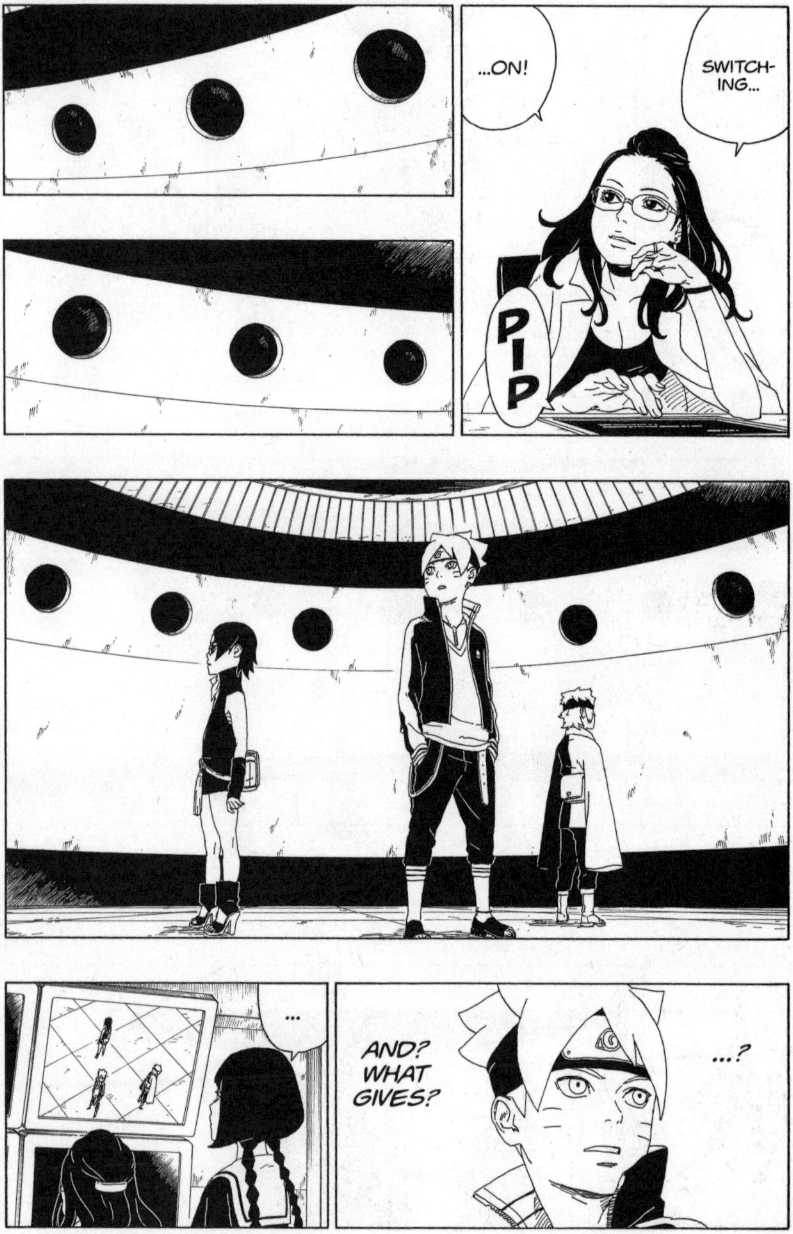
SWITCHING...
...ON!
PIP
...?
AND? WHAT GIVES?
...

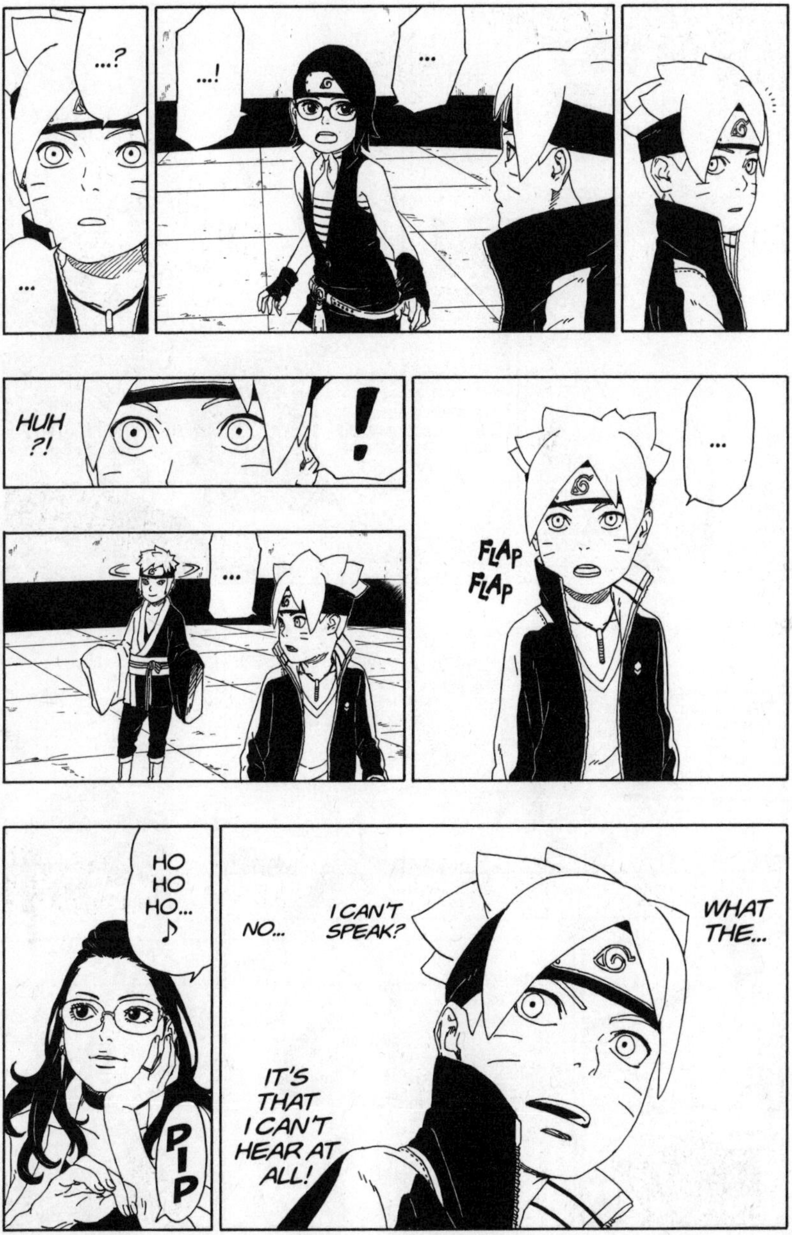
...
...!
...?
...
...
FLAP
FLAP
!
HUH ?!
...
WHAT THE...
I CAN'T SPEAK?
NO...
IT'S THAT I CAN'T HEAR AT ALL!
HO HO HO... ♪
PIP

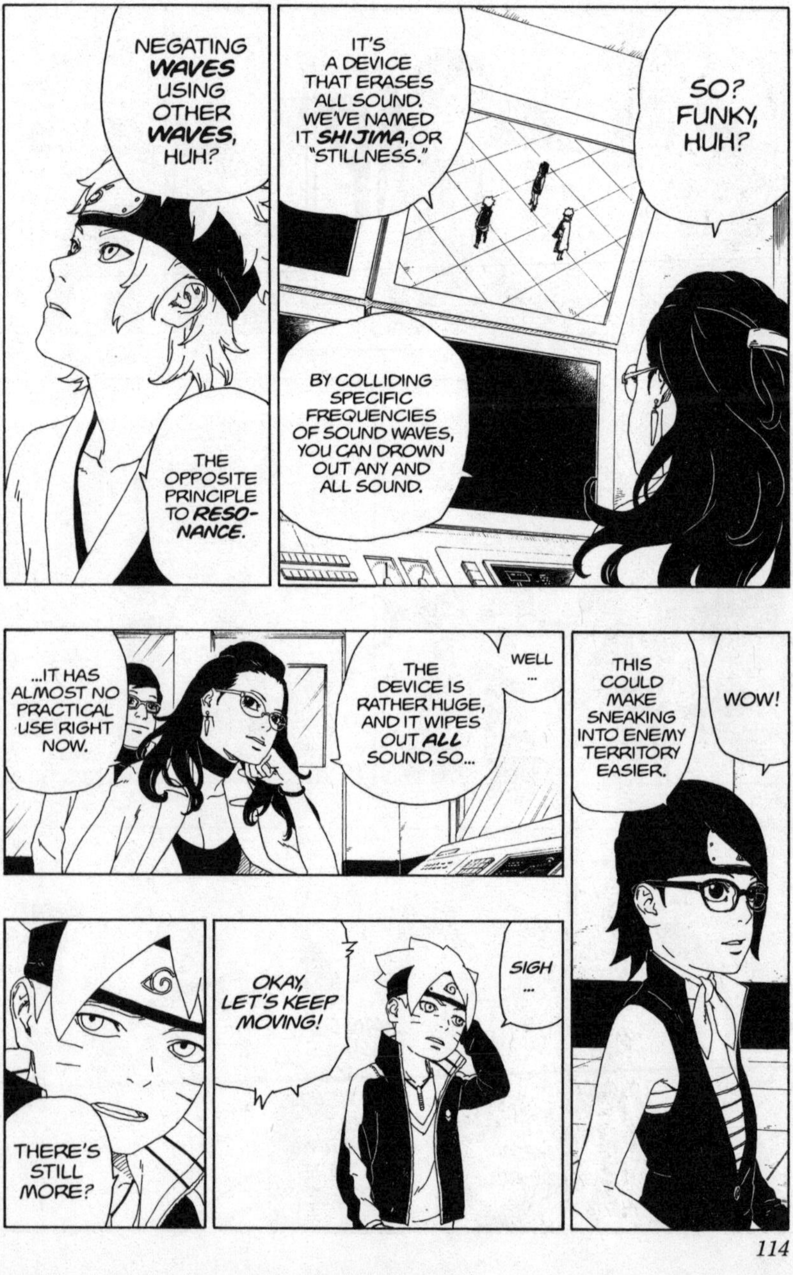
SO? FUNKY, HUH?
IT'S A DEVICE THAT ERASES ALL SOUND. WE'VE NAMED IT SHIJIMA, OR "STILLNESS."
BY COLLIDING SPECIFIC FREQUENCIES OF SOUND WAVES, YOU CAN DROWN OUT ANY AND ALL SOUND.
NEGATING WAVES USING OTHER WAVES, HUH?
THE OPPOSITE PRINCIPLE TO RESONANCE.
WOW!
THIS COULD MAKE SNEAKING INTO ENEMY TERRITORY EASIER.
WELL...
THE DEVICE IS RATHER HUGE, AND IT WIPES OUT ALL SOUND, SO...
...IT HAS ALMOST NO PRACTICAL USE RIGHT NOW.
SIGH...
OKAY, LET'S KEEP MOVING!
THERE'S STILL MORE?

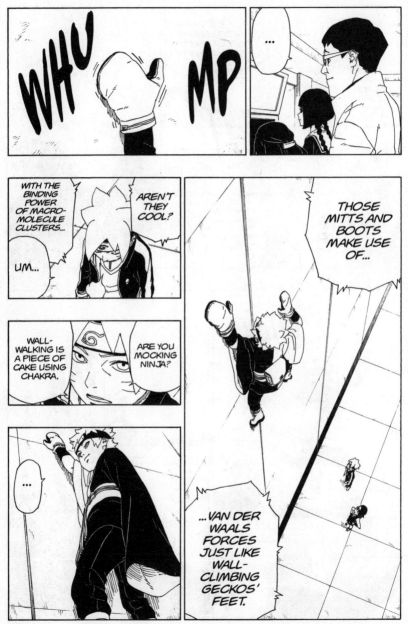

...
WHUMP
THOSE MITTS AND BOOTS MAKE USE OF...
...VAN DER WAALS FORCES JUST LIKE WALL-CLIMBING GECKOS' FEET.
AREN'T THEY COOL?
WITH THE BINDING POWER OF MACRO-MOLECULE CLUSTERS...
UM...
ARE YOU MOCKING NINJA?
WALL-WALKING IS A PIECE OF CAKE USING CHAKRA.
...

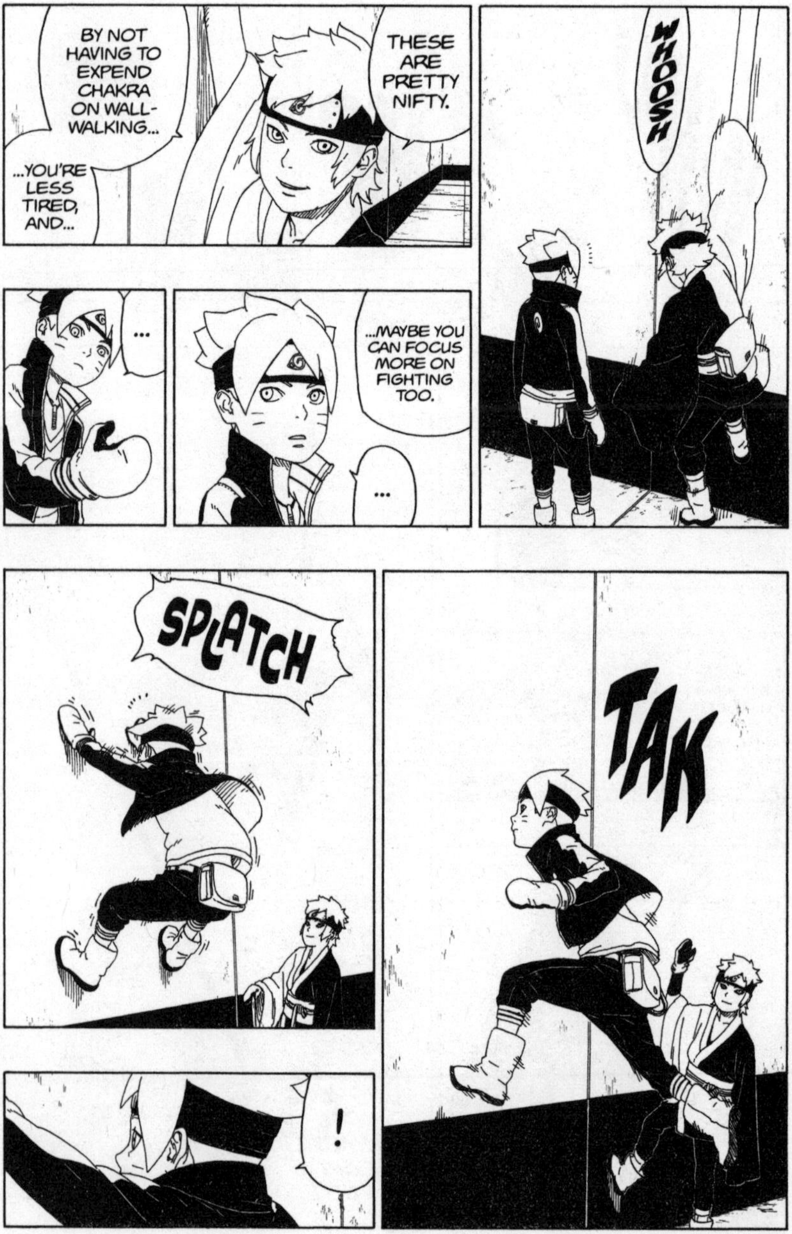
WHOOSH
THESE ARE PRETTY NIFTY.
BY NOT HAVING TO EXPEND CHAKRA ON WALL-WALKING...
...YOU'RE LESS TIRED, AND...
...MAYBE YOU CAN FOCUS MORE ON FIGHTING TOO.
...
...
TAK
SPLATCH
!

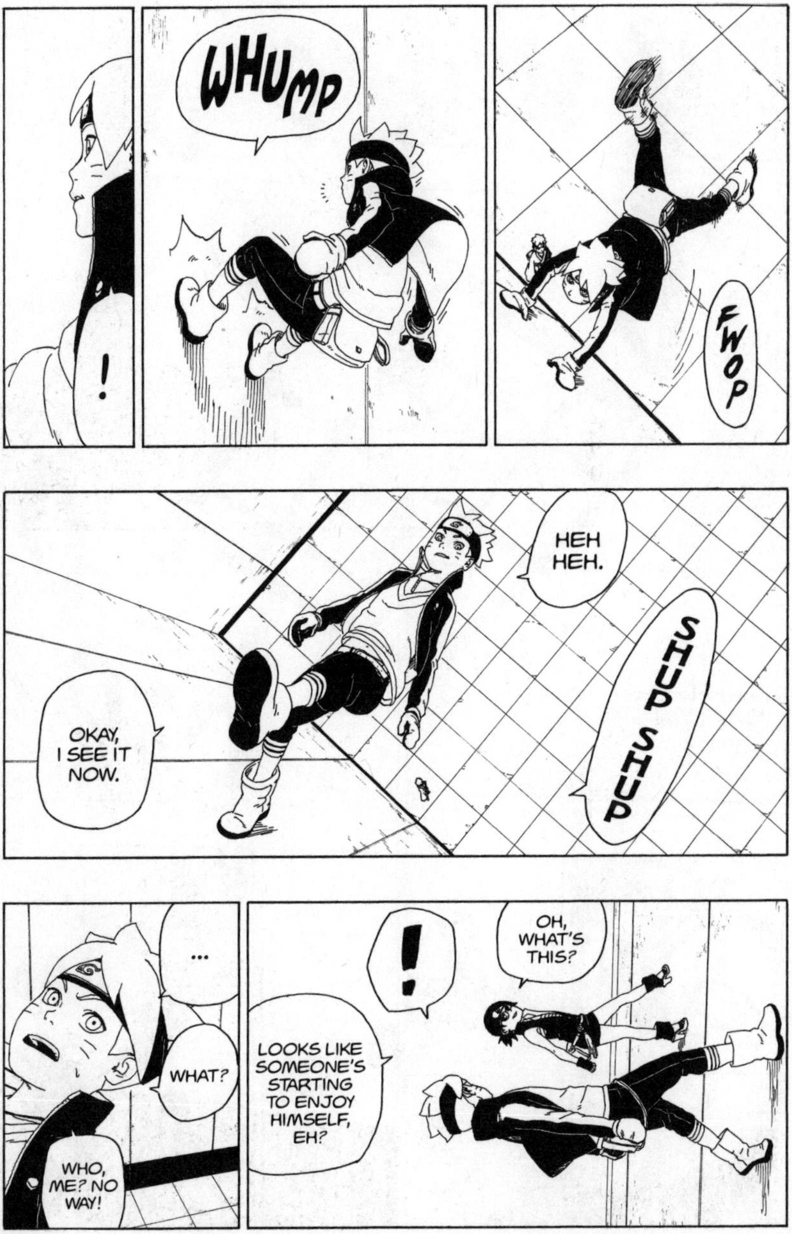
FWOP
WHUMP
!
HEH HEH.
SHUP SHUP
OKAY, I SEE IT NOW.
OH, WHAT'S THIS?
!
LOOKS LIKE SOMEONE'S STARTING TO ENJOY HIMSELF, EH?
...
WHAT?
WHO, ME? NO WAY!

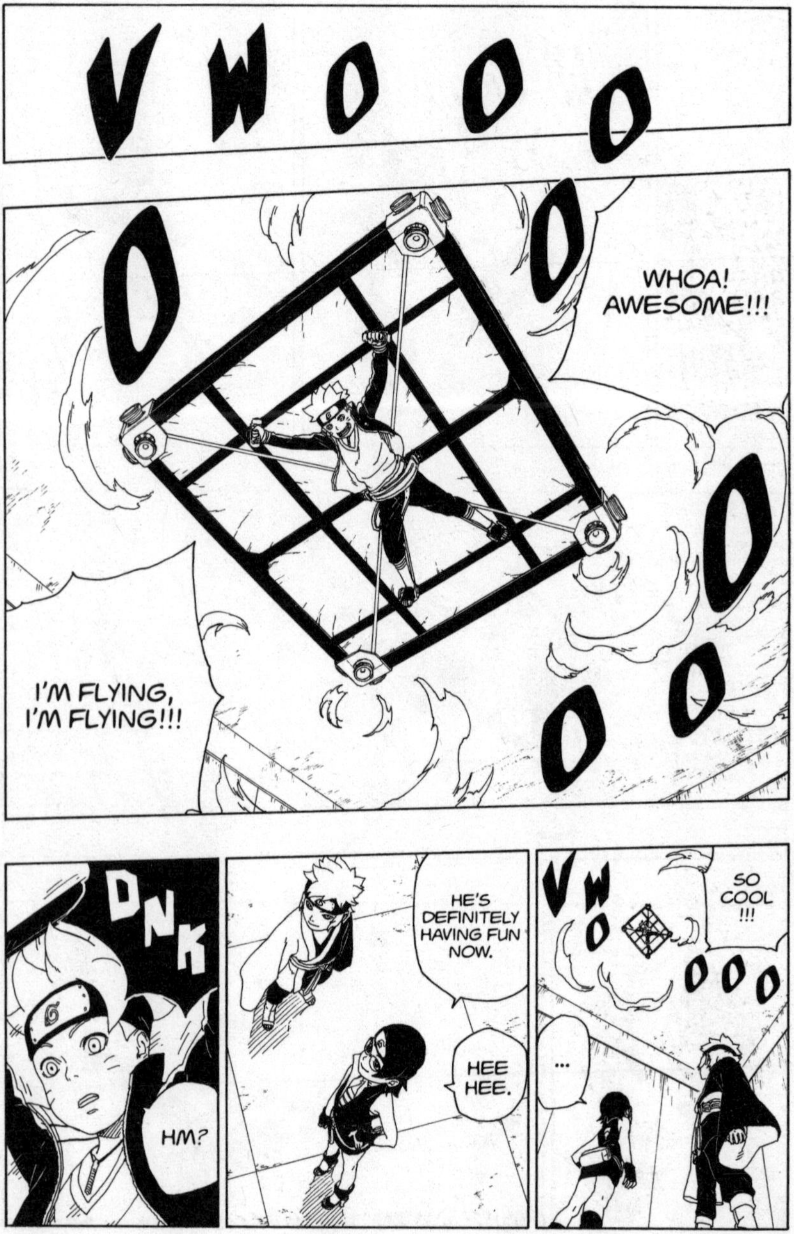
VWOOO
OOOOOOO
WHOA! AWESOME!!!
I'M FLYING, I'M FLYING!!!
SO COOL !!!
VWO
OOO
...
HE'S DEFINITELY HAVING FUN NOW.
HEE HEE.
DNK
HM?

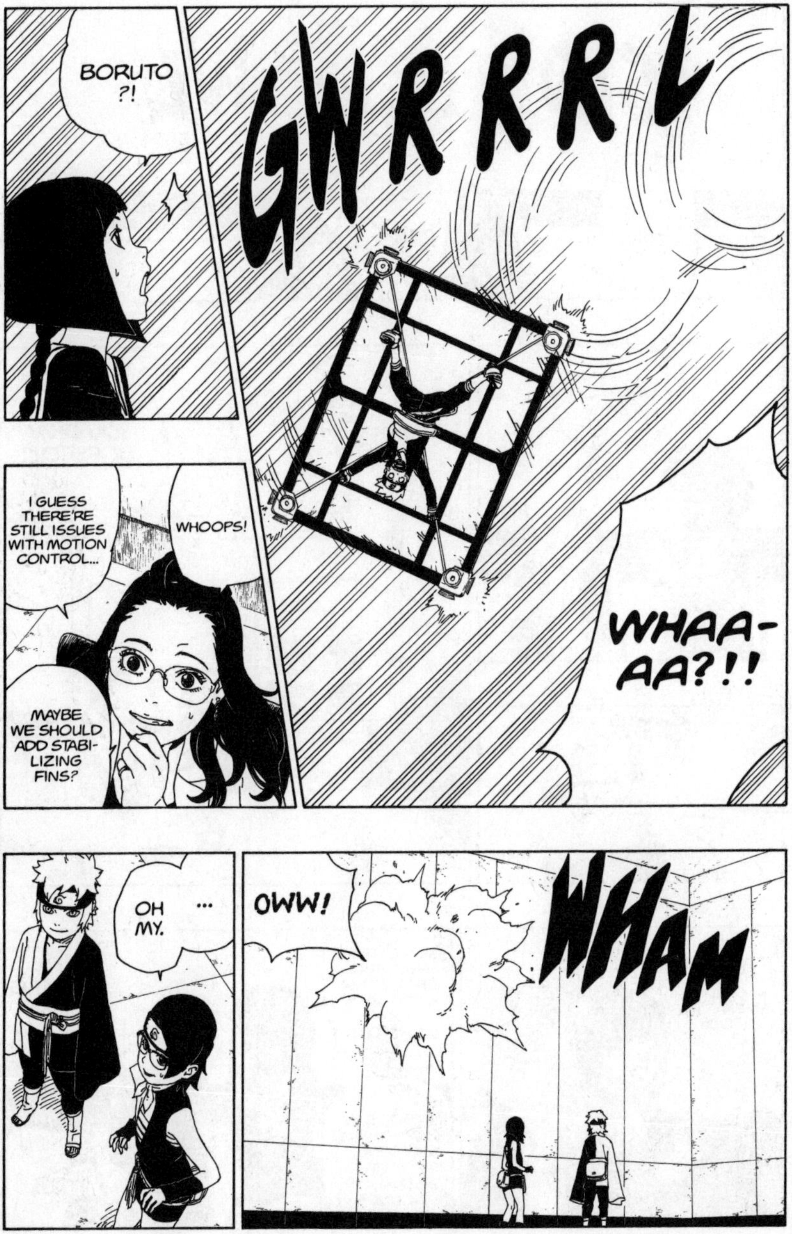
GWRRRL
WHAA-AA?!!
BORUTO?!
WHOOPS!
I GUESS THERE'RE STILL ISSUES WITH MOTION CONTROL...
MAYBE WE SHOULD ADD STABI-LIZING FINS?
WHAM
OWW!
...
OH MY.

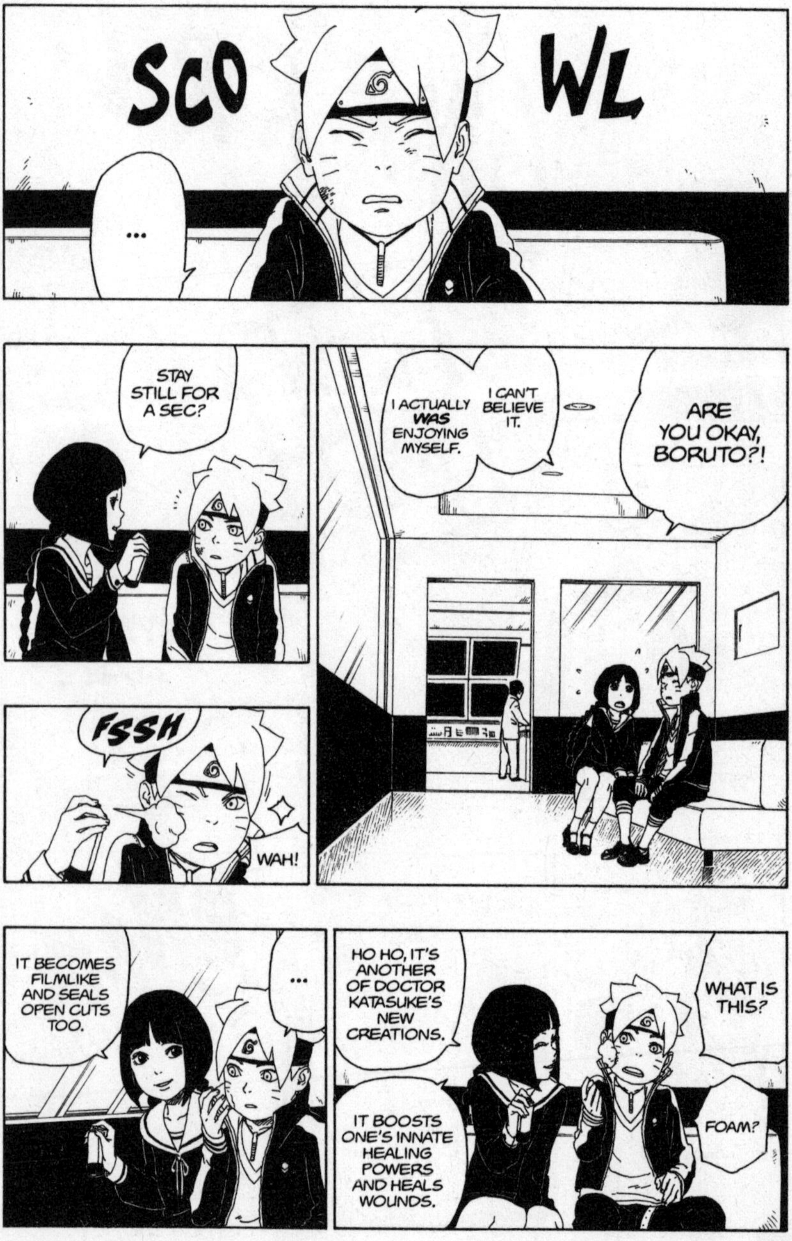
SCOWL
...
ARE YOU OKAY, BORUTO?!
I CAN'T BELIEVE IT.
I ACTUALLY WAS ENJOYING MYSELF.
STAY STILL FOR A SEC?
FSSH
WAH!
WHAT IS THIS?
FOAM?
HO HO, IT'S ANOTHER OF DOCTOR KATASUKE'S NEW CREATIONS.
IT BOOSTS ONE'S INNATE HEALING POWERS AND HEALS WOUNDS.
...
IT BECOMES FILMLIKE AND SEALS OPEN CUTS TOO.

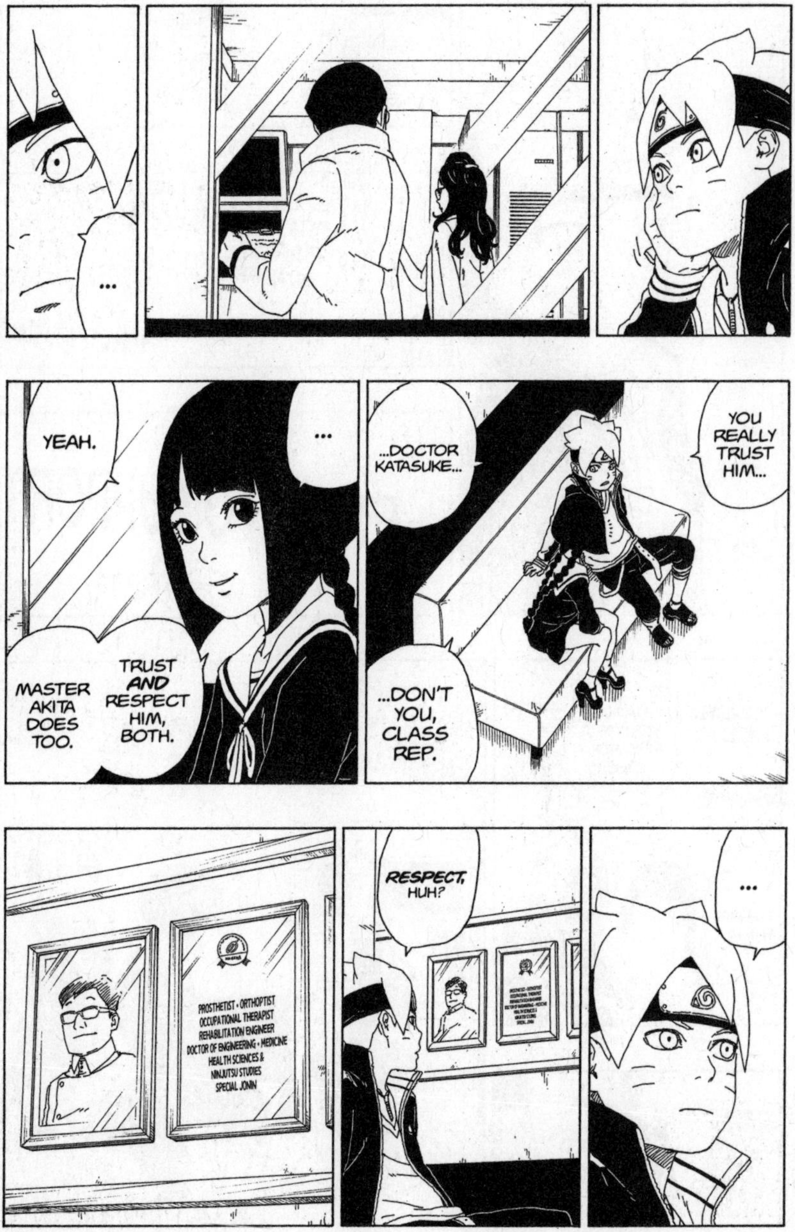
...
YOU REALLY TRUST HIM...
...DOCTOR KATASUKE...
...DON'T YOU, CLASS REP.
...
YEAH.
TRUST AND RESPECT HIM, BOTH.
MASTER AKITA DOES TOO.
...
RESPECT, HUH?
PROSTHETIST • ORTHOPTIST
OCCUPATIONAL THERAPIST
REHABILITATION ENGINEER
DOCTOR OF ENGINEERING • MEDICINE
HEALTH SCIENCES &
NINJUTSU STUDIES
SPECIAL JONIN

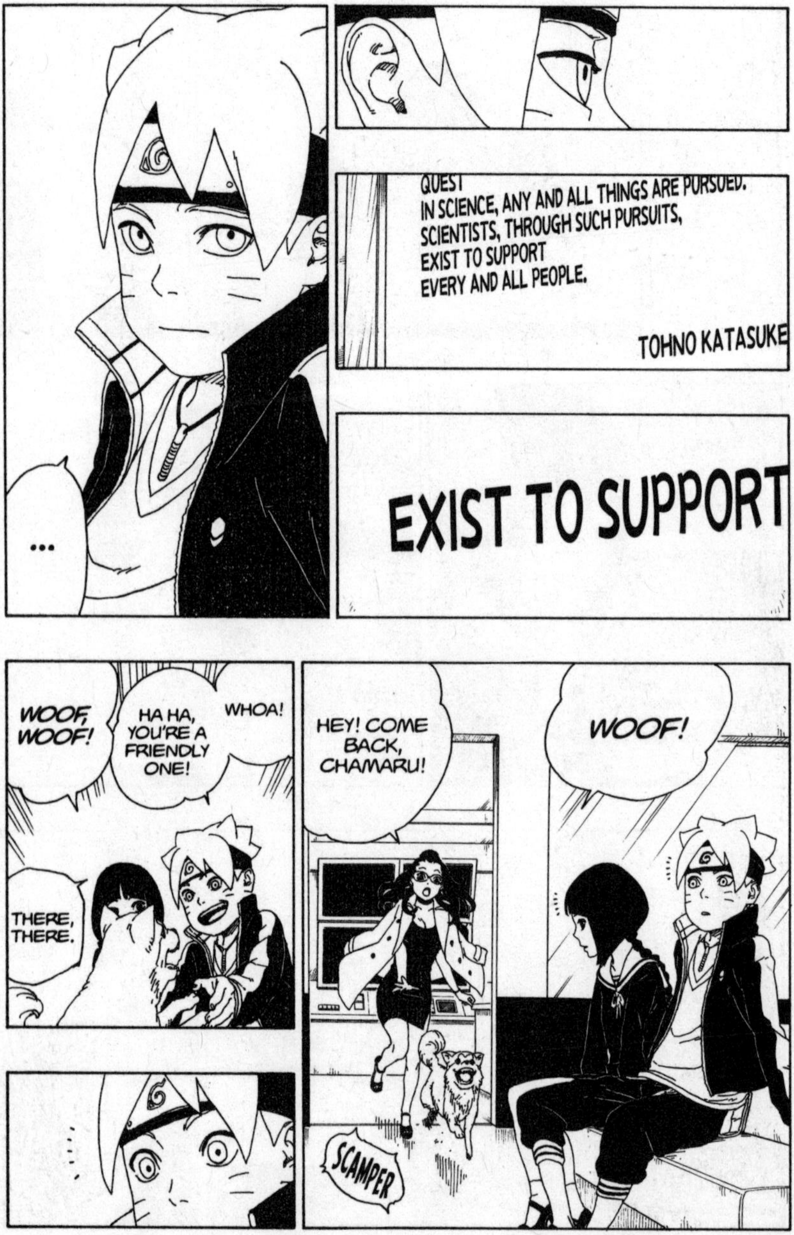
QUEST
IN SCIENCE, ANY AND ALL THINGS ARE PURSUED.
SCIENTISTS, THROUGH SUCH PURSUITS,
EXIST TO SUPPORT
EVERY AND ALL PEOPLE.
TOHNO KATASUKE
EXIST TO SUPPORT
...
WOOF!
HEY! COME BACK, CHAMARU!
SCAMPER
WHOA!
HA HA, YOU'RE A FRIENDLY ONE!
WOOF, WOOF!
THERE, THERE.

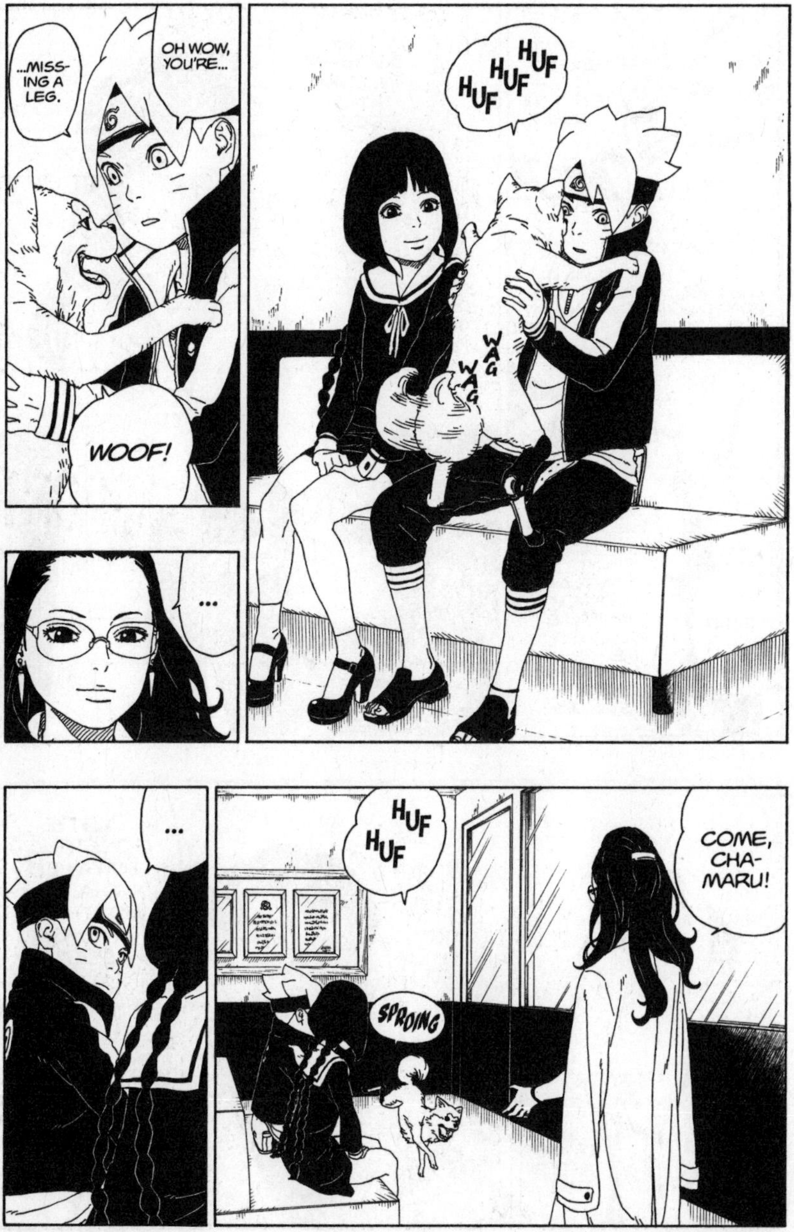
HUF HUF HUF
WAG WAG
OH WOW, YOU'RE...
...MISSING A LEG.
WOOF!
...
COME, CHAMARU!
HUF HUF
SPROING
...

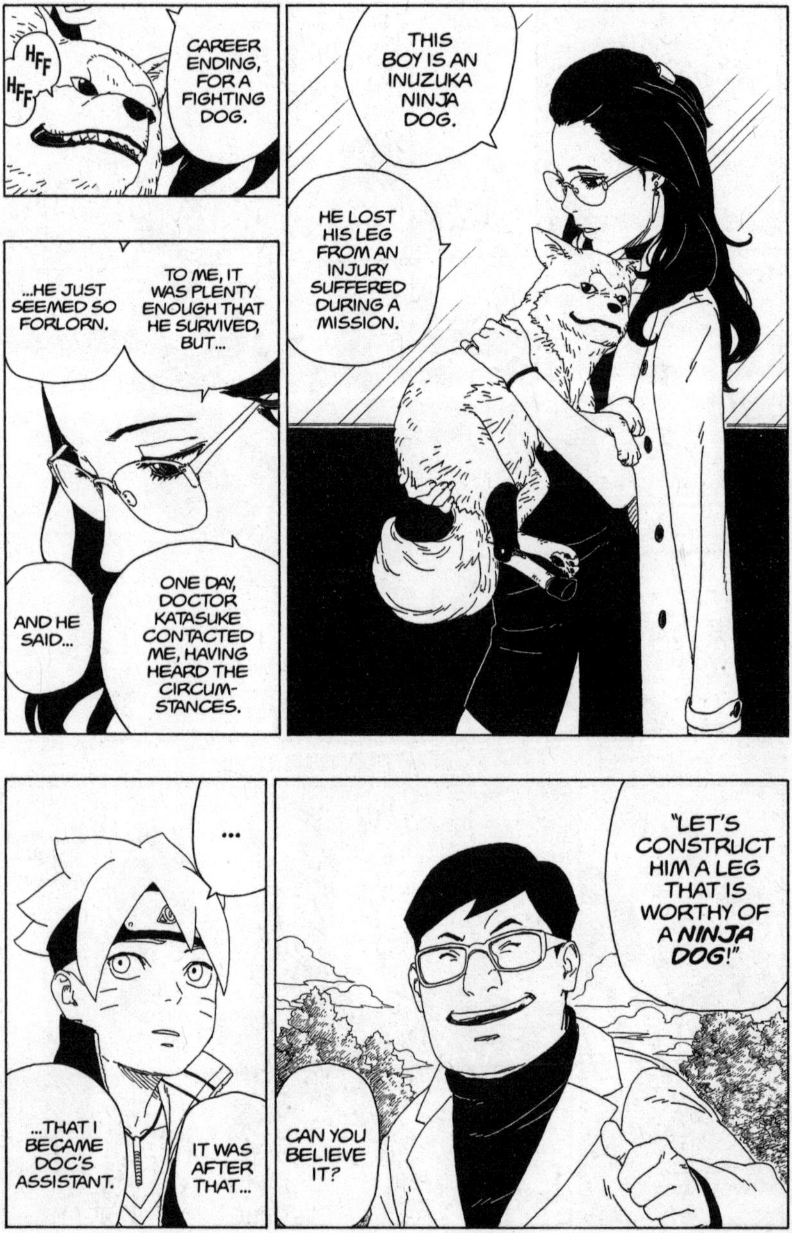
THIS BOY IS AN INUZUKA NINJA DOG.
HE LOST HIS LEG FROM AN INJURY SUFFERED DURING A MISSION.
CAREER ENDING, FOR A FIGHTING DOG.
HFF HFF
TO ME, IT WAS PLENTY ENOUGH THAT HE SURVIVED, BUT...
...HE JUST SEEMED SO FORLORN.
ONE DAY, DOCTOR KATASUKE CONTACTED ME, HAVING HEARD THE CIRCUMSTANCES.
AND HE SAID...
"LET'S CONSTRUCT HIM A LEG THAT IS WORTHY OF A ***NINJA DOG***!"
CAN YOU BELIEVE IT?
...
IT WAS AFTER THAT...
...THAT I BECAME DOC'S ASSISTANT.

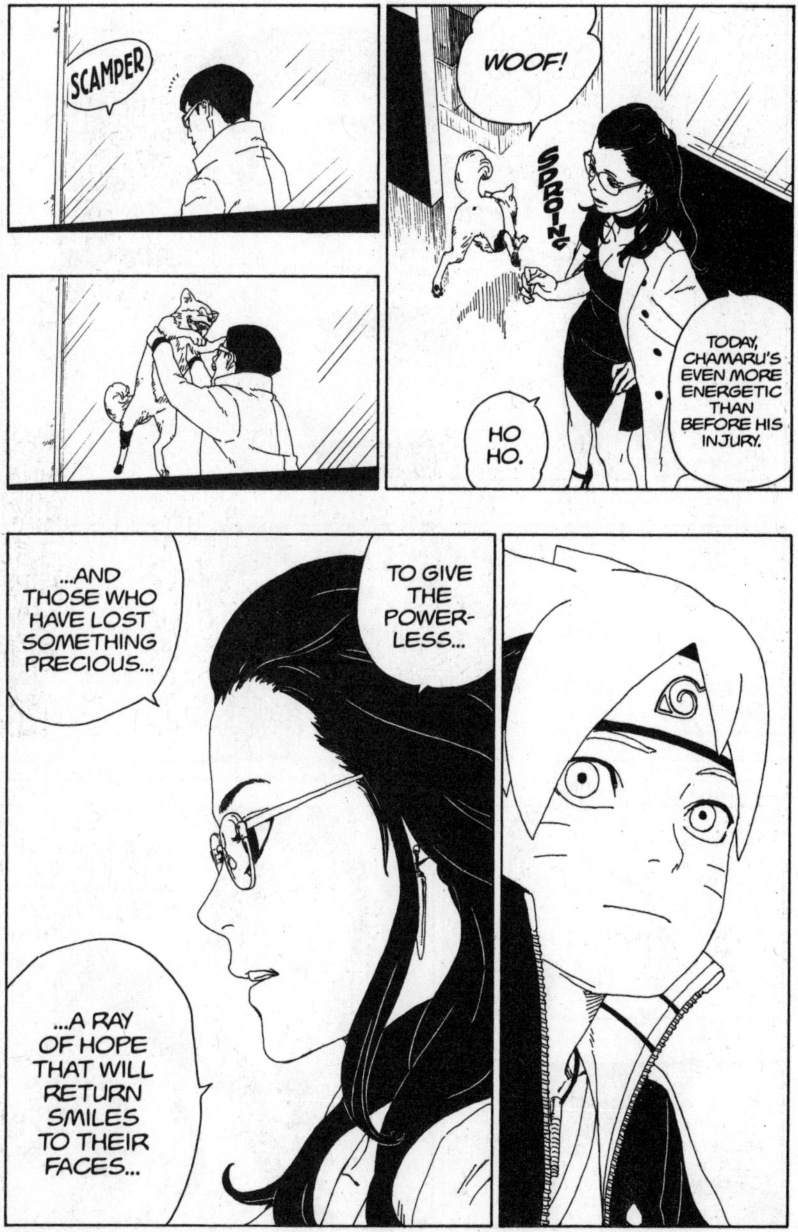
WOOF!
SPROING
TODAY, CHAMARU'S EVEN MORE ENERGETIC THAN BEFORE HIS INJURY.
HO HO.
SCAMPER
TO GIVE THE POWER-LESS...
...AND THOSE WHO HAVE LOST SOMETHING PRECIOUS...
...A RAY OF HOPE THAT WILL RETURN SMILES TO THEIR FACES...

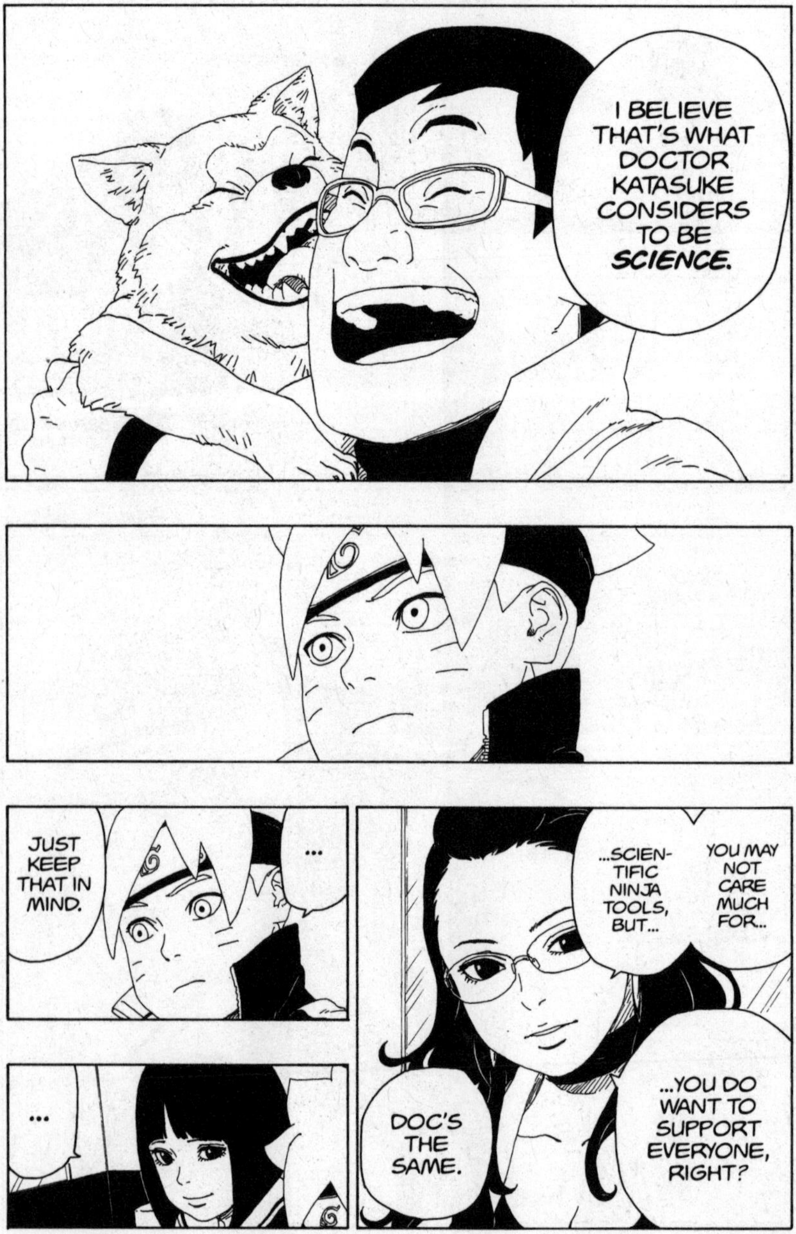
I BELIEVE THAT'S WHAT DOCTOR KATASUKE CONSIDERS TO BE SCIENCE.
YOU MAY NOT CARE MUCH FOR...
...SCIENTIFIC NINJA TOOLS, BUT...
...YOU DO WANT TO SUPPORT EVERYONE, RIGHT?
DOC'S THE SAME.
...
JUST KEEP THAT IN MIND.
...

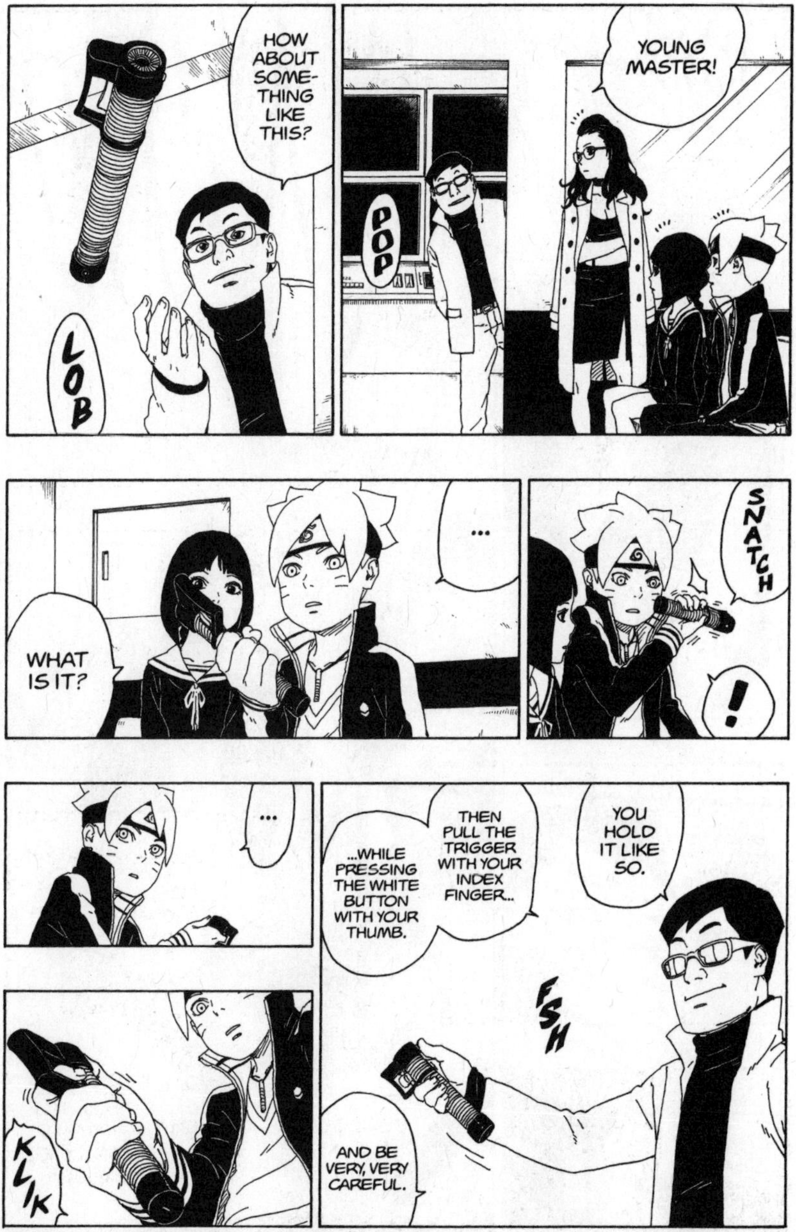
YOUNG MASTER!
POP
HOW ABOUT SOME-THING LIKE THIS?
LOB
SNATCH
!
...
WHAT IS IT?
YOU HOLD IT LIKE SO.
THEN PULL THE TRIGGER WITH YOUR INDEX FINGER..
...WHILE PRESSING THE WHITE BUTTON WITH YOUR THUMB.
FSH
AND BE VERY, VERY CAREFUL.
...
KLIK

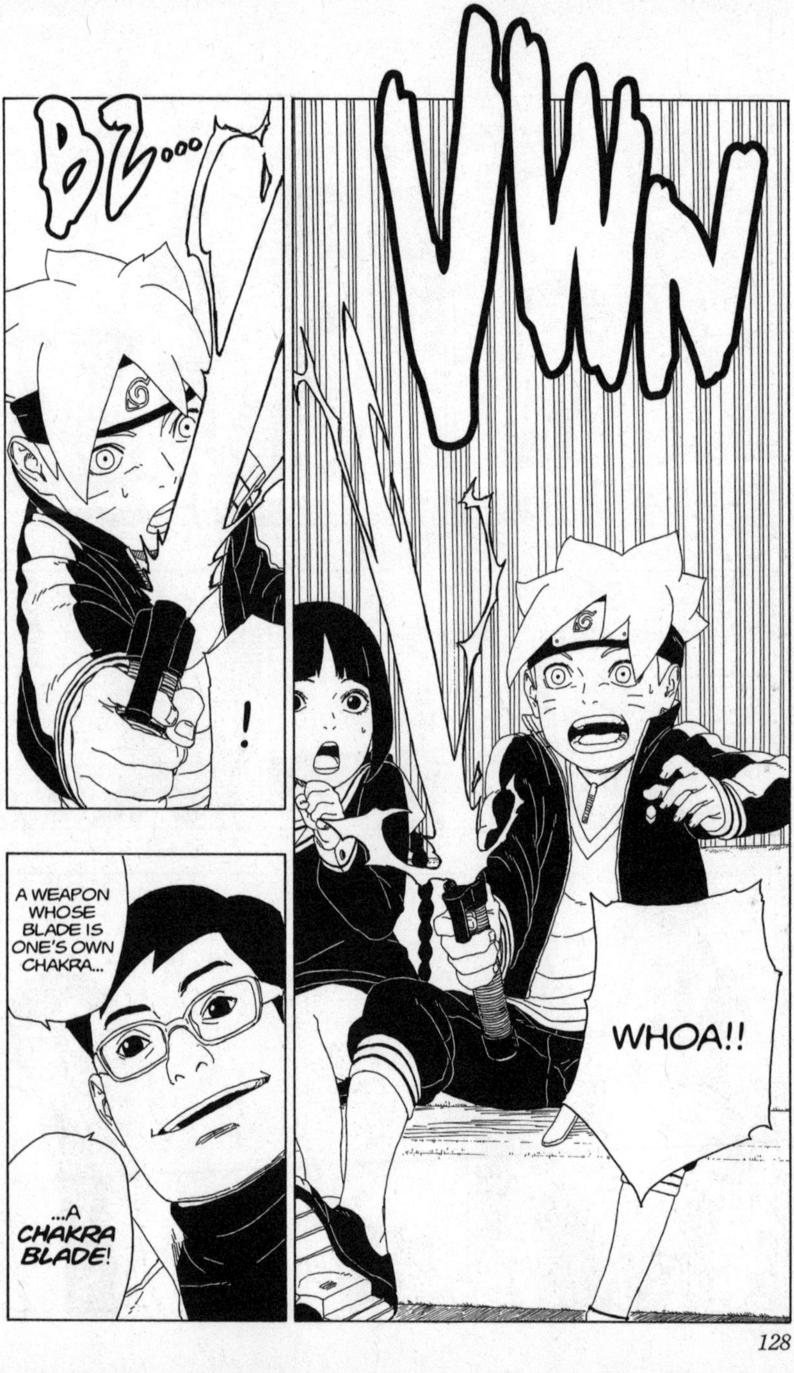
VWN
WHOA!!
BZ...
!
A WEAPON WHOSE BLADE IS ONE'S OWN CHAKRA...
...A CHAKRA BLADE!

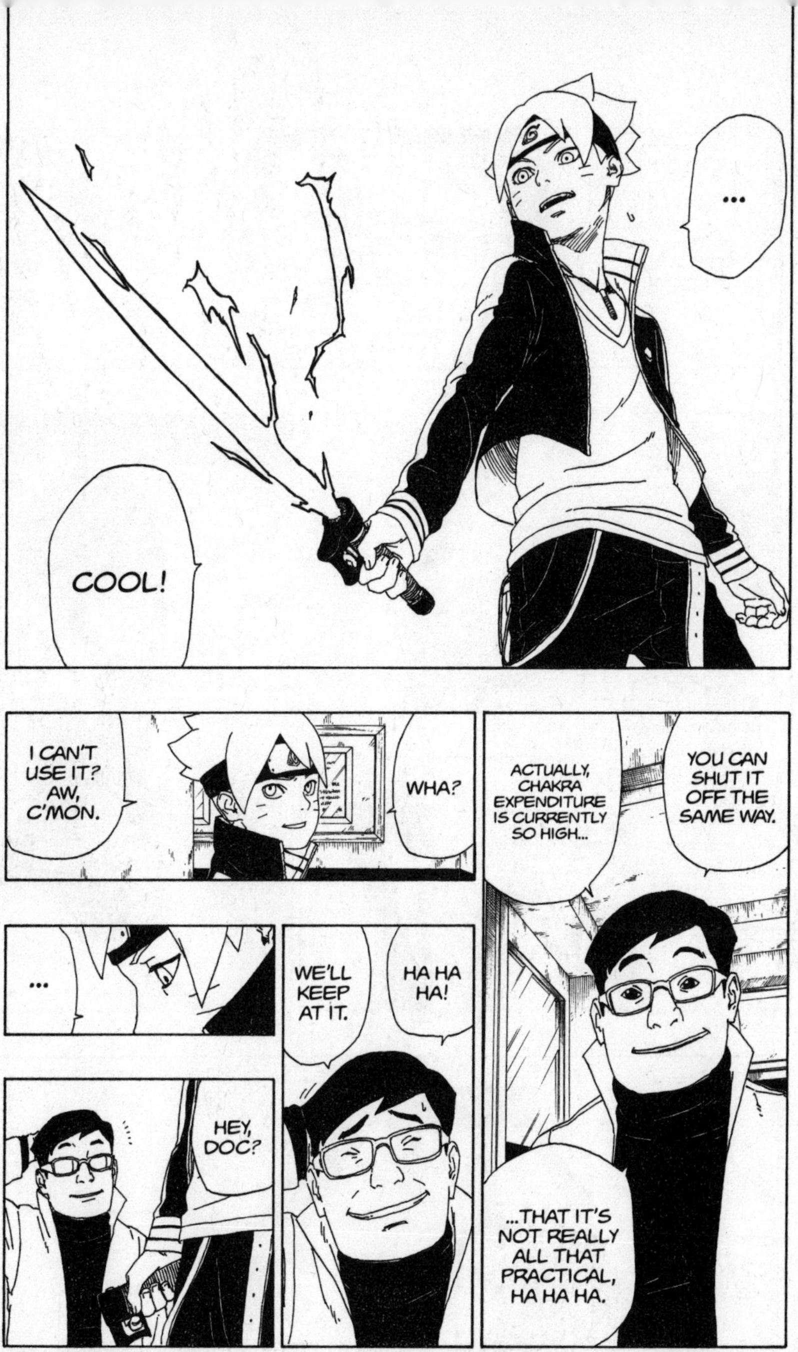
...
COOL!
YOU CAN SHUT IT OFF THE SAME WAY.
ACTUALLY, CHAKRA EXPENDITURE IS CURRENTLY SO HIGH...
...THAT IT'S NOT REALLY ALL THAT PRACTICAL, HA HA HA.
WHA?
I CAN'T USE IT? AW, C'MON.
HA HA HA!
WE'LL KEEP AT IT.
...
HEY, DOC?

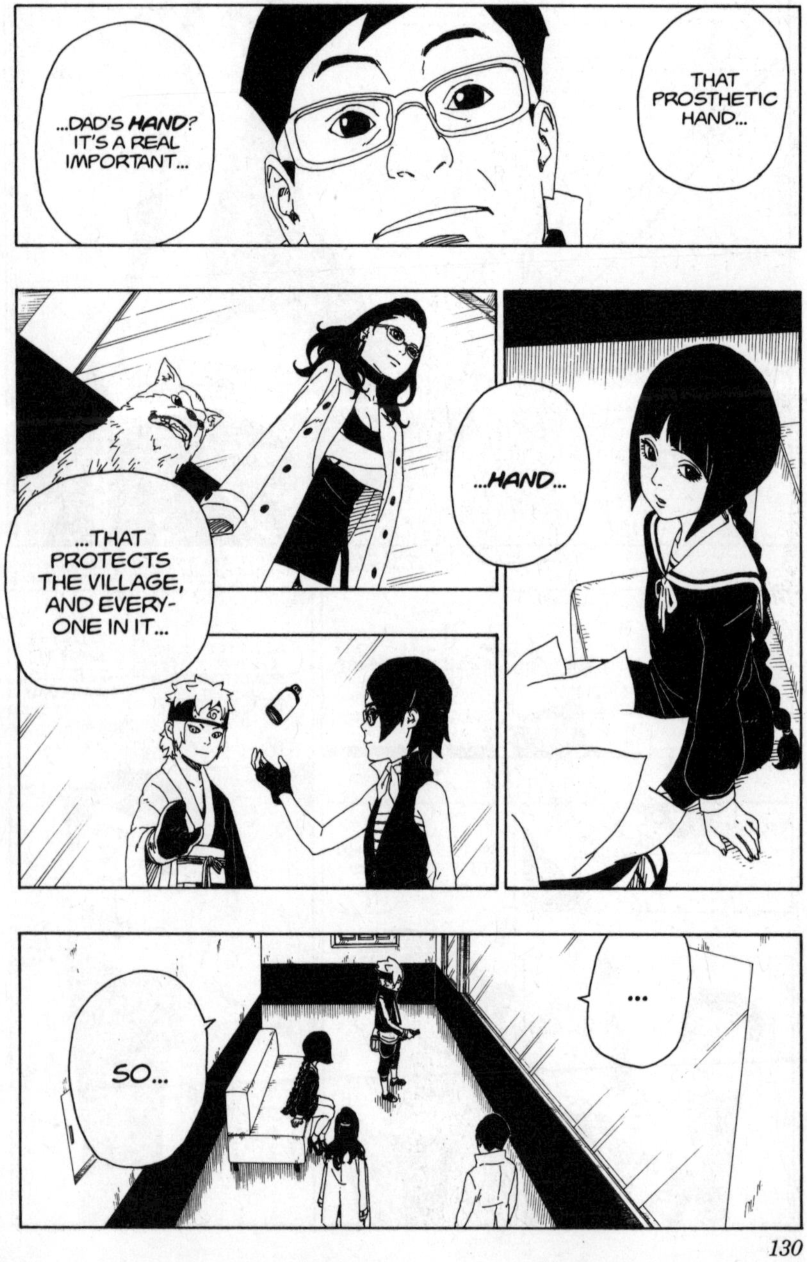
THAT PROSTHETIC HAND...
...DAD'S **HAND**? IT'S A REAL IMPORTANT...
...**HAND**...
...THAT PROTECTS THE VILLAGE, AND EVERY-ONE IN IT...
...
SO...

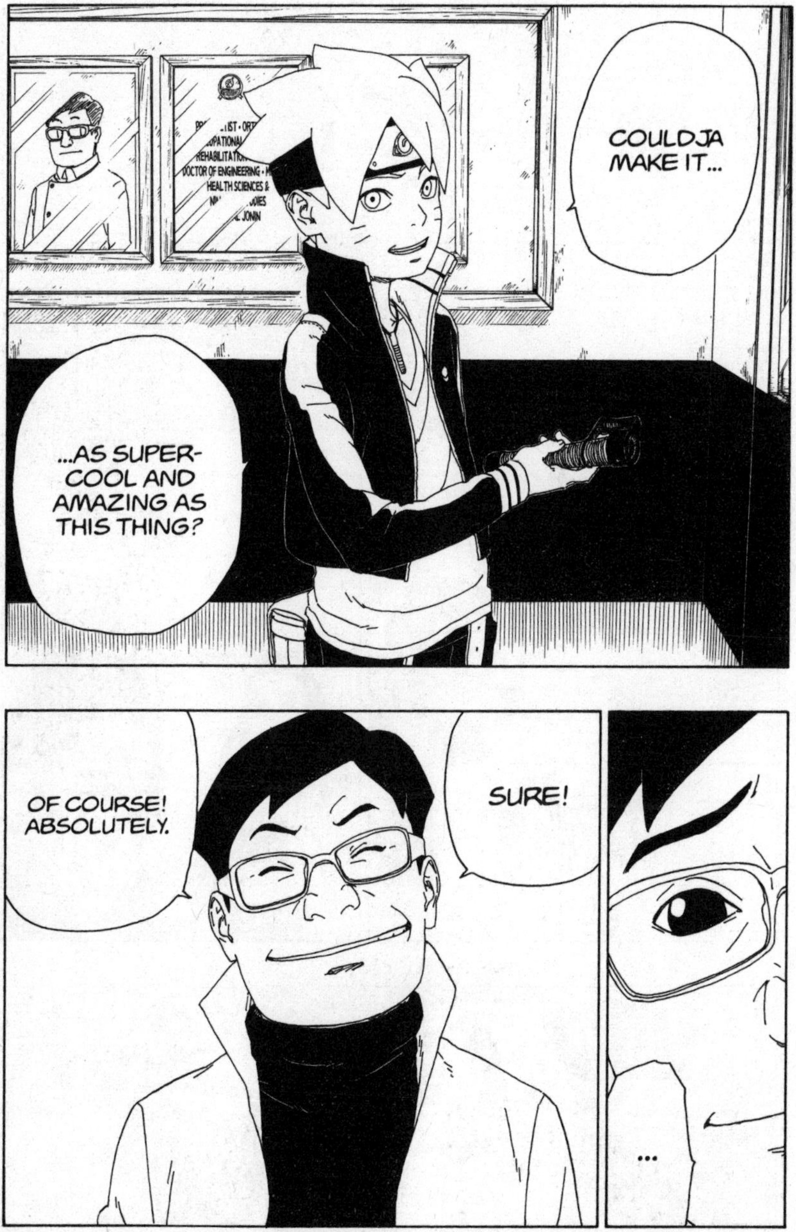
COULDJA MAKE IT...
...AS SUPER-COOL AND AMAZING AS THIS THING?
...
SURE!
OF COURSE! ABSOLUTELY.

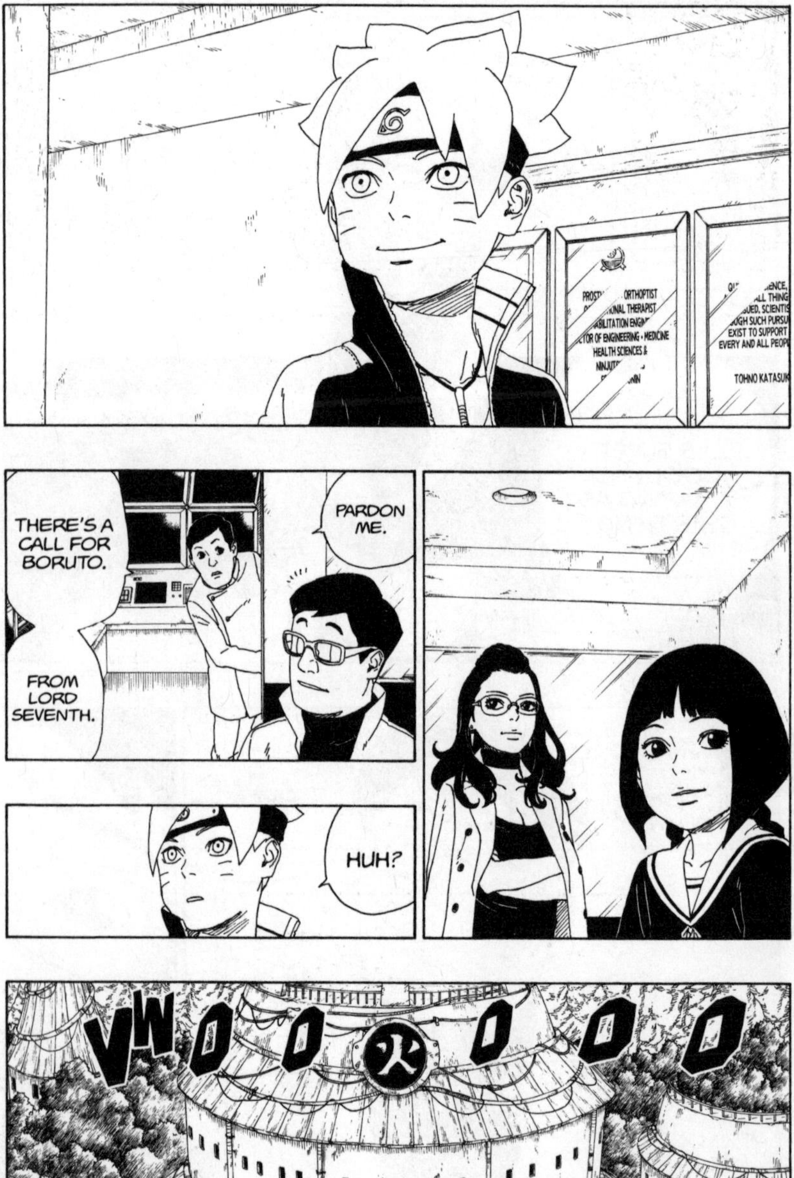
PARDON ME.
THERE'S A CALL FOR BORUTO.
FROM LORD SEVENTH.
HUH?
VWOOOOO

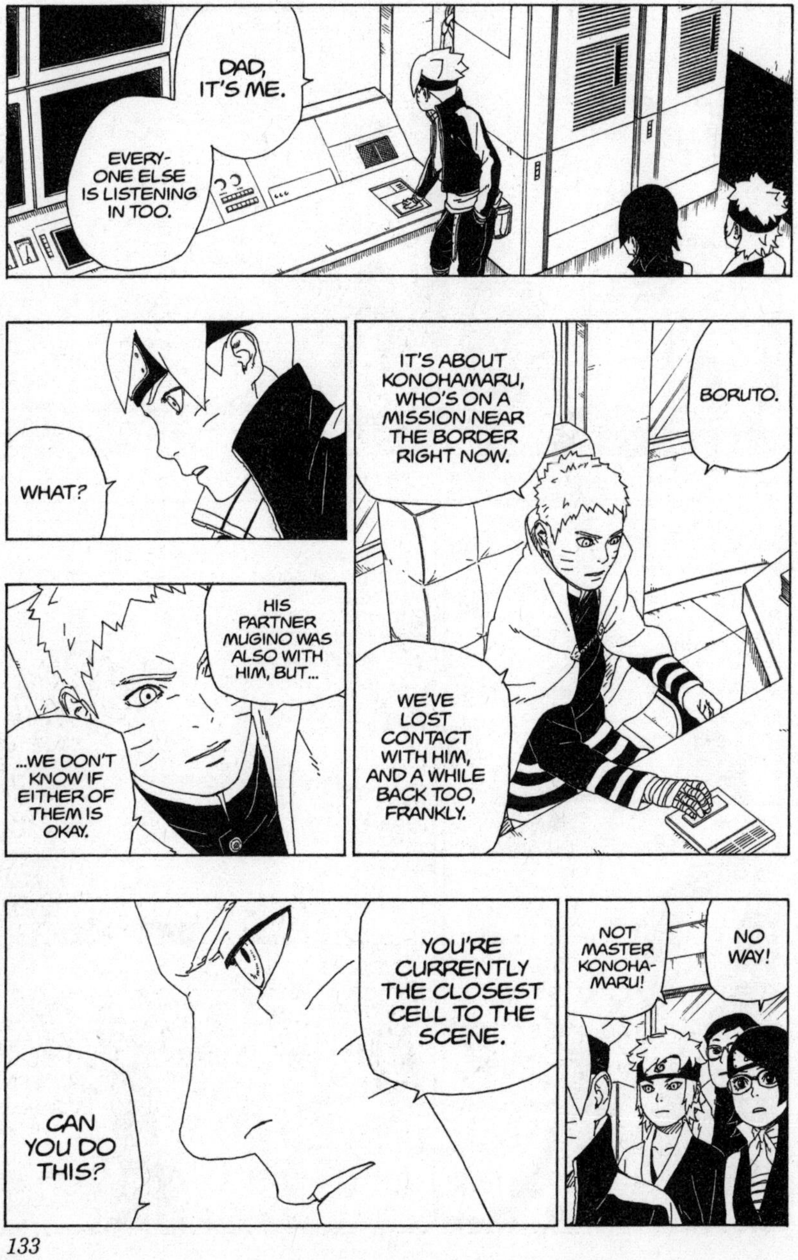
DAD, IT'S ME.
EVERY-ONE ELSE IS LISTENING IN TOO.
BORUTO.
IT'S ABOUT KONOHAMARU, WHO'S ON A MISSION NEAR THE BORDER RIGHT NOW.
WE'VE LOST CONTACT WITH HIM, AND A WHILE BACK TOO, FRANKLY.
WHAT?
HIS PARTNER MUGINO WAS ALSO WITH HIM, BUT...
...WE DON'T KNOW IF EITHER OF THEM IS OKAY.
NO WAY!
NOT MASTER KONOHA-MARU!
YOU'RE CURRENTLY THE CLOSEST CELL TO THE SCENE.
CAN YOU DO THIS?

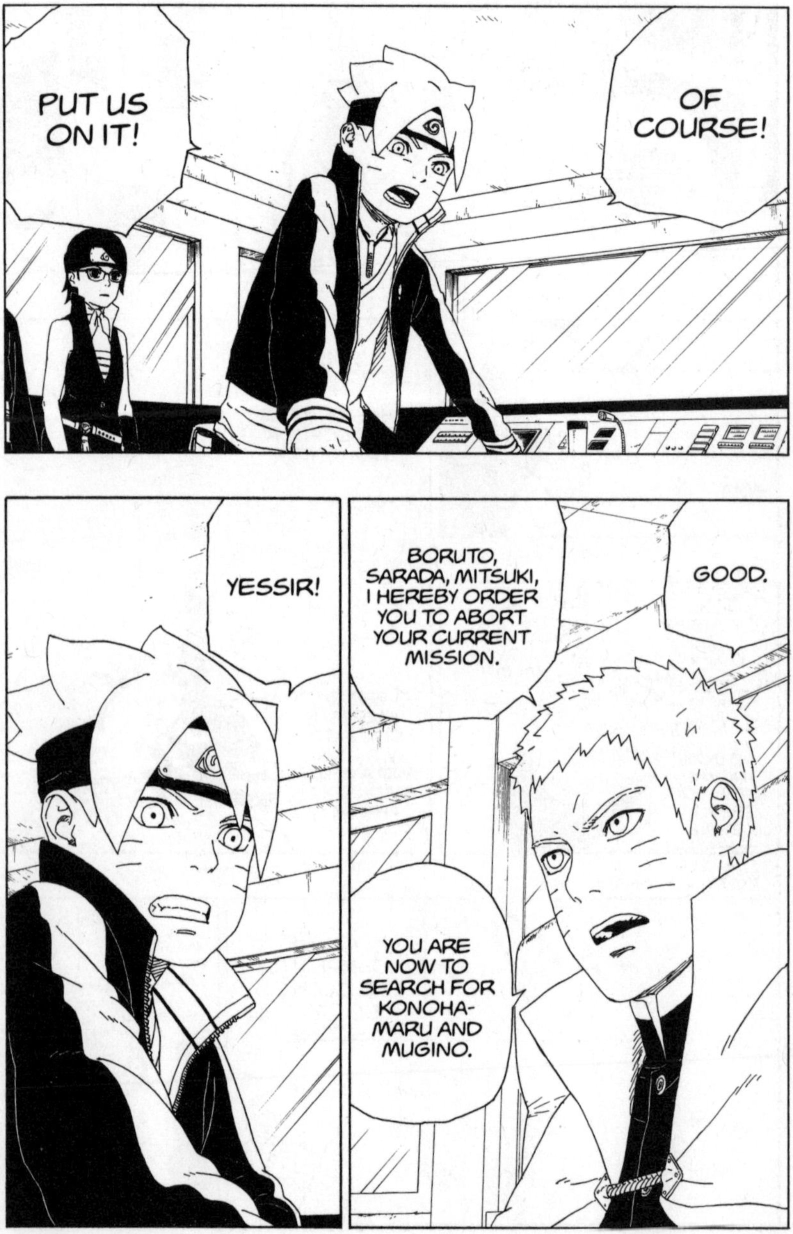
OF COURSE!
PUT US ON IT!
GOOD.
BORUTO, SARADA, MITSUKI, I HEREBY ORDER YOU TO ABORT YOUR CURRENT MISSION.
YOU ARE NOW TO SEARCH FOR KONOHA-MARU AND MUGINO.
YESSIR!

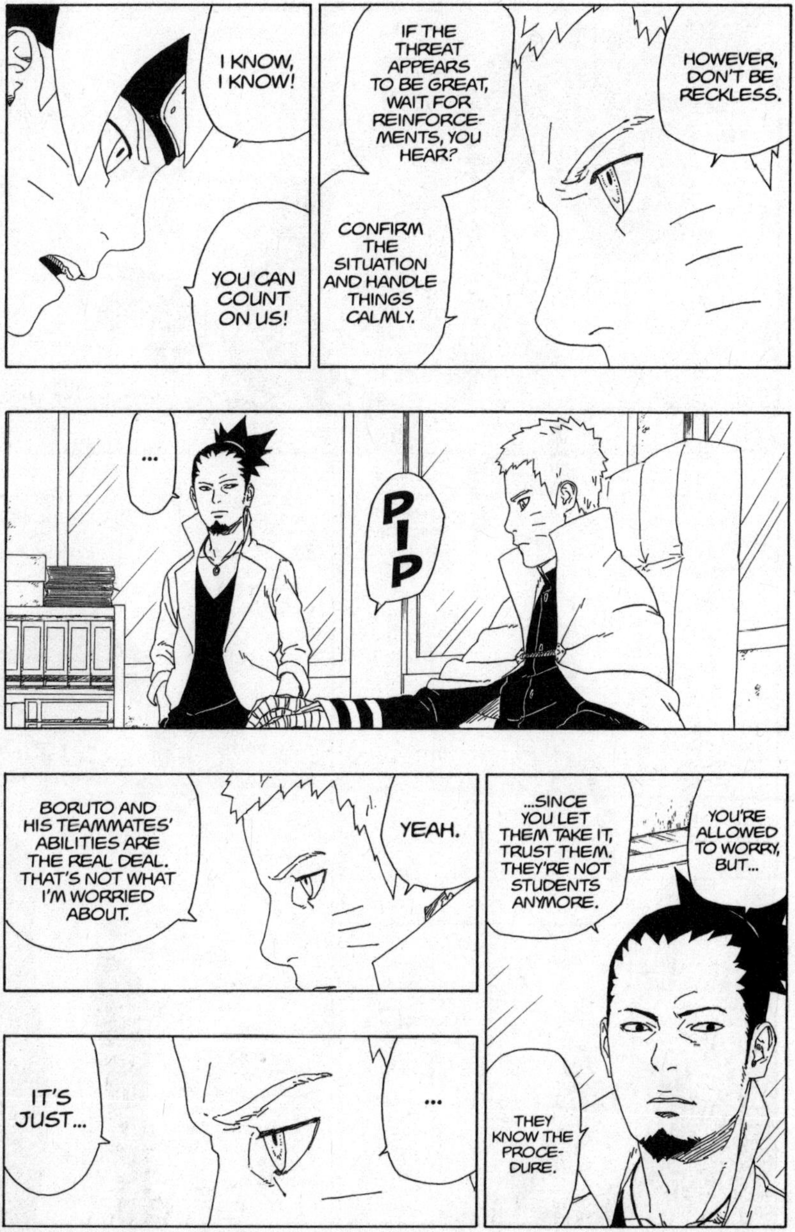
HOWEVER, DON'T BE RECKLESS.
IF THE THREAT APPEARS TO BE GREAT, WAIT FOR REINFORCE-MENTS, YOU HEAR?
CONFIRM THE SITUATION AND HANDLE THINGS CALMLY.
I KNOW, I KNOW!
YOU CAN COUNT ON US!
PIP
...
YOU'RE ALLOWED TO WORRY, BUT...
...SINCE YOU LET THEM TAKE IT, TRUST THEM. THEY'RE NOT STUDENTS ANYMORE.
THEY KNOW THE PROCE-DURE.
YEAH.
BORUTO AND HIS TEAMMATES' ABILITIES ARE THE REAL DEAL. THAT'S NOT WHAT I'M WORRIED ABOUT.
...
IT'S JUST...

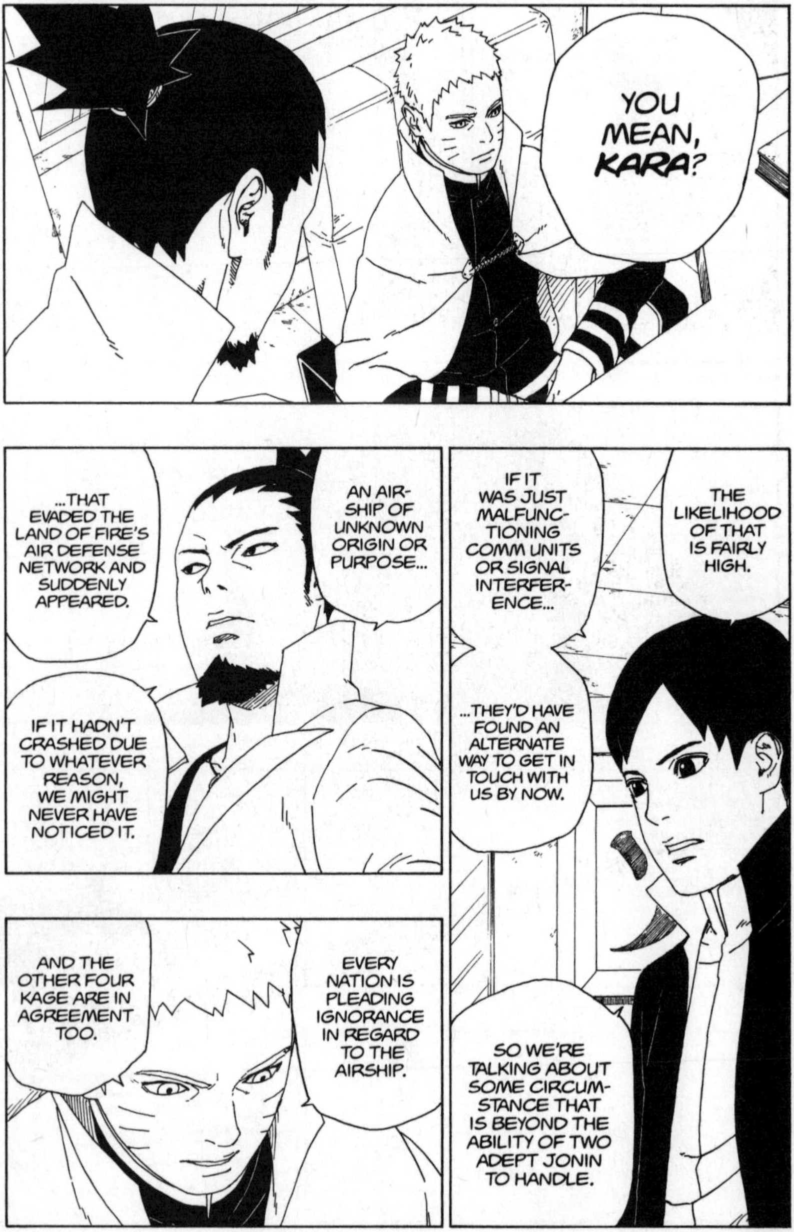
YOU MEAN, KARA?
THE LIKELIHOOD OF THAT IS FAIRLY HIGH.
IF IT WAS JUST MALFUNCTIONING COMM UNITS OR SIGNAL INTERFERENCE...
...THEY'D HAVE FOUND AN ALTERNATE WAY TO GET IN TOUCH WITH US BY NOW.
SO WE'RE TALKING ABOUT SOME CIRCUMSTANCE THAT IS BEYOND THE ABILITY OF TWO ADEPT JONIN TO HANDLE.
AN AIRSHIP OF UNKNOWN ORIGIN OR PURPOSE...
...THAT EVADED THE LAND OF FIRE'S AIR DEFENSE NETWORK AND SUDDENLY APPEARED.
IF IT HADN'T CRASHED DUE TO WHATEVER REASON, WE MIGHT NEVER HAVE NOTICED IT.
EVERY NATION IS PLEADING IGNORANCE IN REGARD TO THE AIRSHIP.
AND THE OTHER FOUR KAGE ARE IN AGREEMENT TOO.

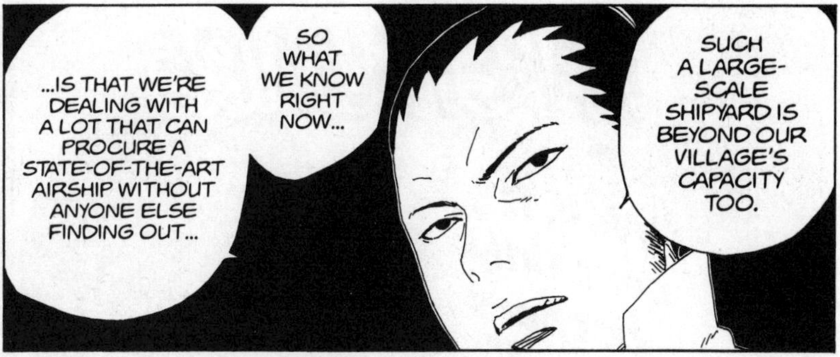
SUCH A LARGE-SCALE SHIPYARD IS BEYOND OUR VILLAGE'S CAPACITY TOO.
SO WHAT WE KNOW RIGHT NOW...
...IS THAT WE'RE DEALING WITH A LOT THAT CAN PROCURE A STATE-OF-THE-ART AIRSHIP WITHOUT ANYONE ELSE FINDING OUT...

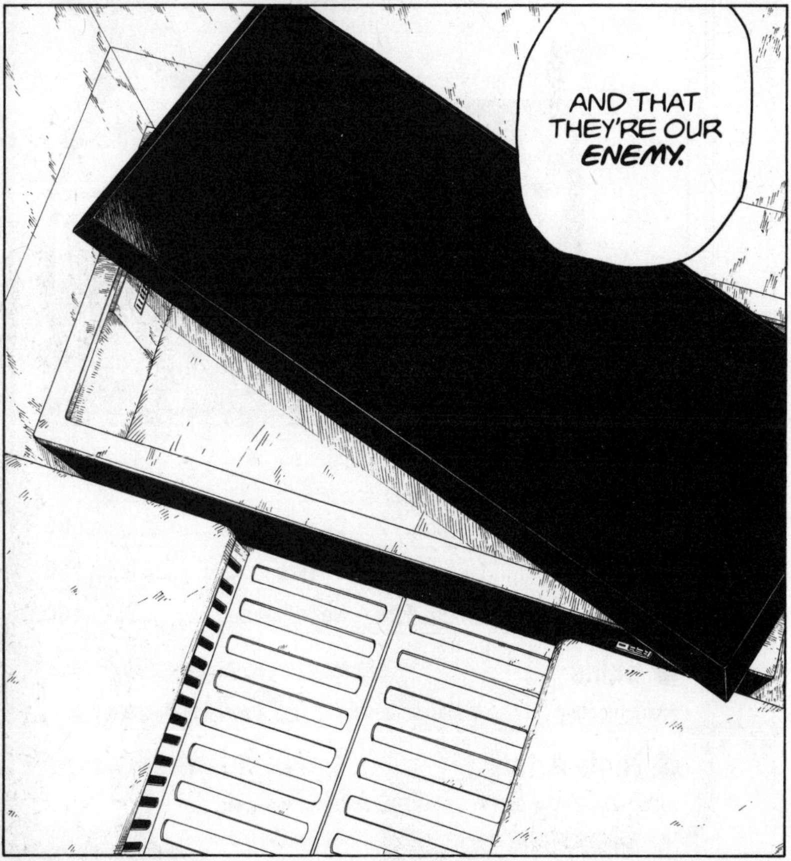
AND THAT THEY'RE OUR *ENEMY.*

NINJA ENCYCLOPEDIA · ENTRY 15

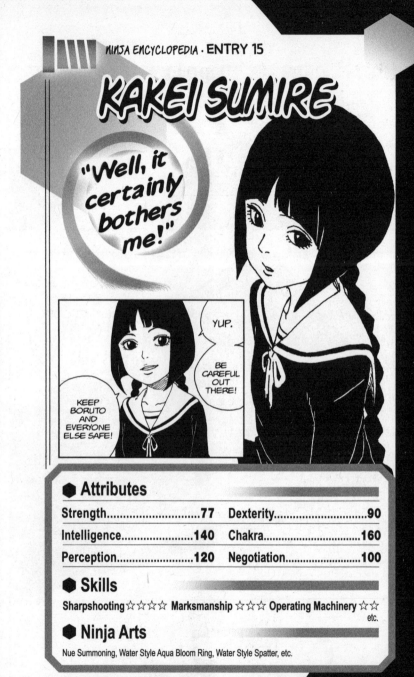

KAKEI SUMIRE

"Well, it certainly bothers me!"

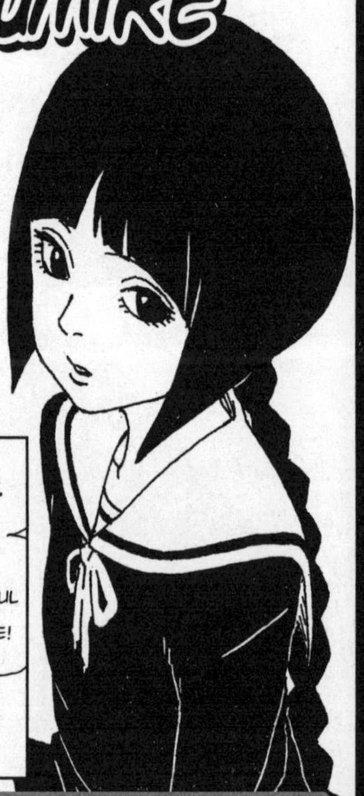

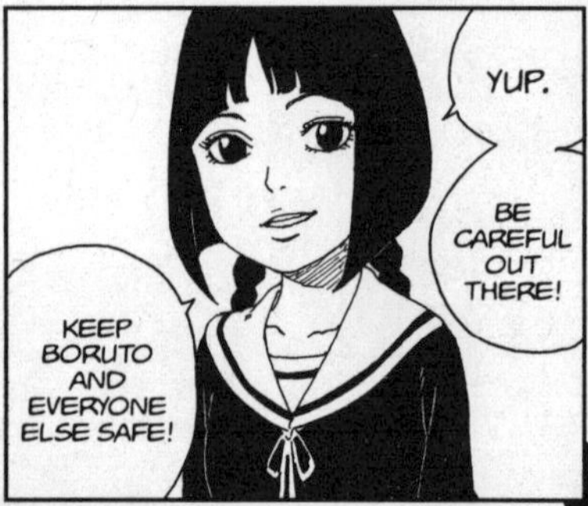
YUP.
BE CAREFUL OUT THERE!
KEEP BORUTO AND EVERYONE ELSE SAFE!

● Attributes

Strength............................77	Dexterity..............................90
Intelligence......................140	Chakra.................................160
Perception........................120	Negotiation.........................100

● Skills

Sharpshooting☆☆☆☆ Marksmanship ☆☆☆ Operating Machinery ☆☆ etc.

● Ninja Arts

Nue Summoning, Water Style Aqua Bloom Ring, Water Style Spatter, etc.

*Average attribute value is 60 for ordinary people and 90 for genin. Skill values range from 1 to 5☆with 5☆signifying super top-notch.

Number 19: Puppets

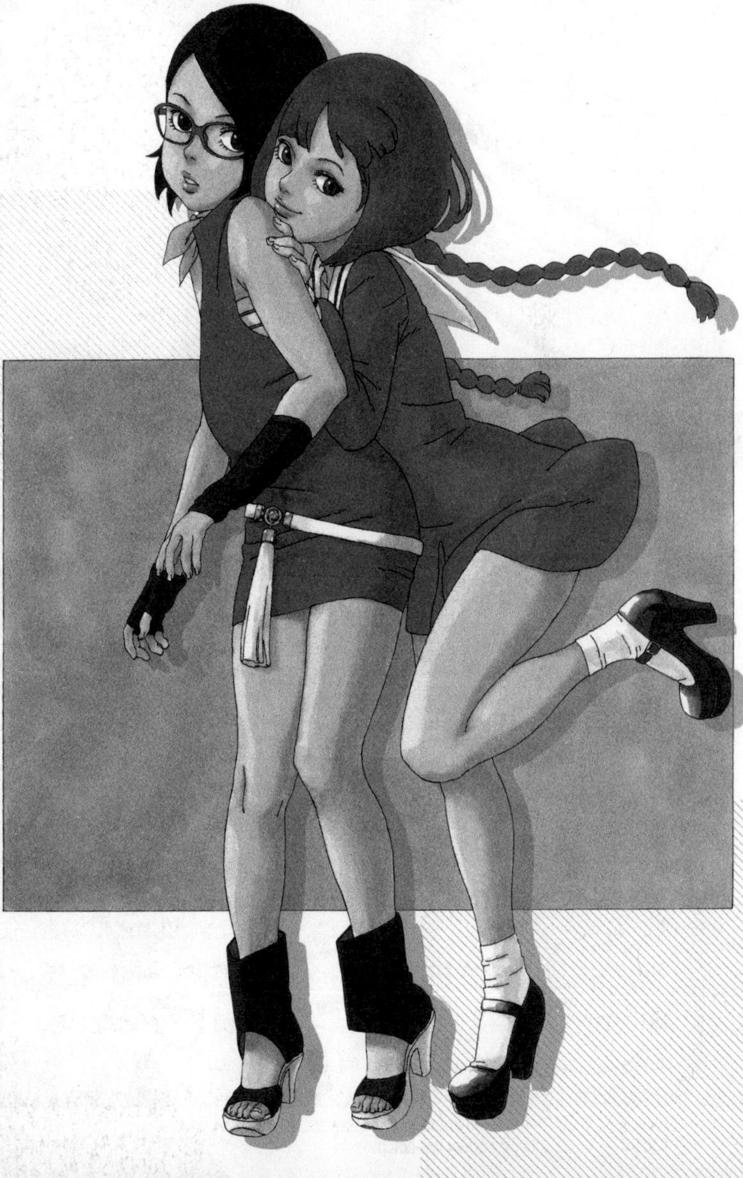

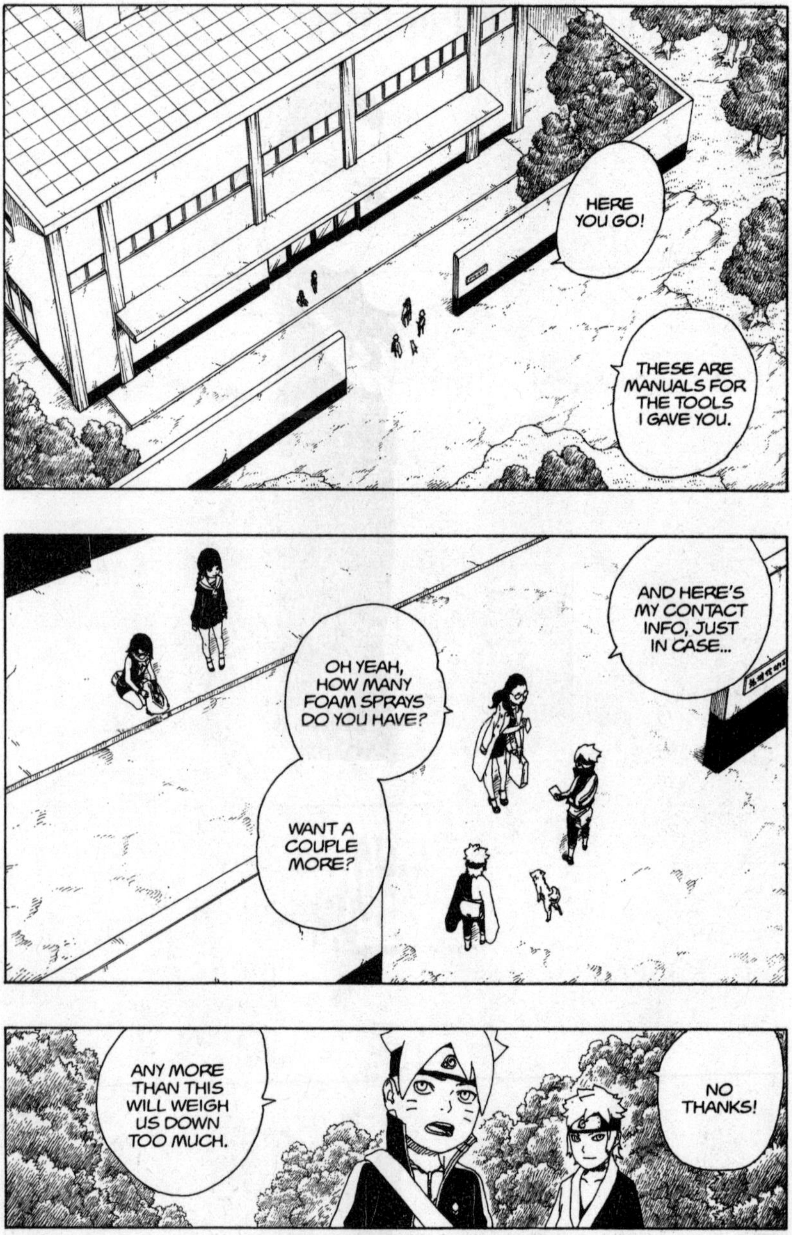
HERE YOU GO!
THESE ARE MANUALS FOR THE TOOLS I GAVE YOU.
AND HERE'S MY CONTACT INFO, JUST IN CASE...
OH YEAH, HOW MANY FOAM SPRAYS DO YOU HAVE?
WANT A COUPLE MORE?
NO THANKS!
ANY MORE THAN THIS WILL WEIGH US DOWN TOO MUCH.

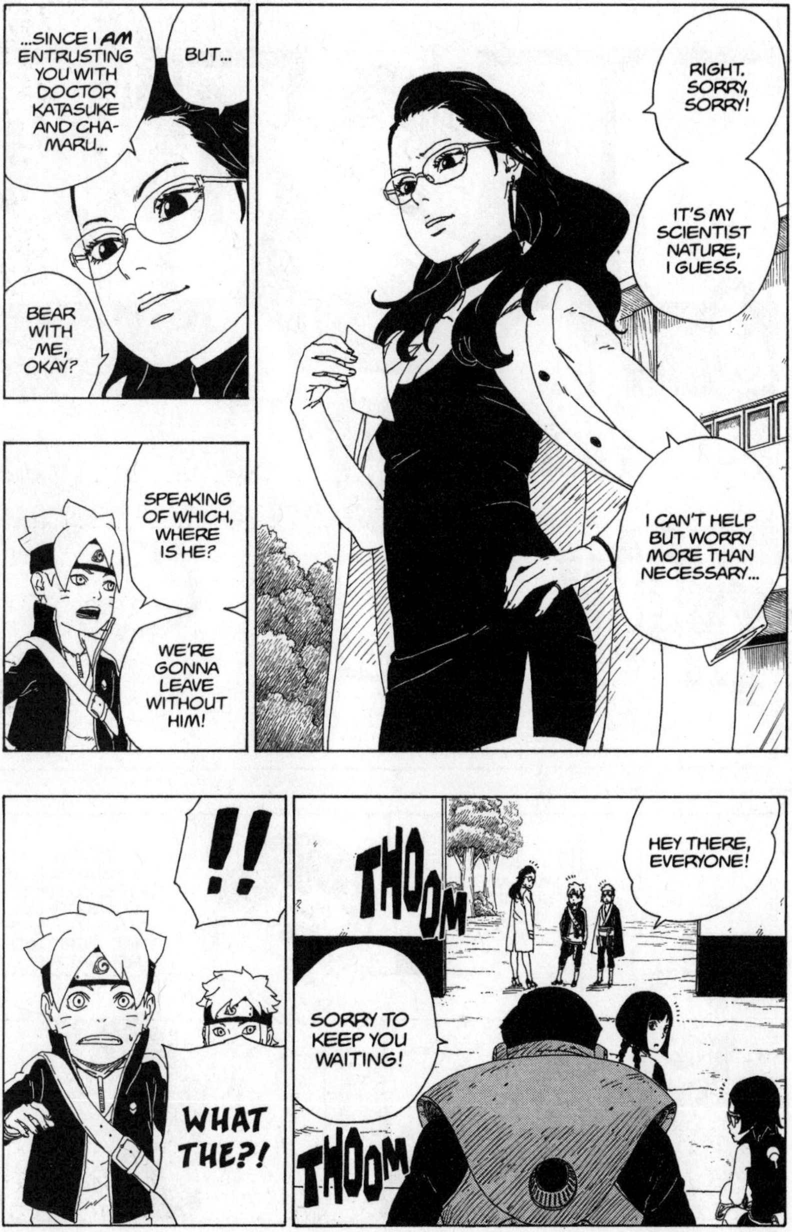
RIGHT. SORRY, SORRY!
IT'S MY SCIENTIST NATURE, I GUESS.
I CAN'T HELP BUT WORRY MORE THAN NECESSARY...
BUT...
...SINCE I AM ENTRUSTING YOU WITH DOCTOR KATASUKE AND CHA-MARU...
BEAR WITH ME, OKAY?
SPEAKING OF WHICH, WHERE IS HE?
WE'RE GONNA LEAVE WITHOUT HIM!
HEY THERE, EVERYONE!
THOOM
SORRY TO KEEP YOU WAITING!
THOOM
!!
WHAT THE?!

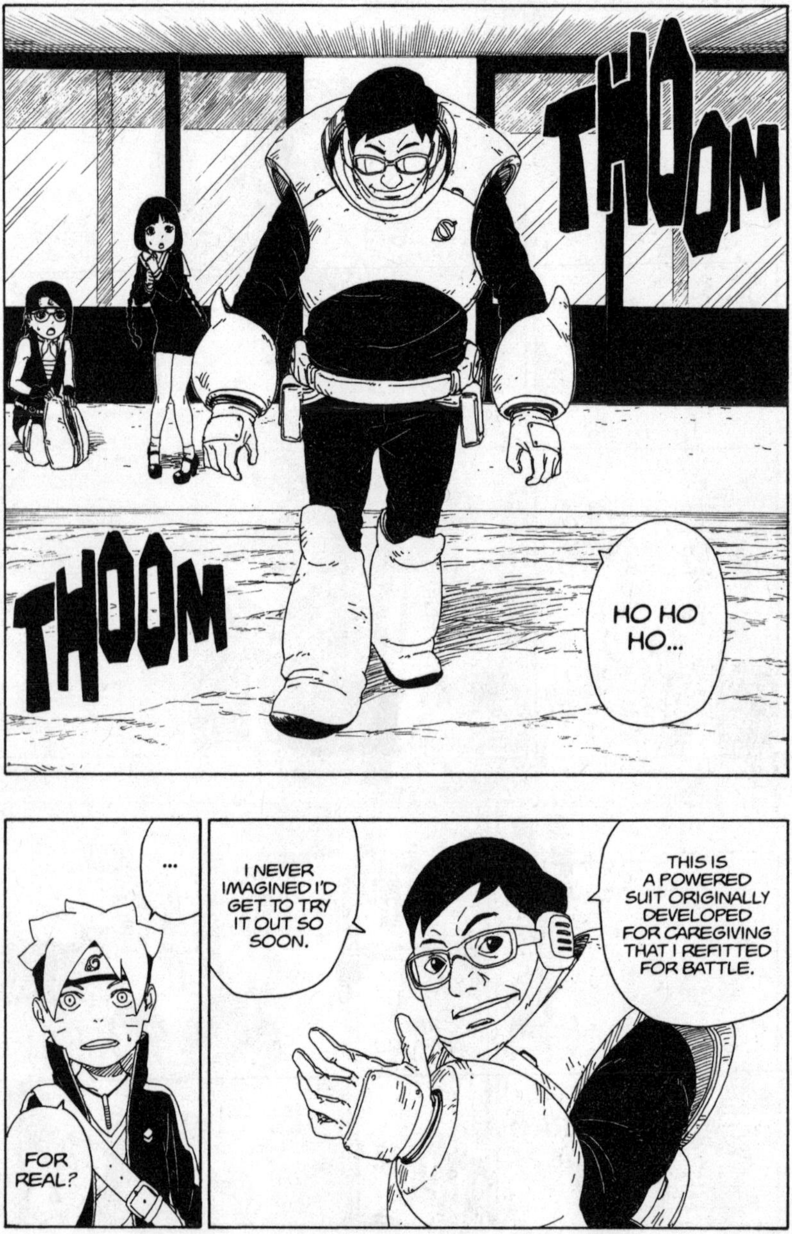
THOOM
HO HO HO...
THOOM
THIS IS A POWERED SUIT ORIGINALLY DEVELOPED FOR CAREGIVING THAT I REFITTED FOR BATTLE.
I NEVER IMAGINED I'D GET TO TRY IT OUT SO SOON.
...
FOR REAL?

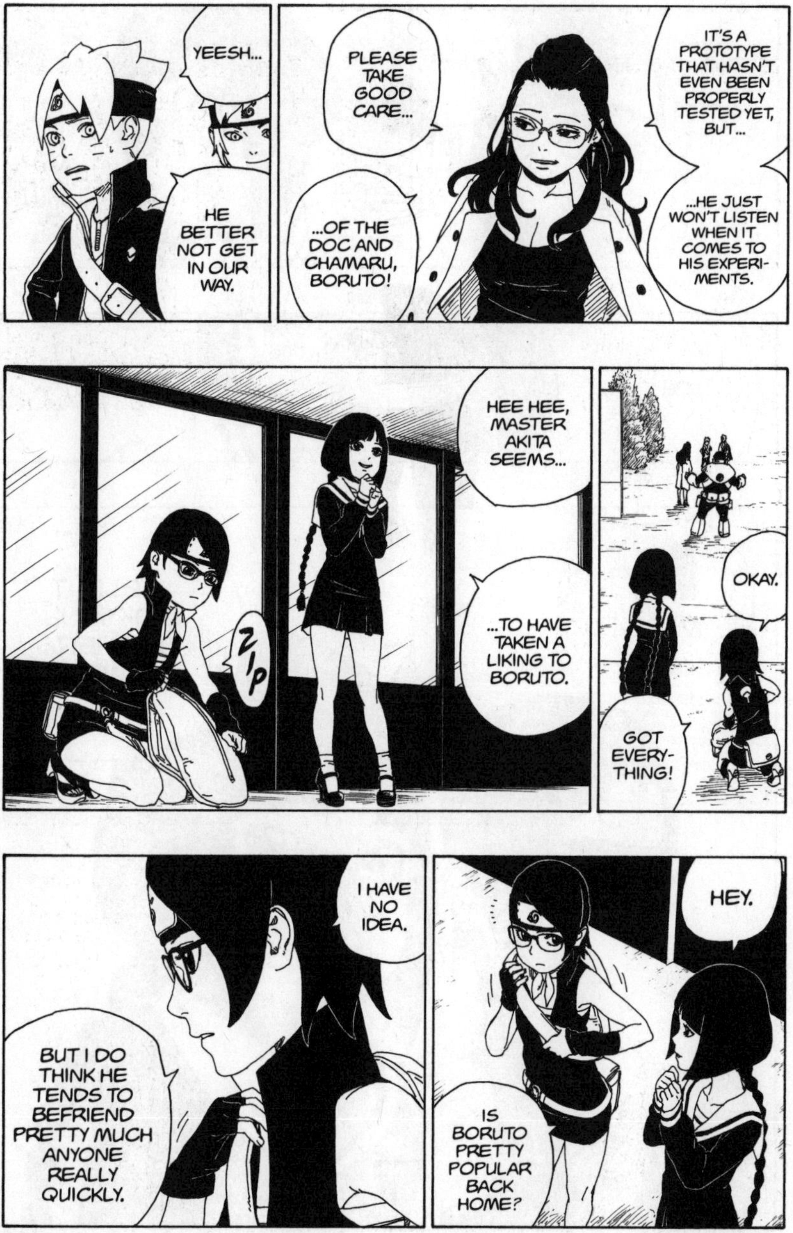
IT'S A PROTOTYPE THAT HASN'T EVEN BEEN PROPERLY TESTED YET, BUT...
...HE JUST WON'T LISTEN WHEN IT COMES TO HIS EXPERIMENTS.
PLEASE TAKE GOOD CARE...
...OF THE DOC AND CHAMARU, BORUTO!
YEESH...
HE BETTER NOT GET IN OUR WAY.
OKAY.
GOT EVERYTHING!
HEE HEE, MASTER AKITA SEEMS...
...TO HAVE TAKEN A LIKING TO BORUTO.
ZIP
HEY.
IS BORUTO PRETTY POPULAR BACK HOME?
I HAVE NO IDEA.
BUT I DO THINK HE TENDS TO BEFRIEND PRETTY MUCH ANYONE REALLY QUICKLY.

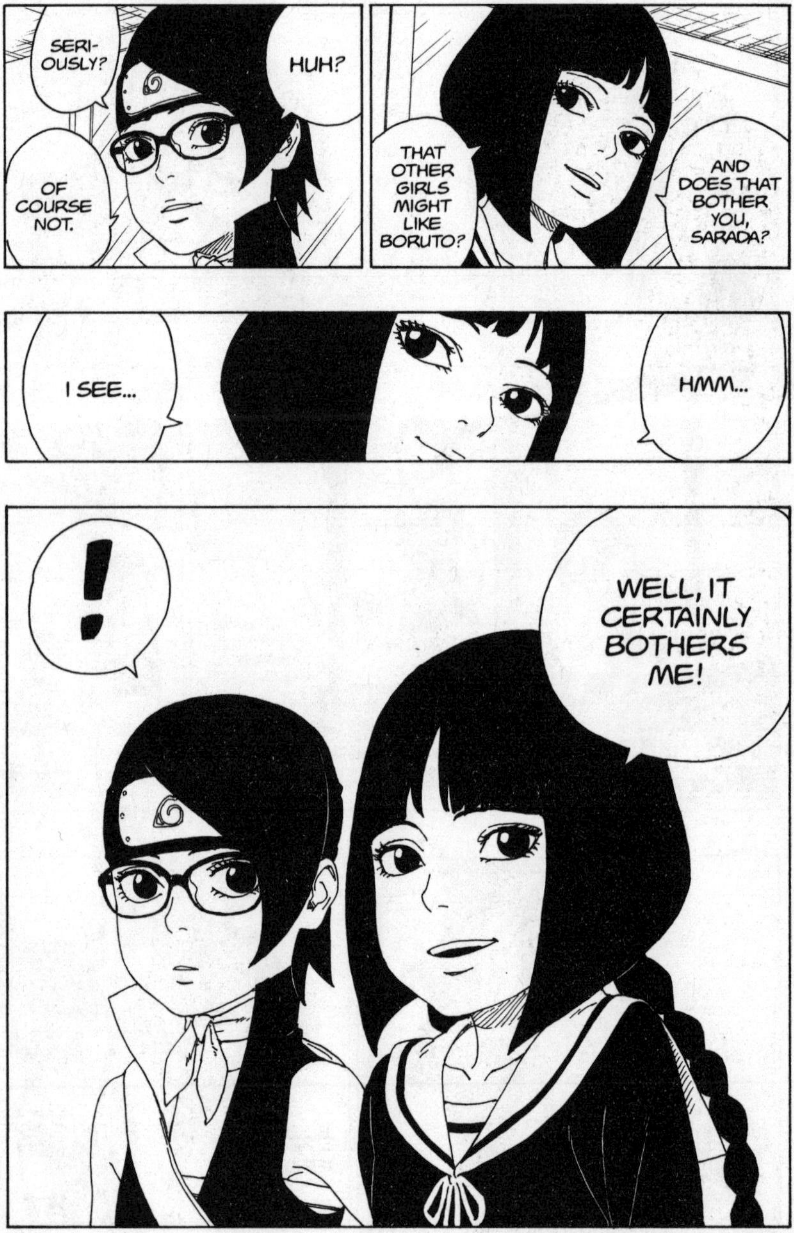

AND DOES THAT BOTHER YOU, SARADA?
THAT OTHER GIRLS MIGHT LIKE BORUTO?
HUH?
SERI-OUSLY?
OF COURSE NOT.
HMM...
I SEE...
WELL, IT CERTAINLY BOTHERS ME!
!

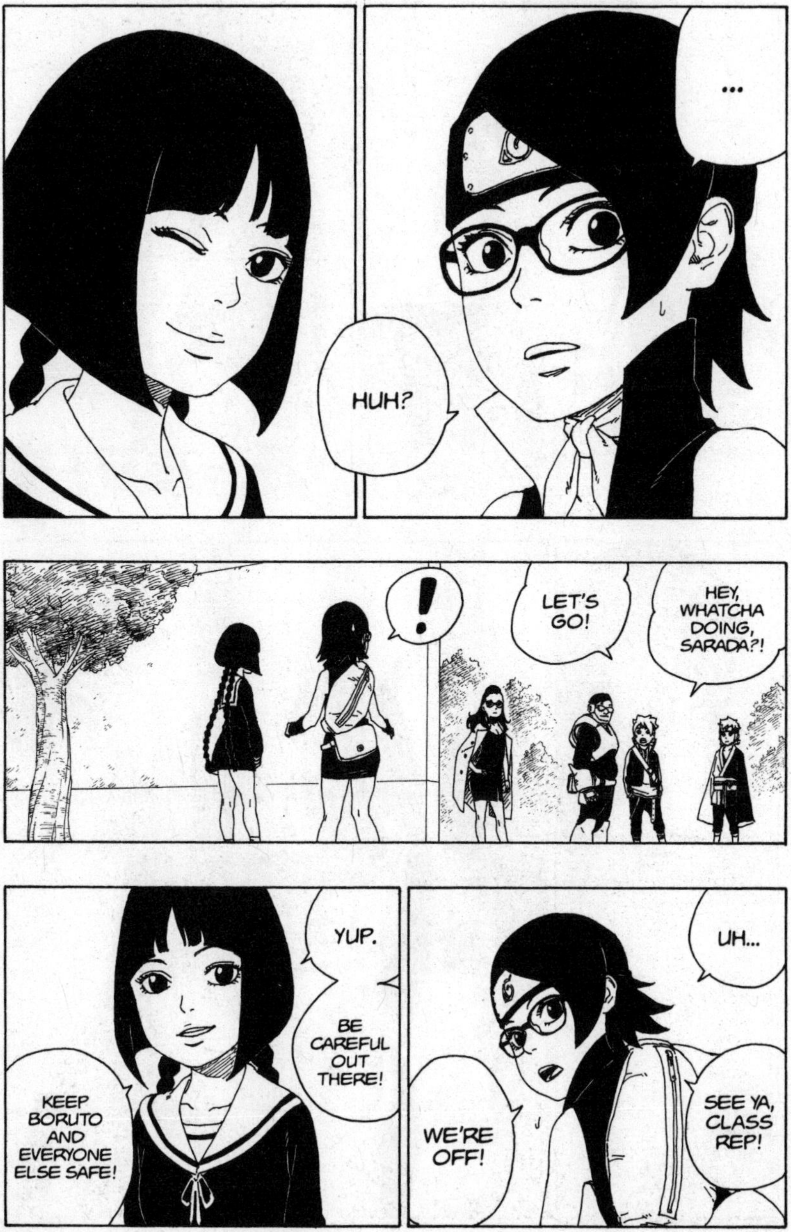
...
HUH?
HEY, WHATCHA DOING, SARADA?!
LET'S GO!
!
UH...
SEE YA, CLASS REP!
WE'RE OFF!
YUP.
BE CAREFUL OUT THERE!
KEEP BORUTO AND EVERYONE ELSE SAFE!

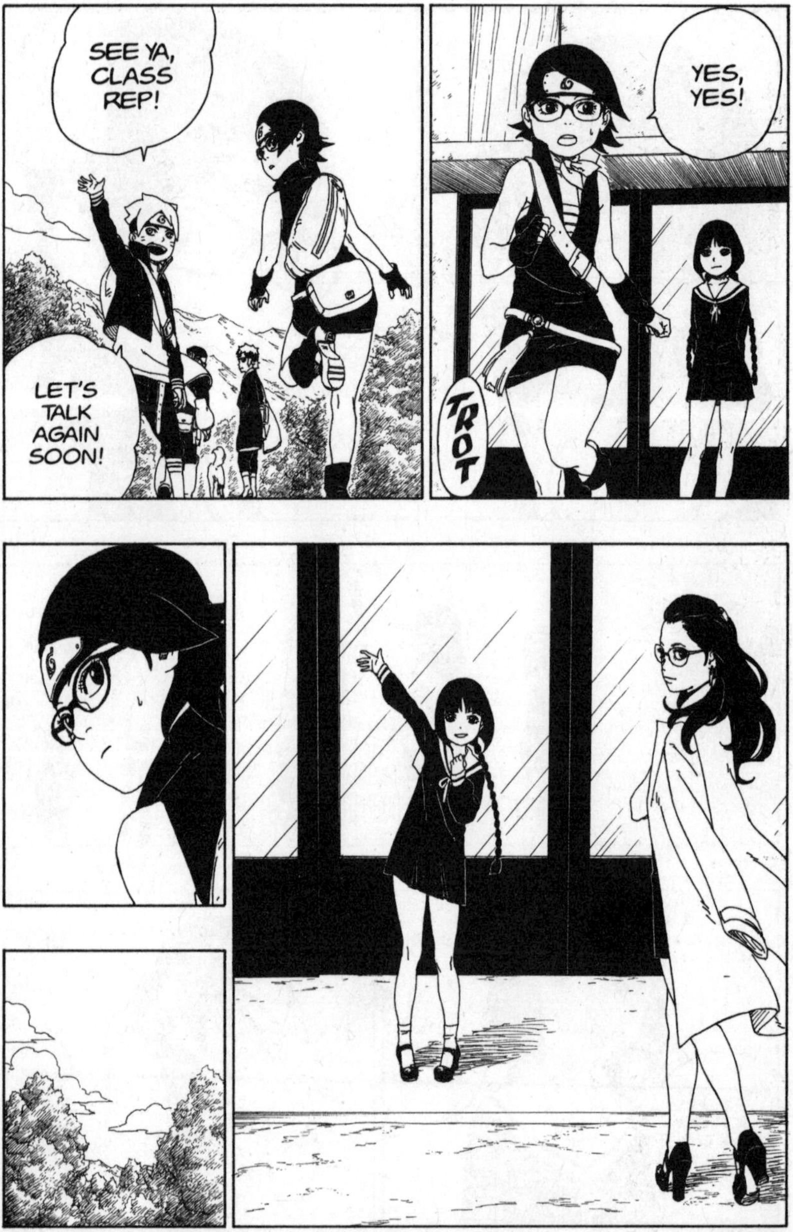
YES, YES!
TROT
SEE YA, CLASS REP!
LET'S TALK AGAIN SOON!

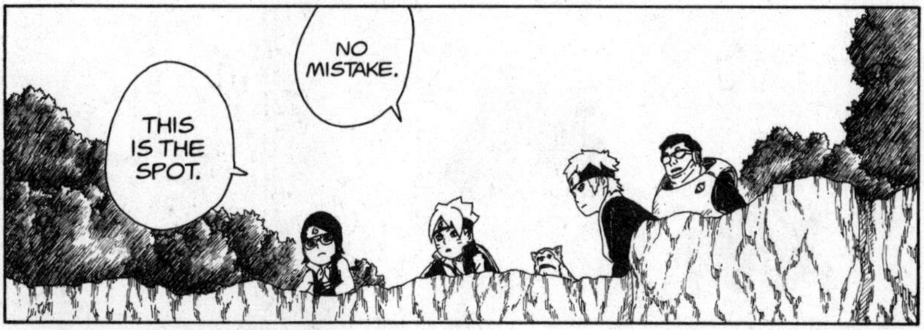
NO MISTAKE.
THIS IS THE SPOT.

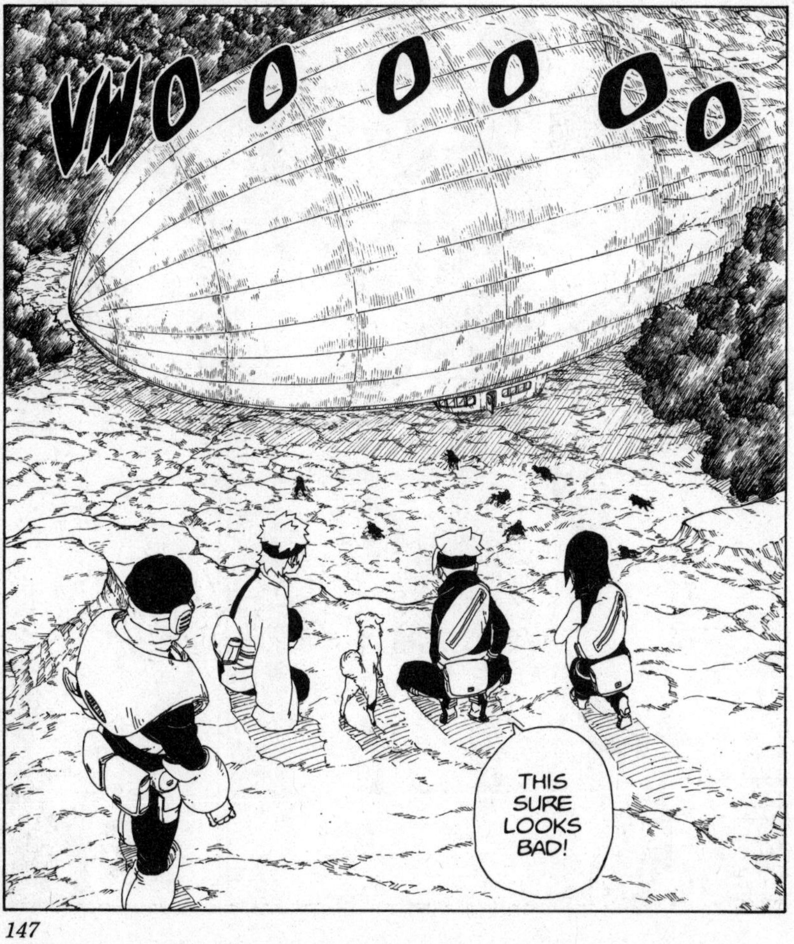
VWOOOOOO
THIS SURE LOOKS BAD!

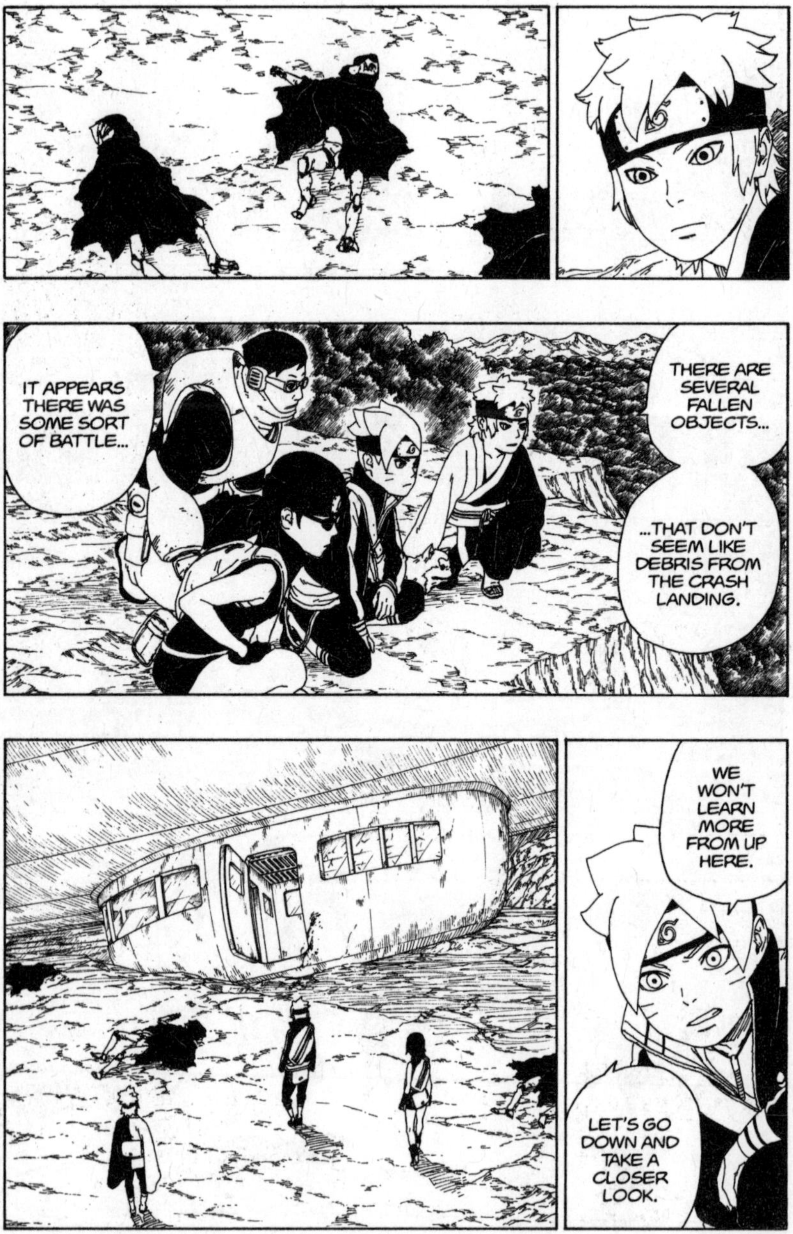
THERE ARE SEVERAL FALLEN OBJECTS...
...THAT DON'T SEEM LIKE DEBRIS FROM THE CRASH LANDING.
IT APPEARS THERE WAS SOME SORT OF BATTLE...
WE WON'T LEARN MORE FROM UP HERE.
LET'S GO DOWN AND TAKE A CLOSER LOOK.

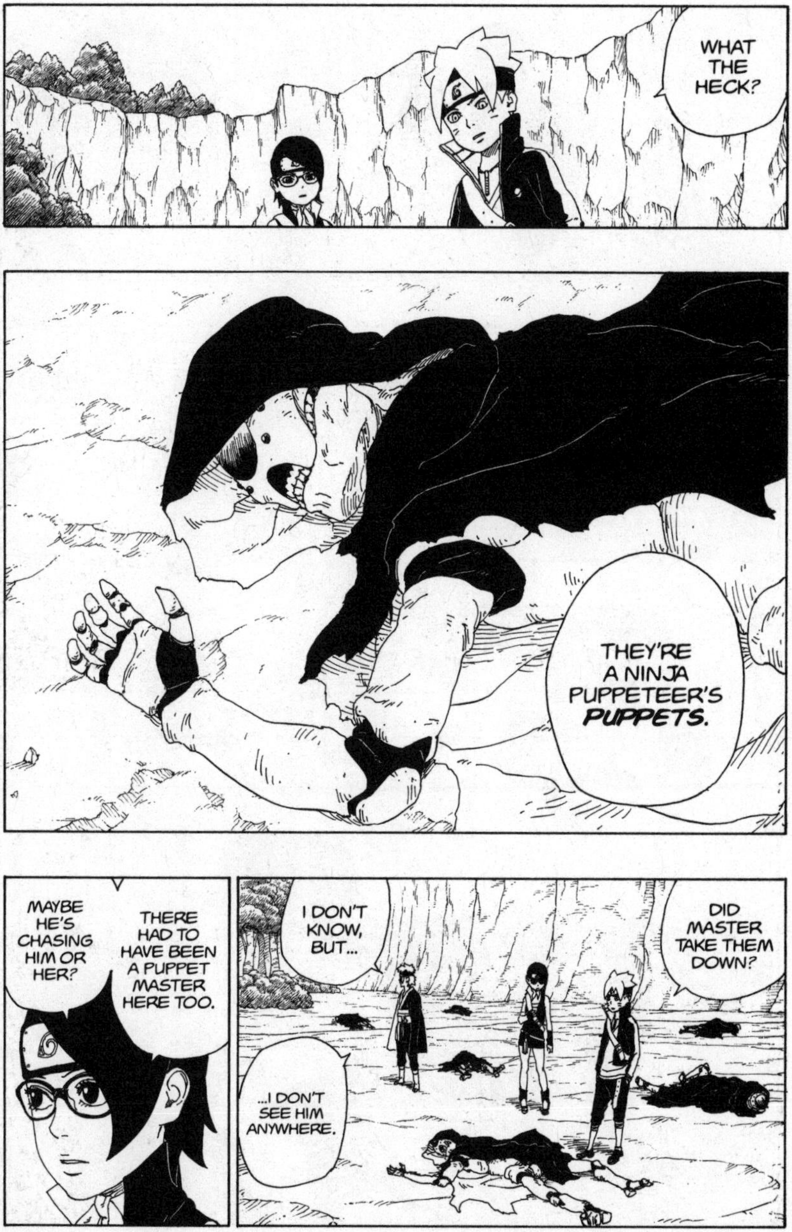
WHAT THE HECK?
THEY'RE A NINJA PUPPETEER'S *PUPPETS.*
DID MASTER TAKE THEM DOWN?
I DON'T KNOW, BUT...
...I DON'T SEE HIM ANYWHERE.
THERE HAD TO HAVE BEEN A PUPPET MASTER HERE TOO.
MAYBE HE'S CHASING HIM OR HER?

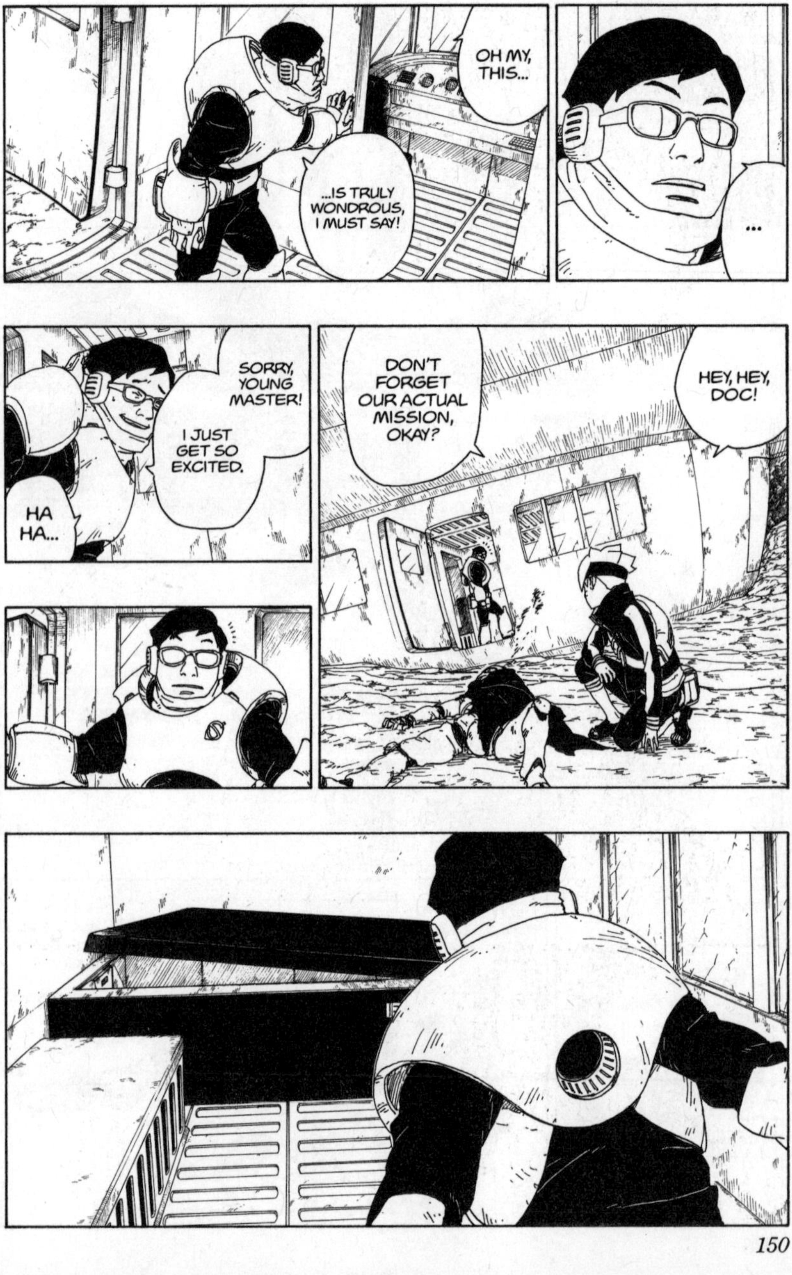
...
OH MY, THIS...
...IS TRULY WONDROUS, I MUST SAY!
HEY, HEY, DOC!
DON'T FORGET OUR ACTUAL MISSION, OKAY?
SORRY, YOUNG MASTER!
I JUST GET SO EXCITED.
HA HA...

THIS CON- TAINER...

...

COULD IT BE...?

KR!!

JERK

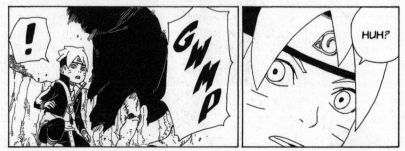

!

GWMP

HUH?

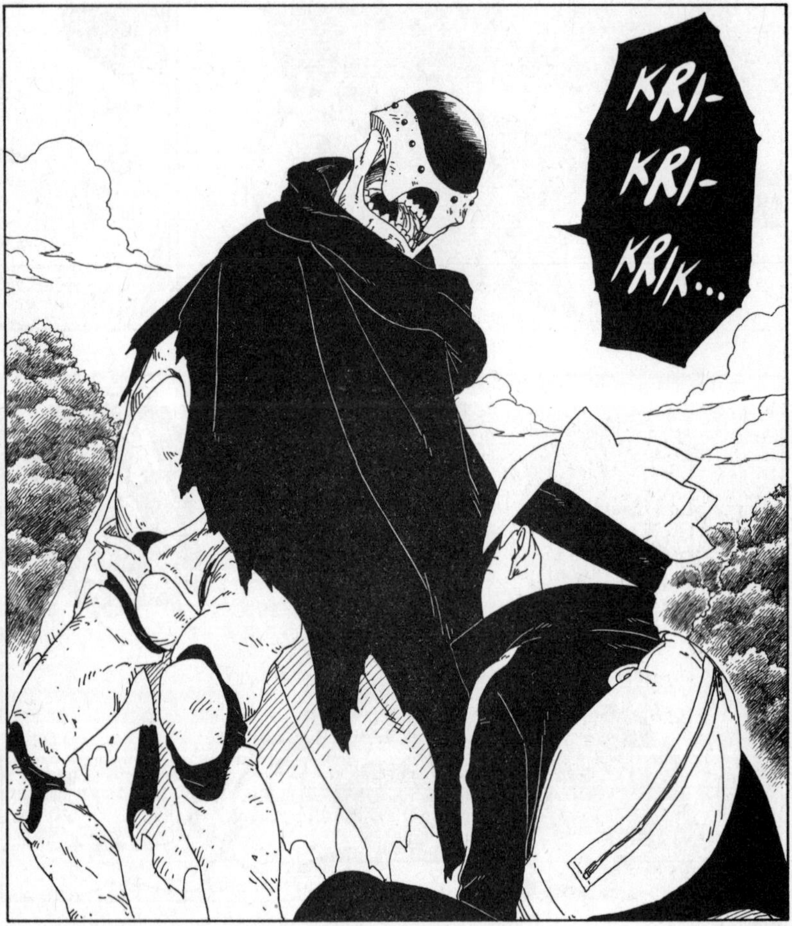
KRI-
KRI-
KRIK...

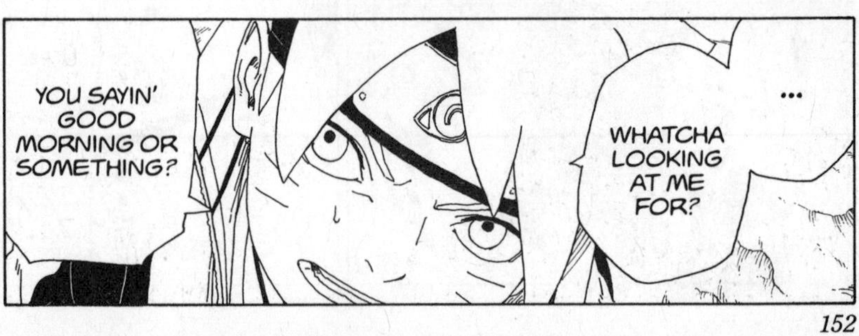
...
WHATCHA LOOKING AT ME FOR?
YOU SAYIN' GOOD MORNING OR SOMETHING?

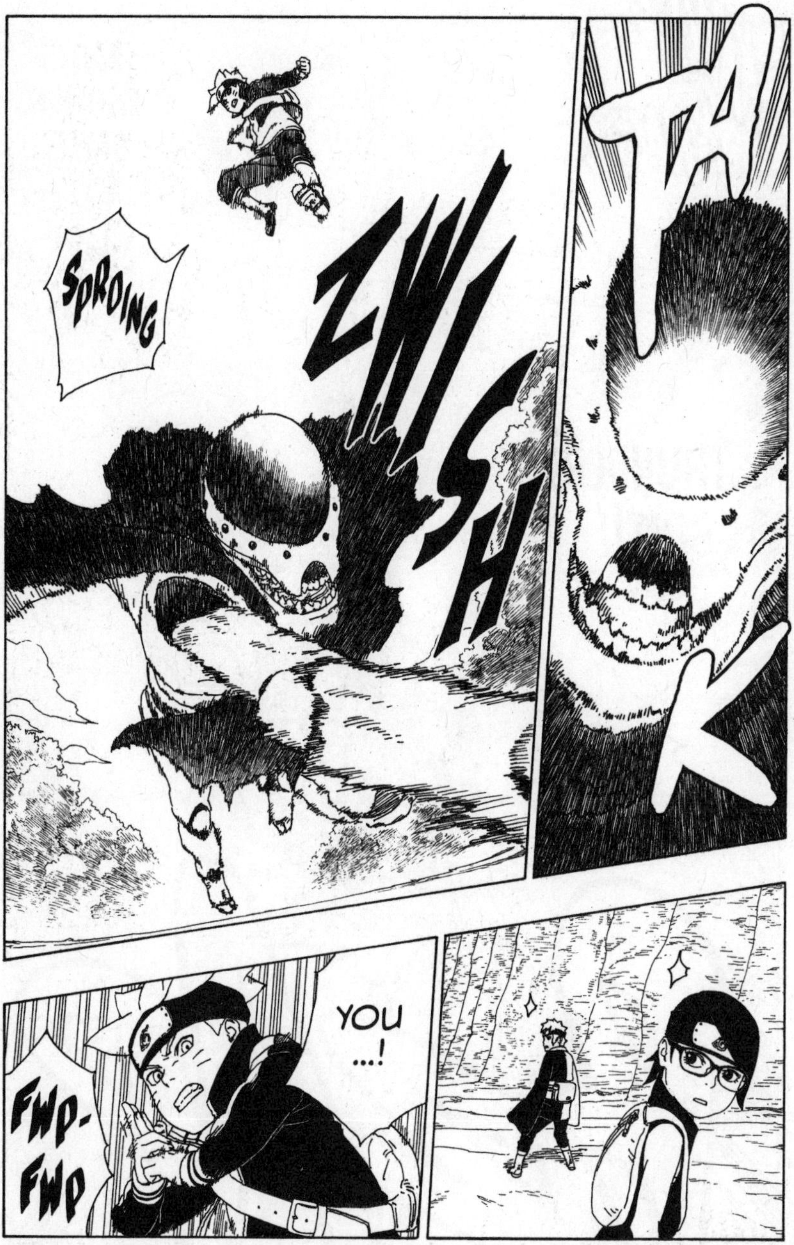
TAK
ZWISH
SPROING
YOU ...!
FWP-FWP

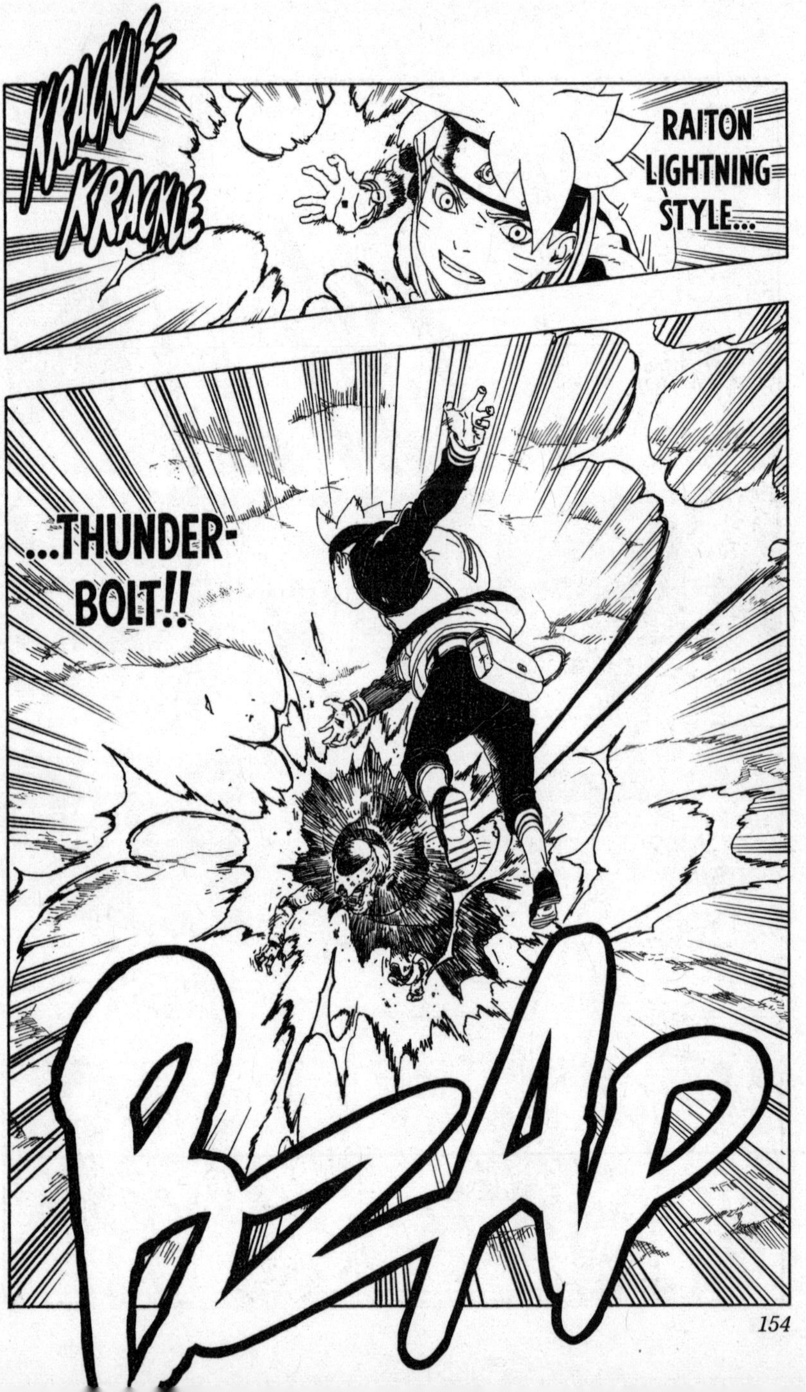
RAITON LIGHTNING STYLE...
KRACKLE KRACKLE
...THUNDER-BOLT!!
BZAP

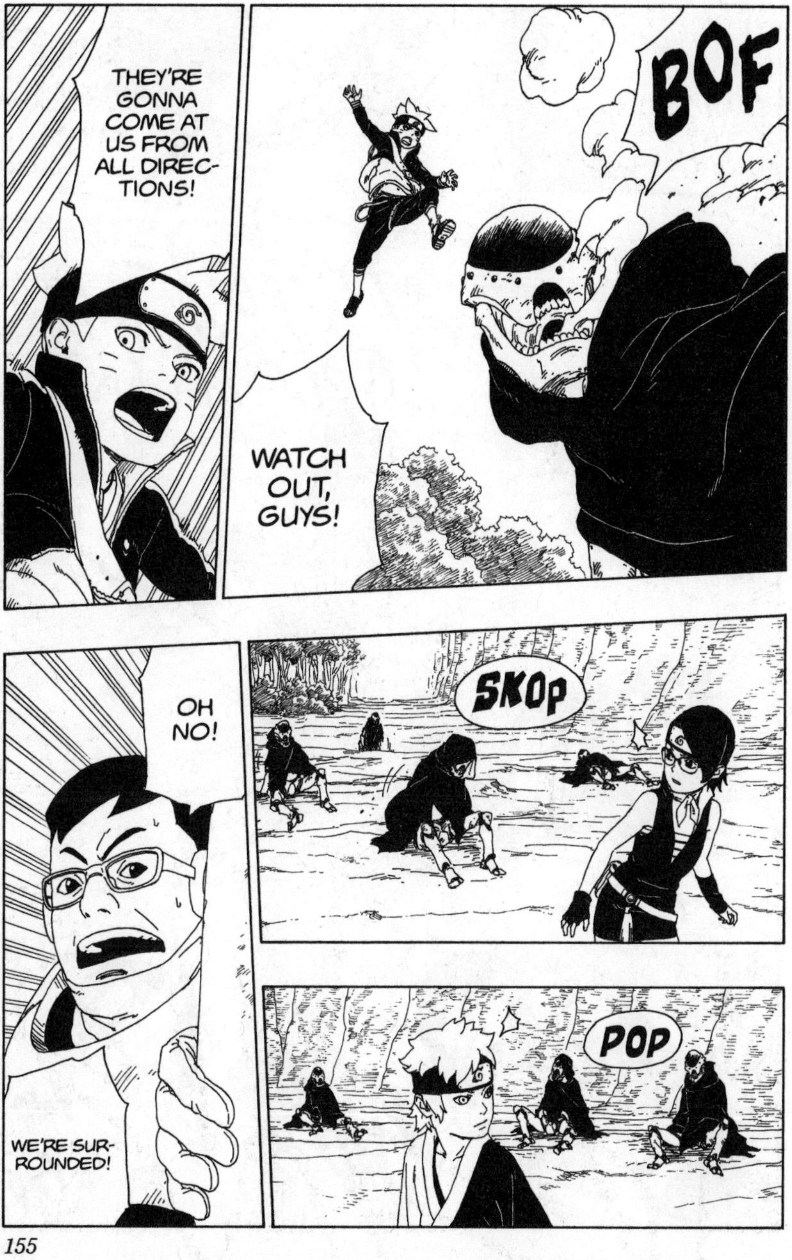
BOF
WATCH OUT, GUYS!
THEY'RE GONNA COME AT US FROM ALL DIREC-TIONS!
SKOP
POP
OH NO!
WE'RE SUR-ROUNDED!

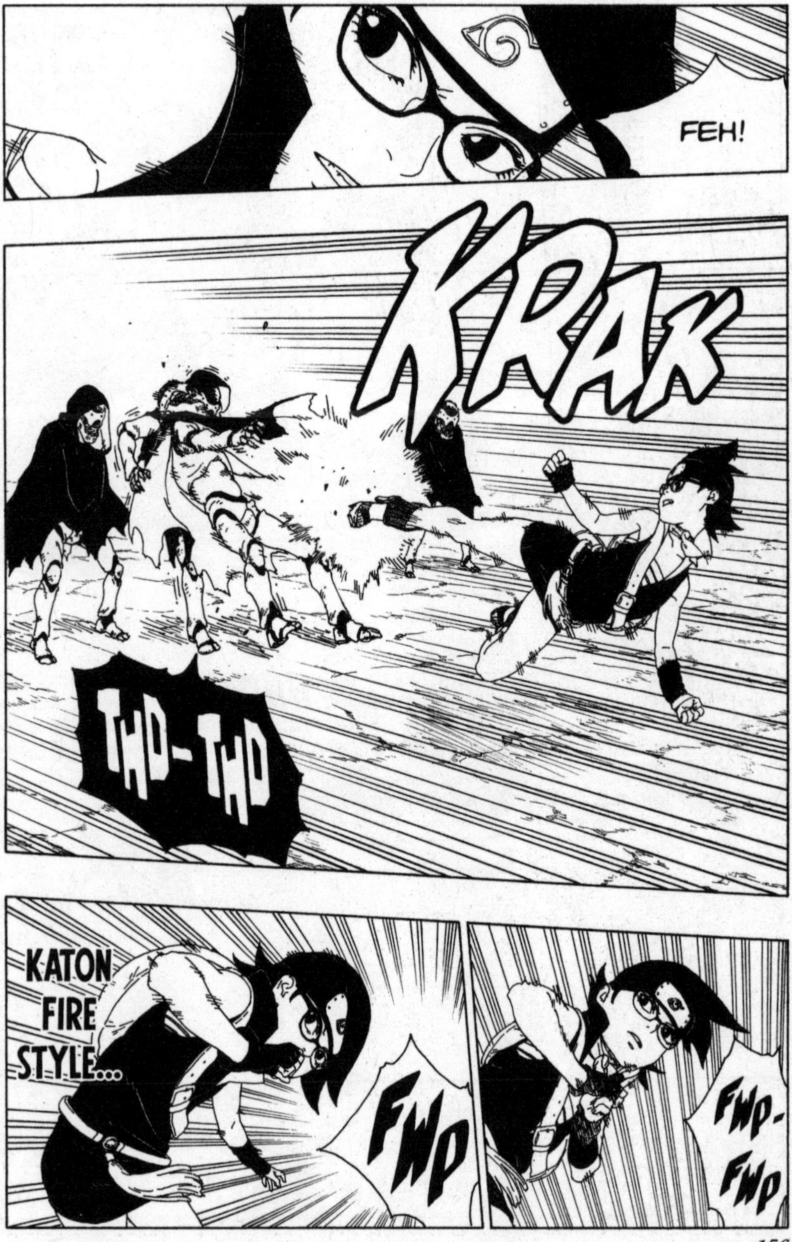
FEH!
KRAK
THD-THD
FWP-FWP
KATON FIRE STYLE...
FWP

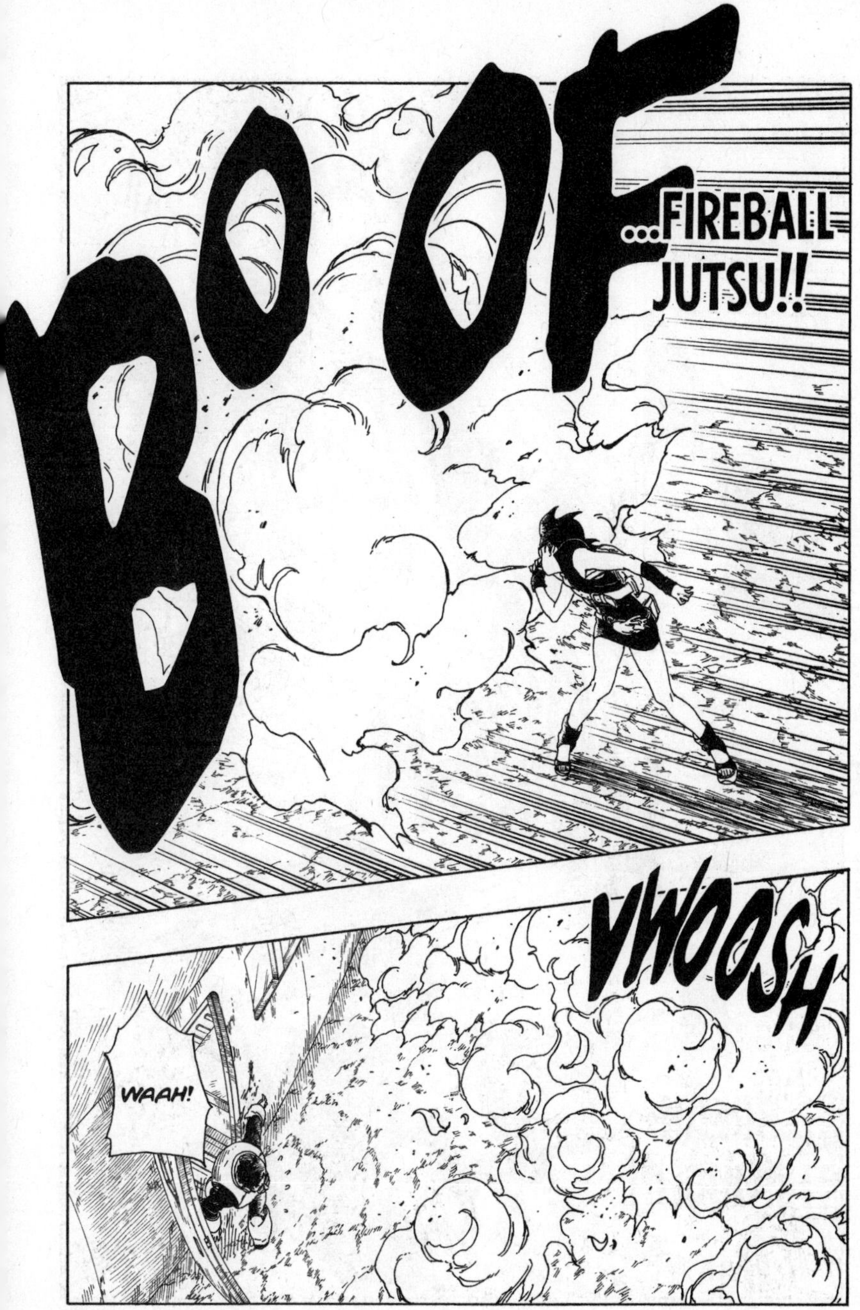
BOOF
...FIREBALL JUTSU!!
VWOOSH
WAAH!

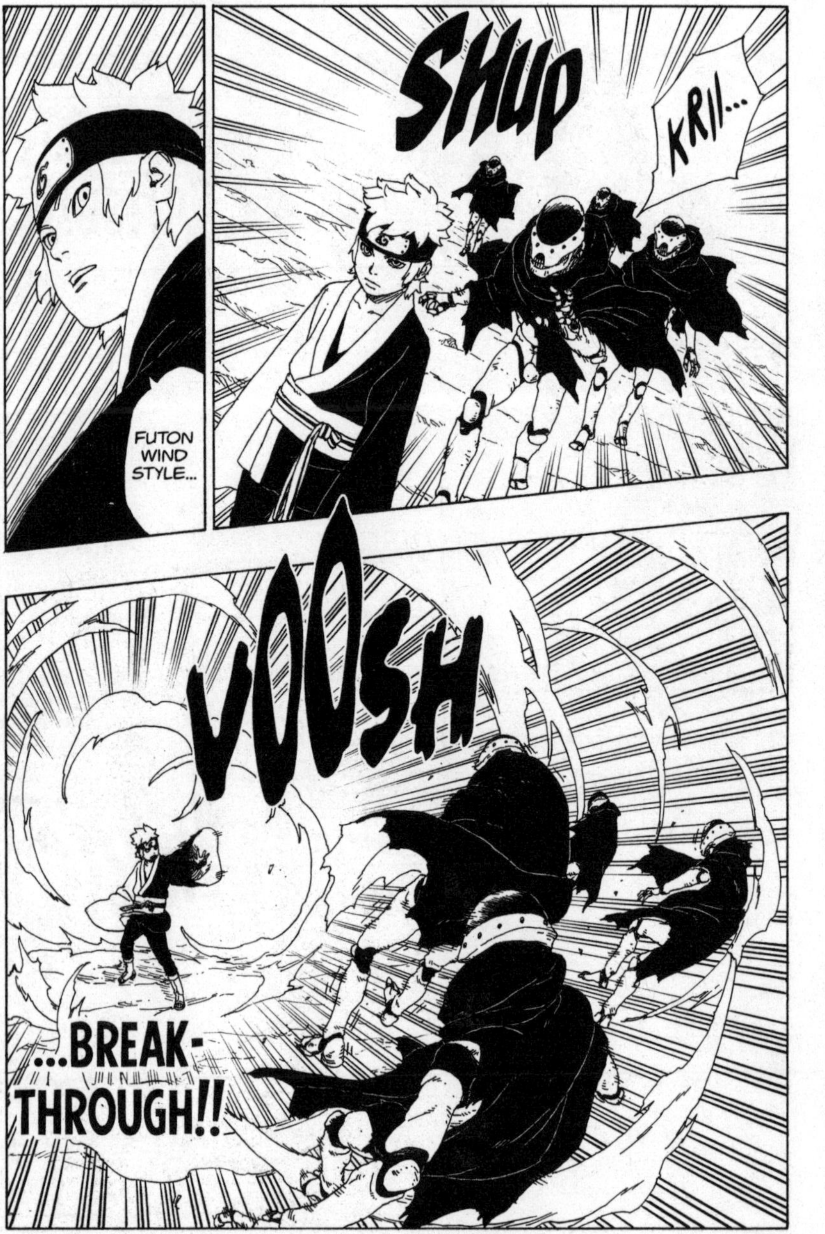
SHUP
KRII...
FUTON WIND STYLE...
VOOSH
...BREAK-THROUGH!!

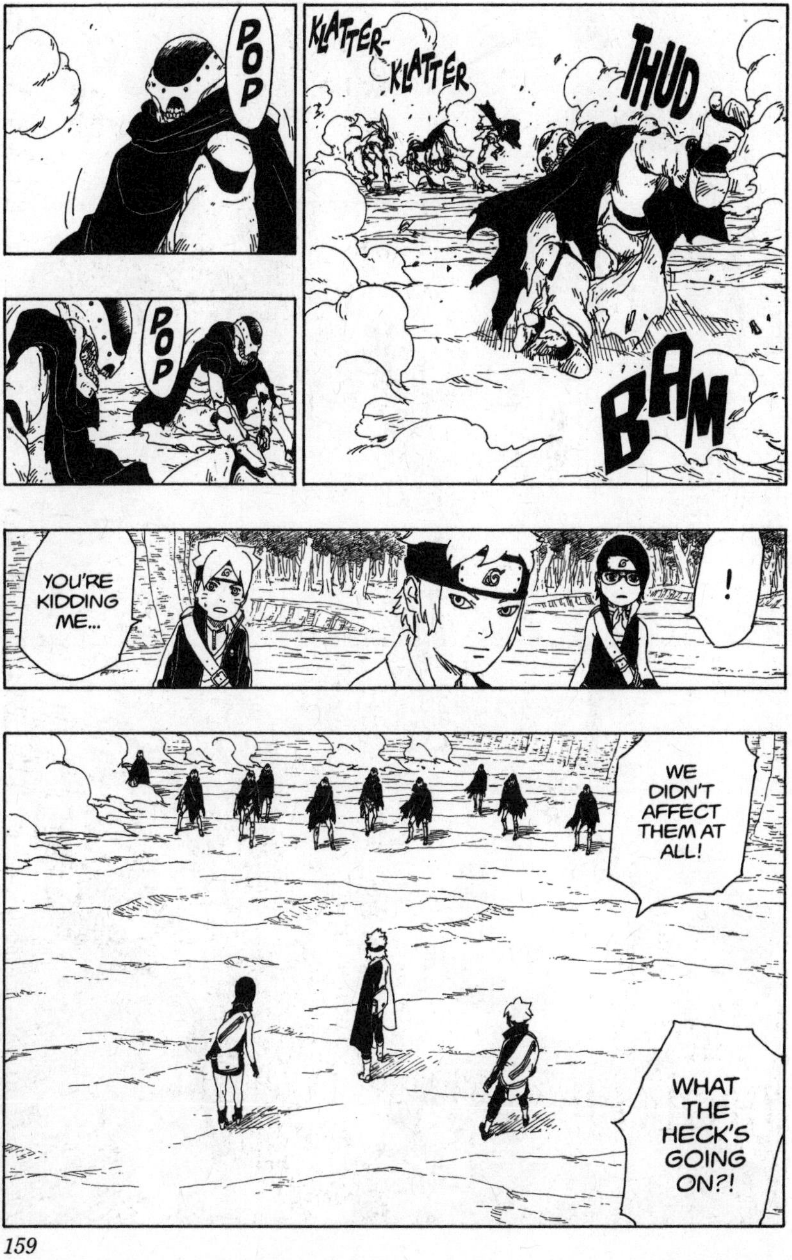
KLATTER-KLATTER
THUD
BAM
POP
POP
!
YOU'RE KIDDING ME...
WE DIDN'T AFFECT THEM AT ALL!
WHAT THE HECK'S GOING ON?!

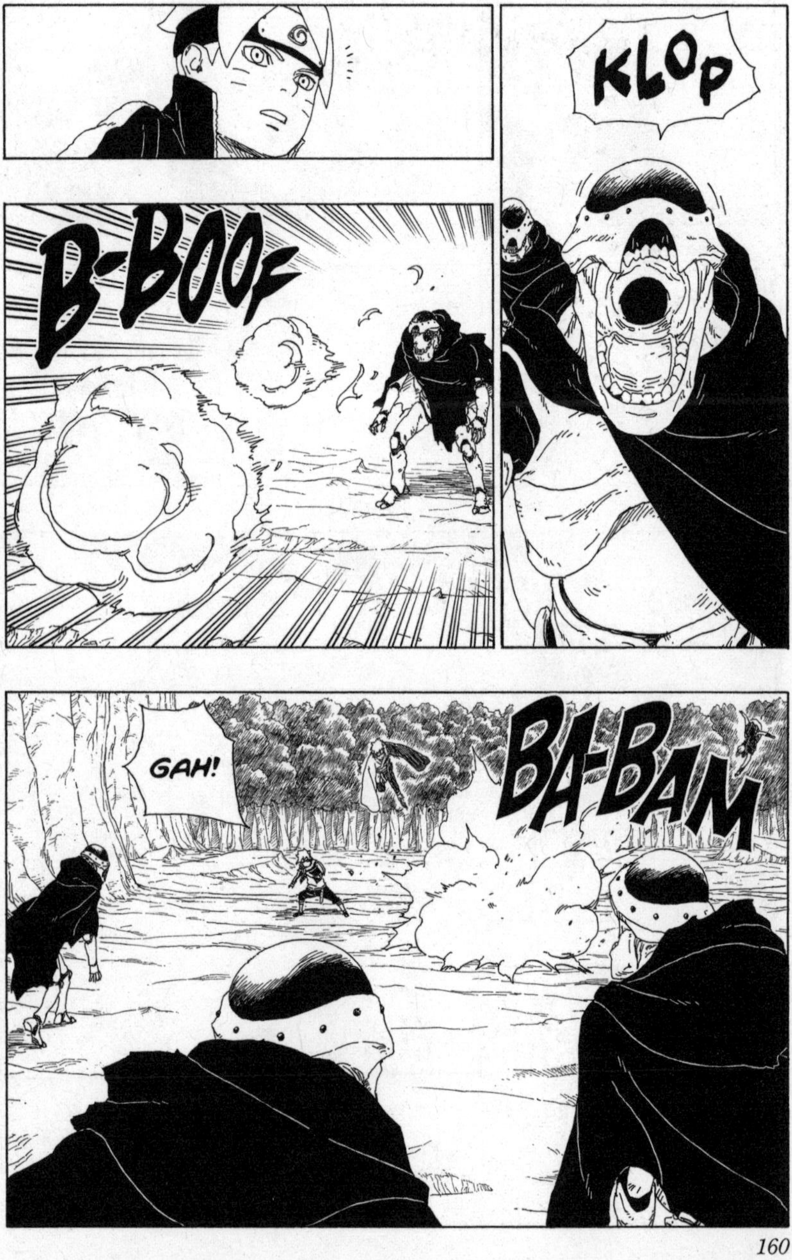
KLOP
B-BOOF
BA-BAM
GAH!

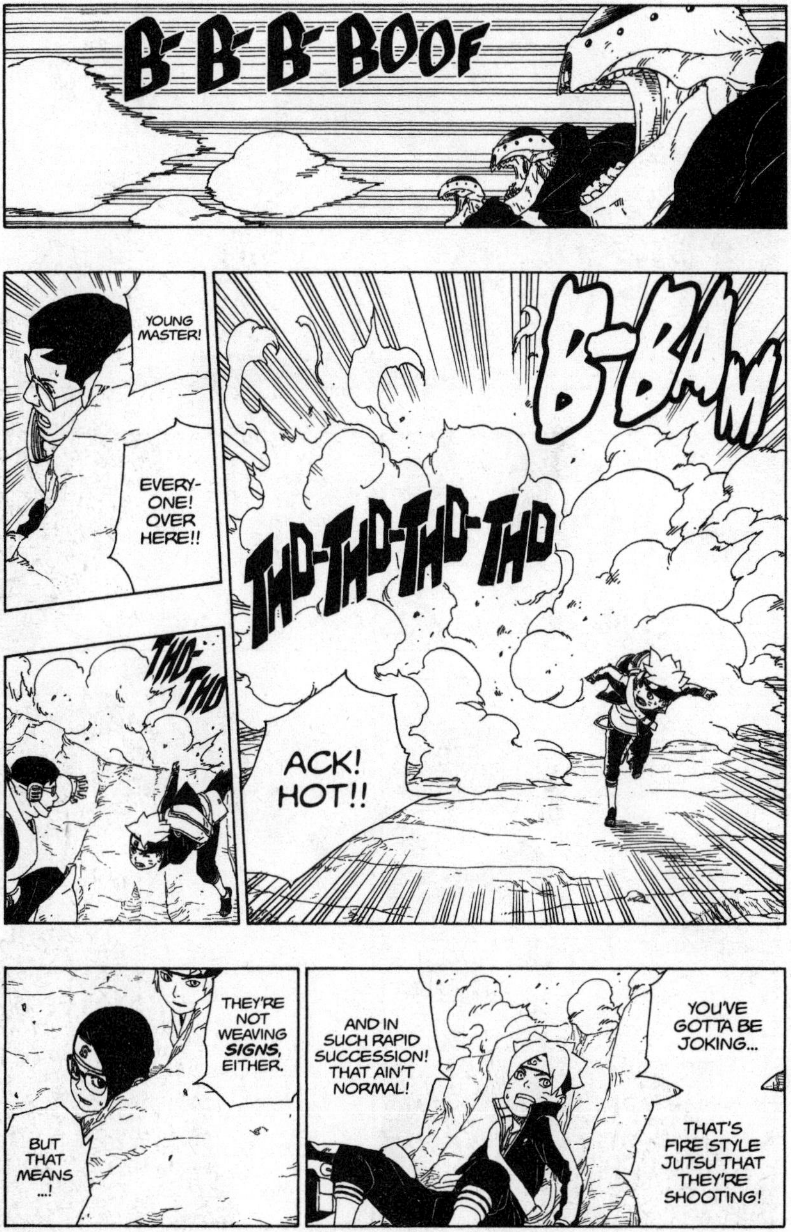
B-B-B-BOOF
B-BAM
THD-THD-THD-THD-THD
ACK! HOT!!
YOUNG MASTER!
EVERY-ONE! OVER HERE!!
THD-THD
YOU'VE GOTTA BE JOKING...
THAT'S FIRE STYLE JUTSU THAT THEY'RE SHOOTING!
AND IN SUCH RAPID SUCCESSION! THAT AIN'T NORMAL!
THEY'RE NOT WEAVING SIGNS, EITHER.
BUT THAT MEANS ...!

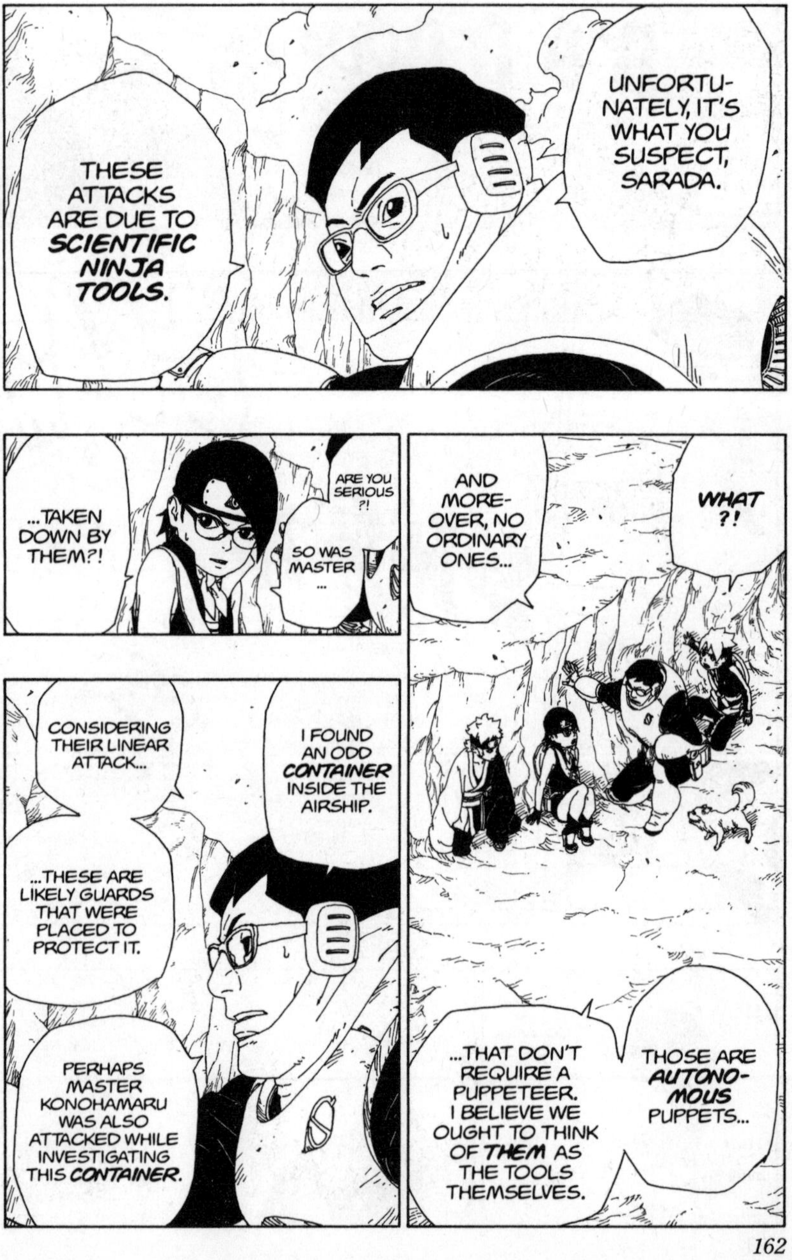
UNFORTUNATELY, IT'S WHAT YOU SUSPECT, SARADA.
THESE ATTACKS ARE DUE TO **SCIENTIFIC NINJA TOOLS.**
WHAT ?!
AND MOREOVER, NO ORDINARY ONES...
THOSE ARE **AUTONOMOUS** PUPPETS...
...THAT DON'T REQUIRE A PUPPETEER. I BELIEVE WE OUGHT TO THINK OF **THEM** AS THE TOOLS THEMSELVES.
ARE YOU SERIOUS ?!
SO WAS MASTER ...
...TAKEN DOWN BY THEM?!
I FOUND AN ODD **CONTAINER** INSIDE THE AIRSHIP.
CONSIDERING THEIR LINEAR ATTACK...
...THESE ARE LIKELY GUARDS THAT WERE PLACED TO PROTECT IT.
PERHAPS MASTER KONOHAMARU WAS ALSO ATTACKED WHILE INVESTIGATING THIS **CONTAINER.**

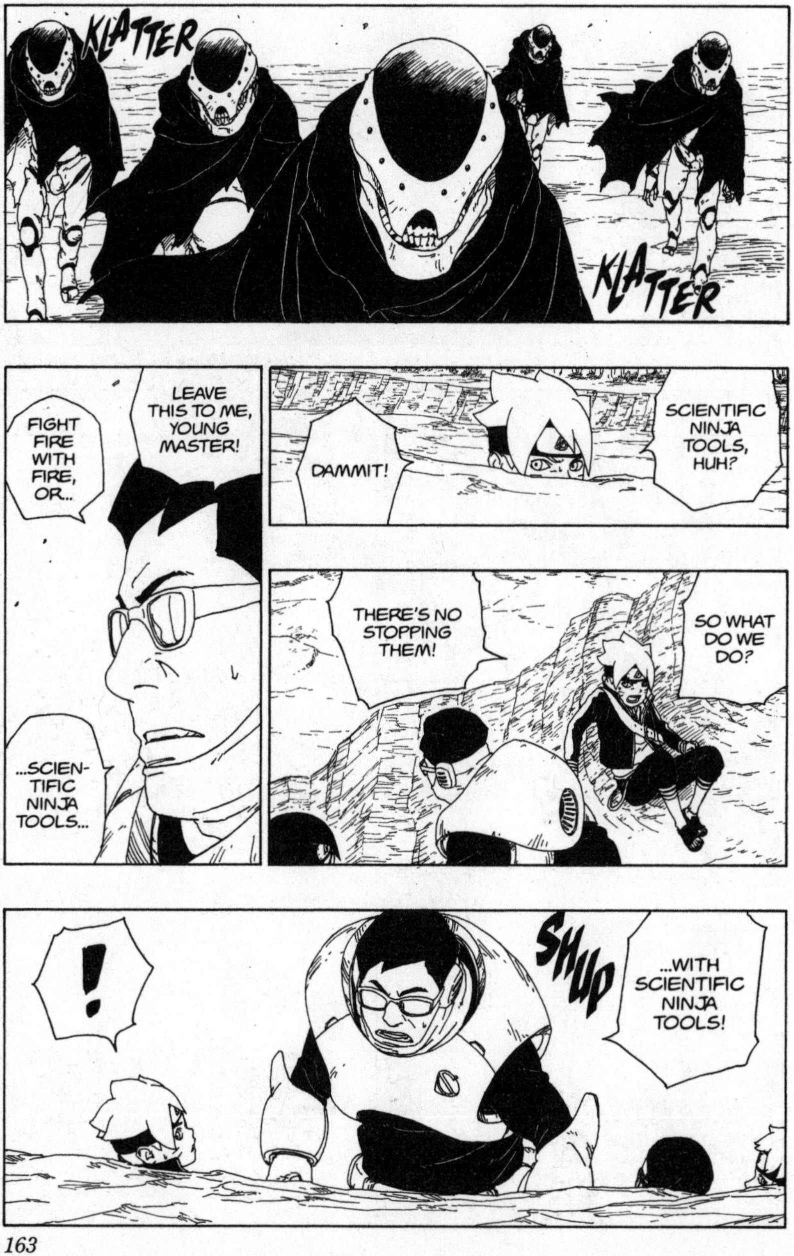
KLATTER
KLATTER
SCIENTIFIC NINJA TOOLS, HUH?
DAMMIT!
SO WHAT DO WE DO?
THERE'S NO STOPPING THEM!
LEAVE THIS TO ME, YOUNG MASTER!
FIGHT FIRE WITH FIRE, OR...
...SCIENTIFIC NINJA TOOLS...
...WITH SCIENTIFIC NINJA TOOLS!
SHUP
!

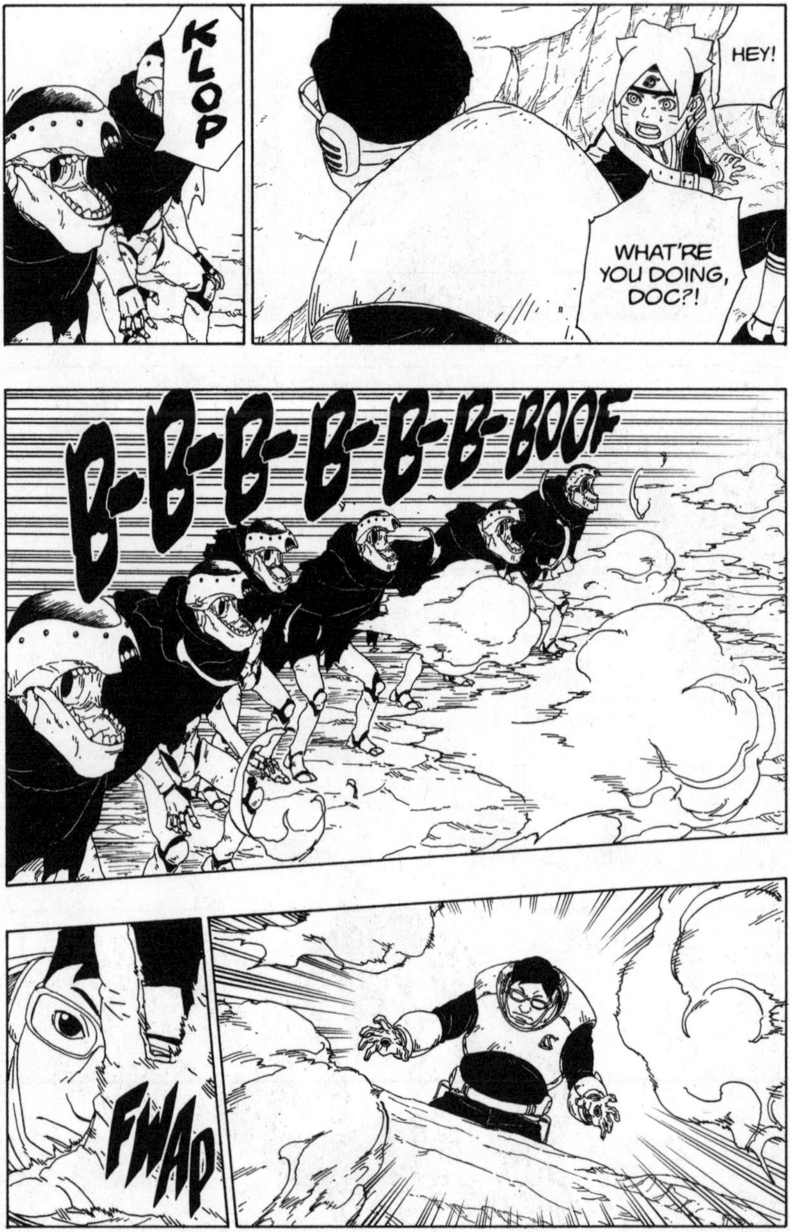
HEY!
WHAT'RE YOU DOING, DOC?!
KLOP
B-B-B-B-B-B-BOOF
FWAP

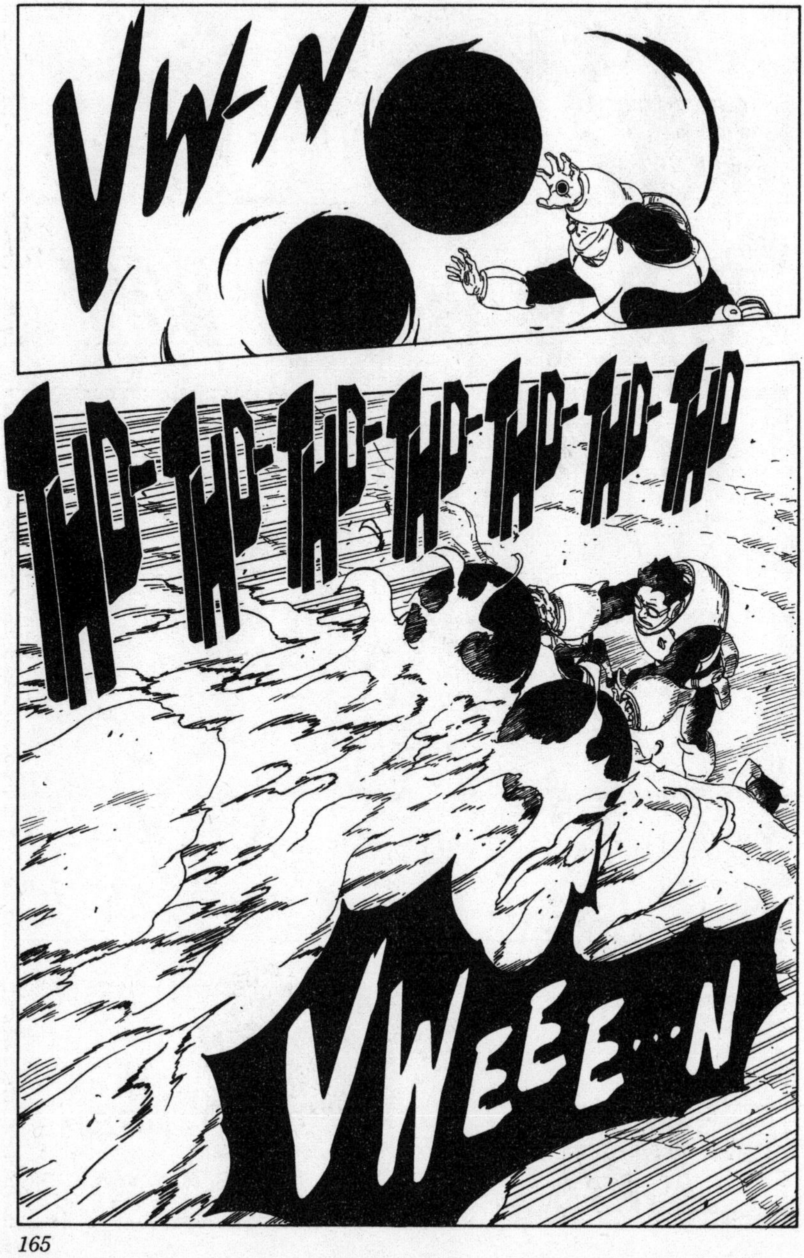
VW-N
THD-THD-THD-THD-THD-THD-THD
VWEEE..N

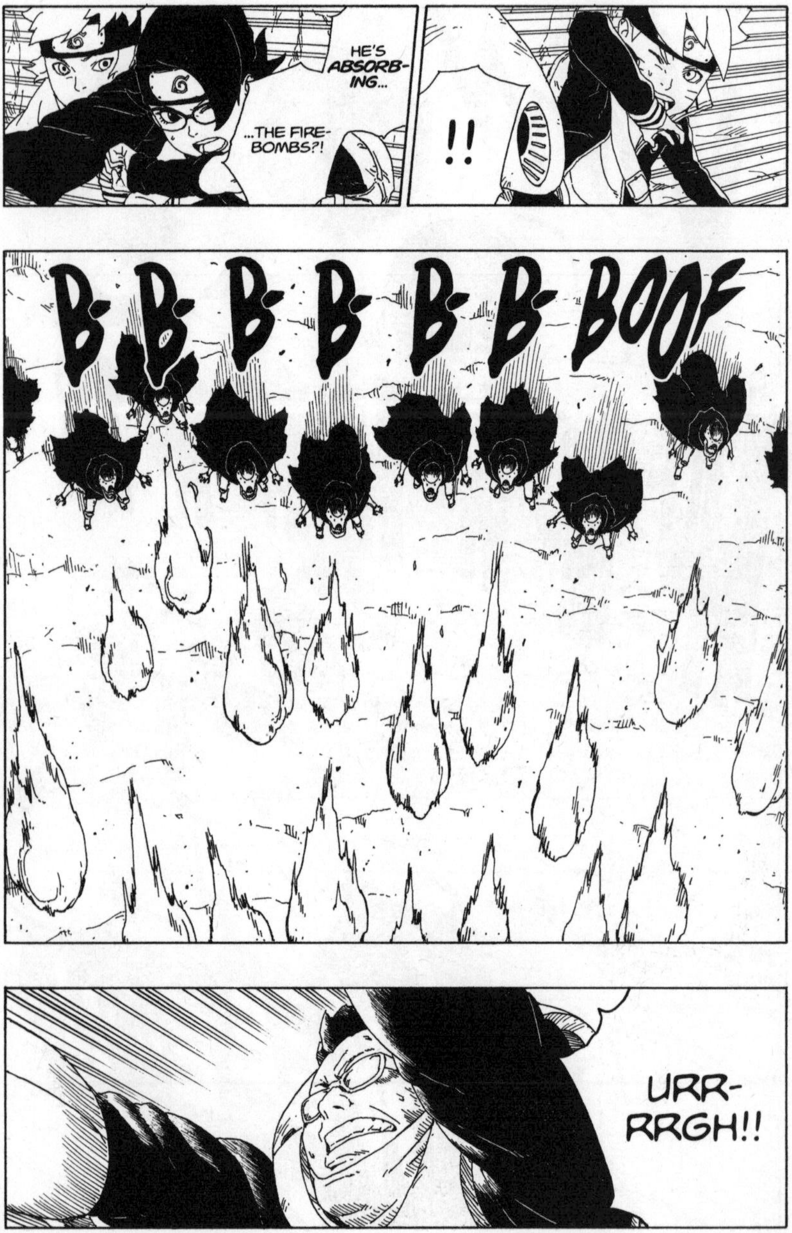
!!
HE'S ABSORBING...
...THE FIRE-BOMBS?!
B-B-B-B-B-B-BOOF
URR-RRGH!!

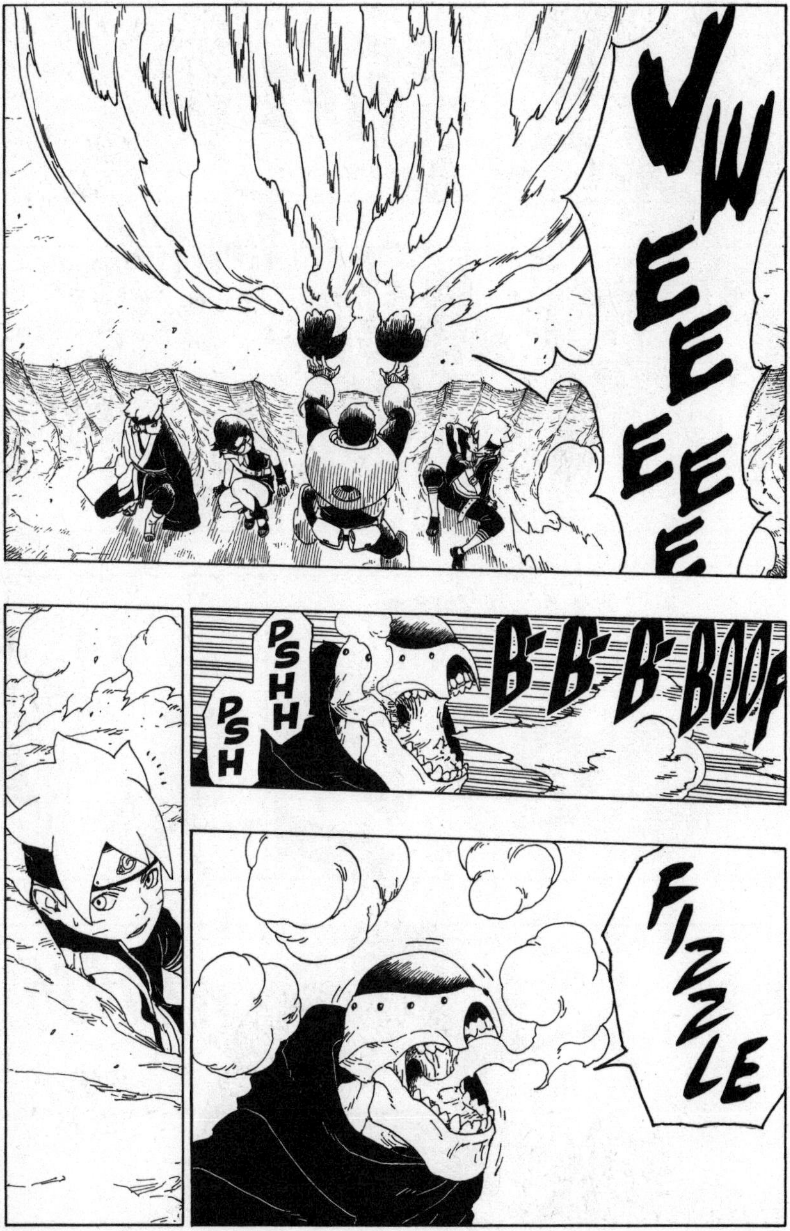
VWEEEEEE
B-B-B-BOOF
PSHH
PSH
FIZZLE

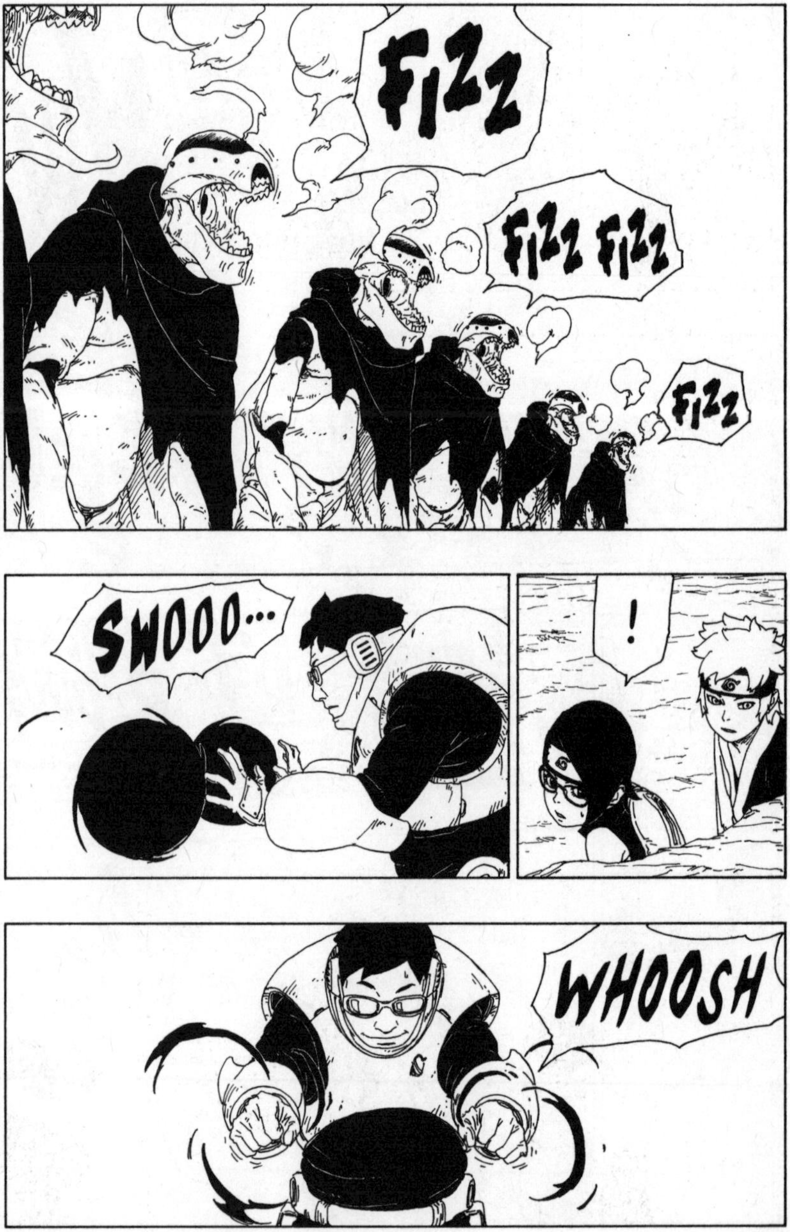
FIZZ
FIZZ FIZZ
FIZZ
!
SWOOO...
WHOOSH

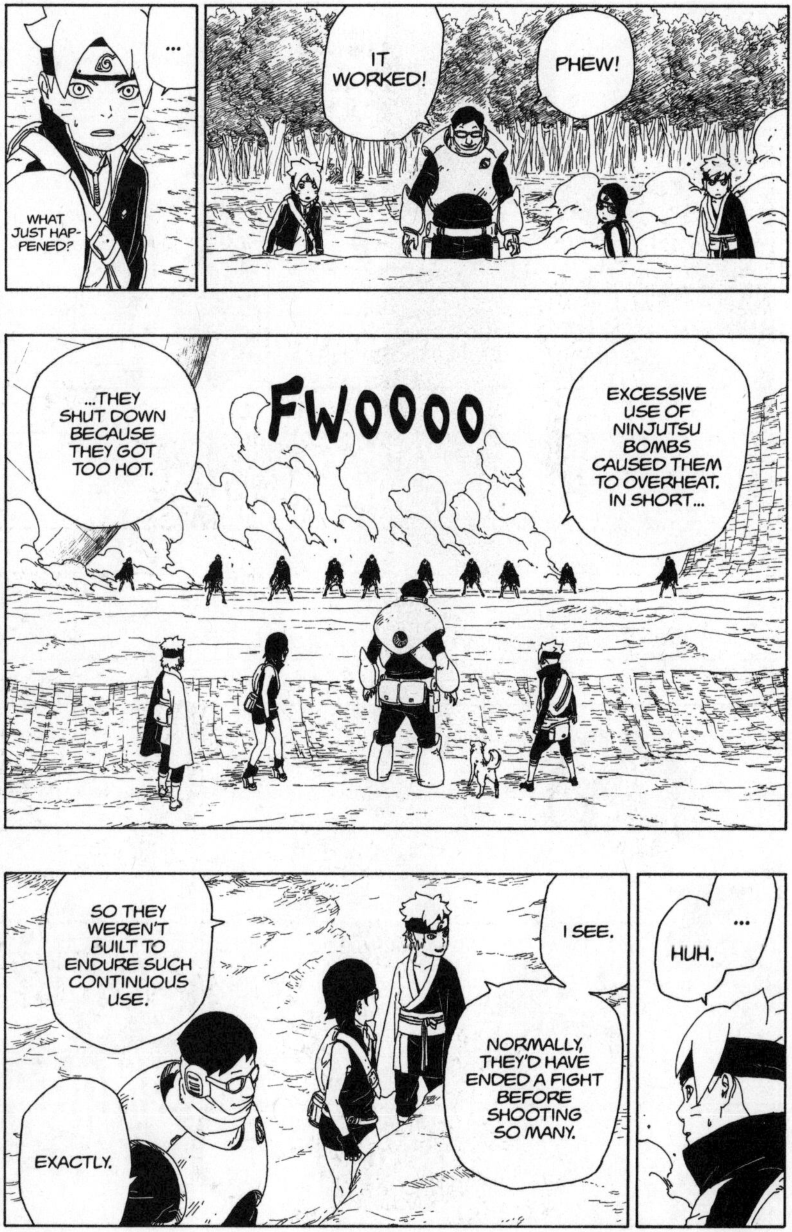
PHEW!
IT WORKED!
...
WHAT JUST HAPPENED?
EXCESSIVE USE OF NINJUTSU BOMBS CAUSED THEM TO OVERHEAT. IN SHORT...
FWOOOO
...THEY SHUT DOWN BECAUSE THEY GOT TOO HOT.
...
HUH.
I SEE.
SO THEY WEREN'T BUILT TO ENDURE SUCH CONTINUOUS USE.
NORMALLY, THEY'D HAVE ENDED A FIGHT BEFORE SHOOTING SO MANY.
EXACTLY.

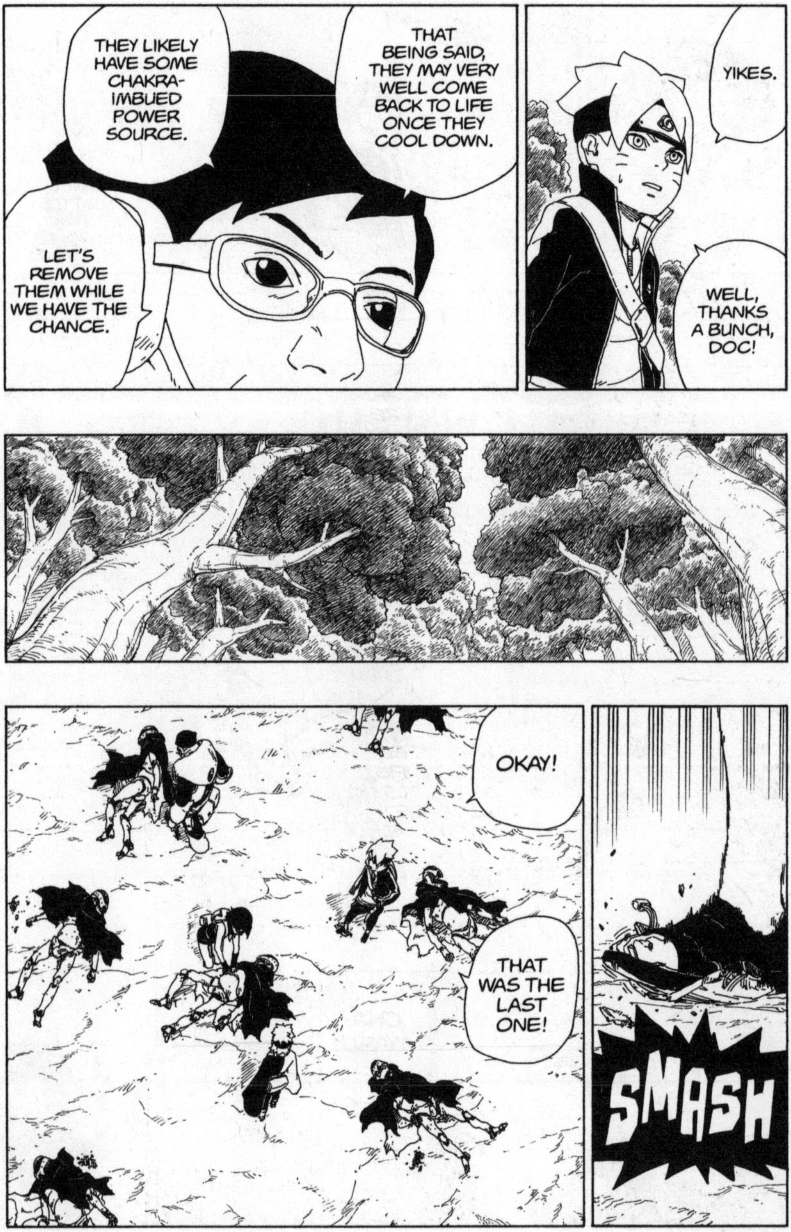
YIKES.
WELL, THANKS A BUNCH, DOC!
THAT BEING SAID, THEY MAY VERY WELL COME BACK TO LIFE ONCE THEY COOL DOWN.
THEY LIKELY HAVE SOME CHAKRA-IMBUED POWER SOURCE.
LET'S REMOVE THEM WHILE WE HAVE THE CHANCE.
SMASH
OKAY!
THAT WAS THE LAST ONE!

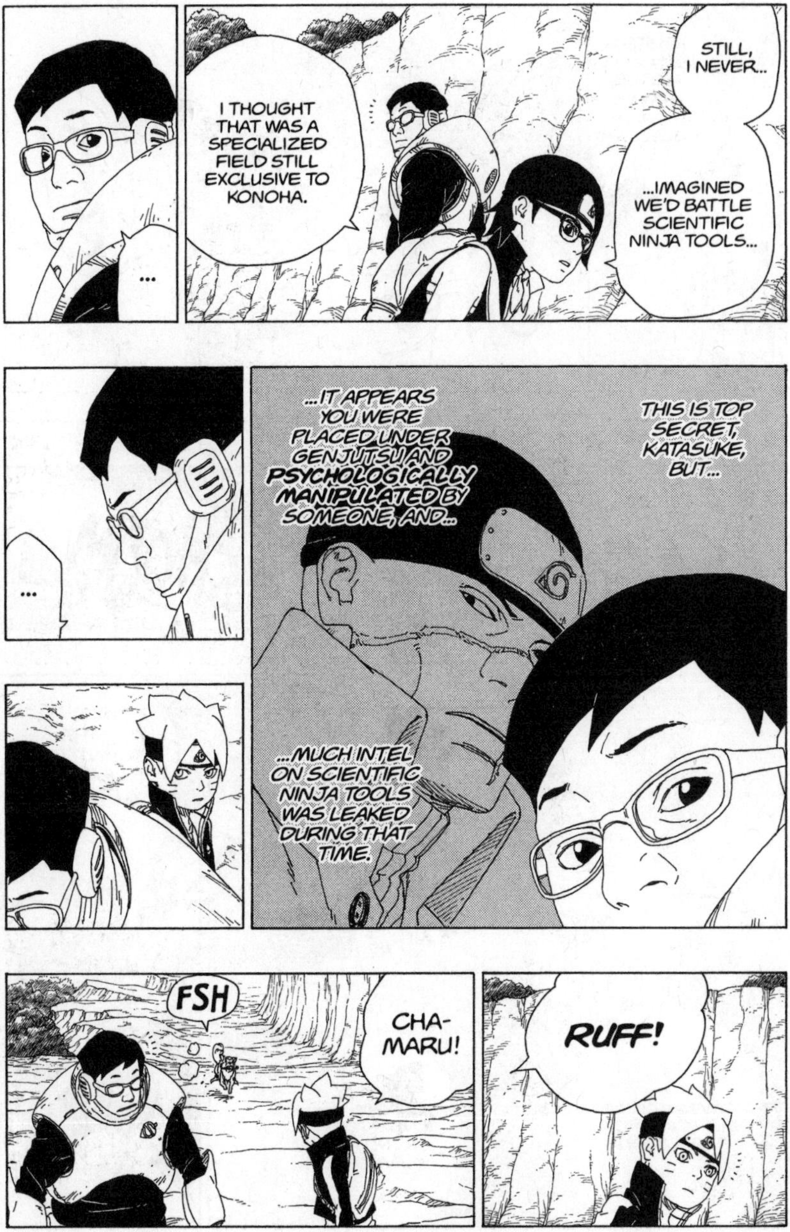
STILL, I NEVER...
...IMAGINED WE'D BATTLE SCIENTIFIC NINJA TOOLS...
I THOUGHT THAT WAS A SPECIALIZED FIELD STILL EXCLUSIVE TO KONOHA.
...
THIS IS TOP SECRET, KATASUKE, BUT...
...IT APPEARS YOU WERE PLACED UNDER GENJUTSU AND PSYCHOLOGICALLY MANIPULATED BY SOMEONE, AND...
...MUCH INTEL ON SCIENTIFIC NINJA TOOLS WAS LEAKED DURING THAT TIME.
...
RUFF!
CHA-MARU!
FSH

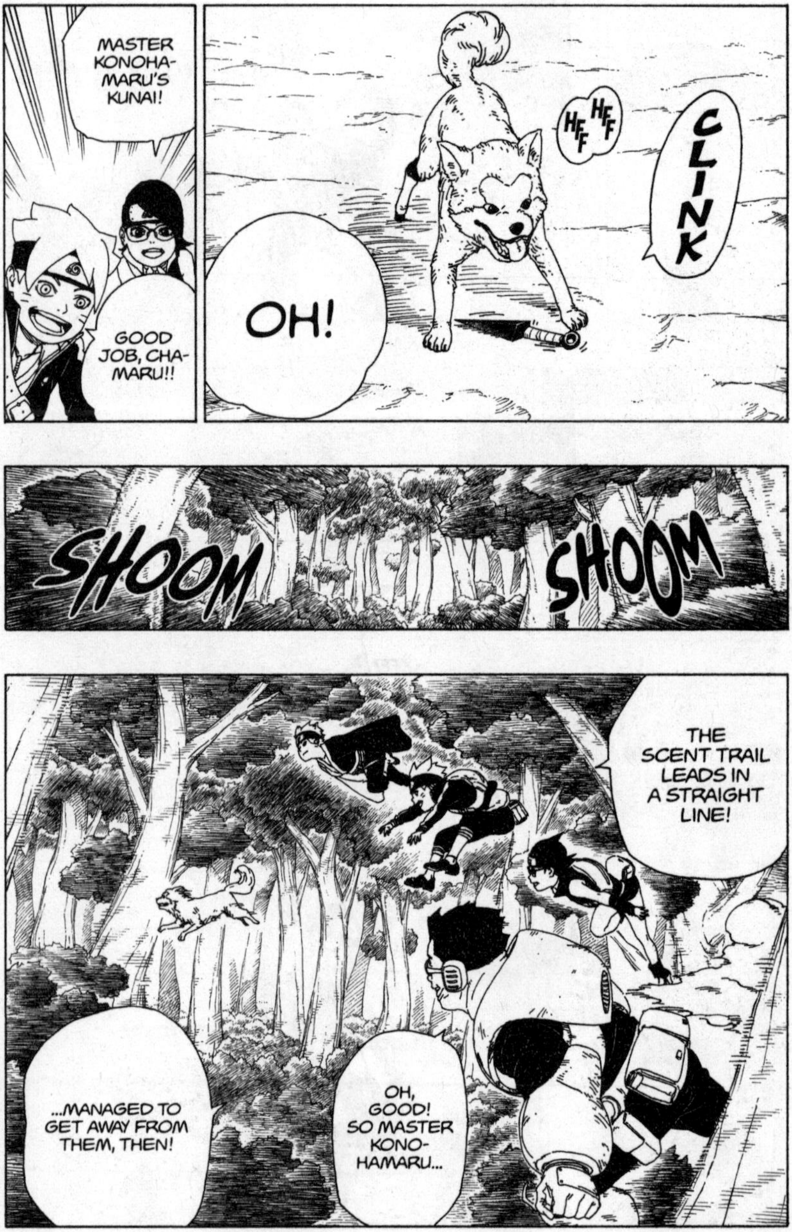
CLINK
HEFF HEFF
OH!
MASTER KONOHA-MARU'S KUNAI!
GOOD JOB, CHA-MARU!!
SHOOM
SHOOM
THE SCENT TRAIL LEADS IN A STRAIGHT LINE!
OH, GOOD! SO MASTER KONO-HAMARU...
...MANAGED TO GET AWAY FROM THEM, THEN!

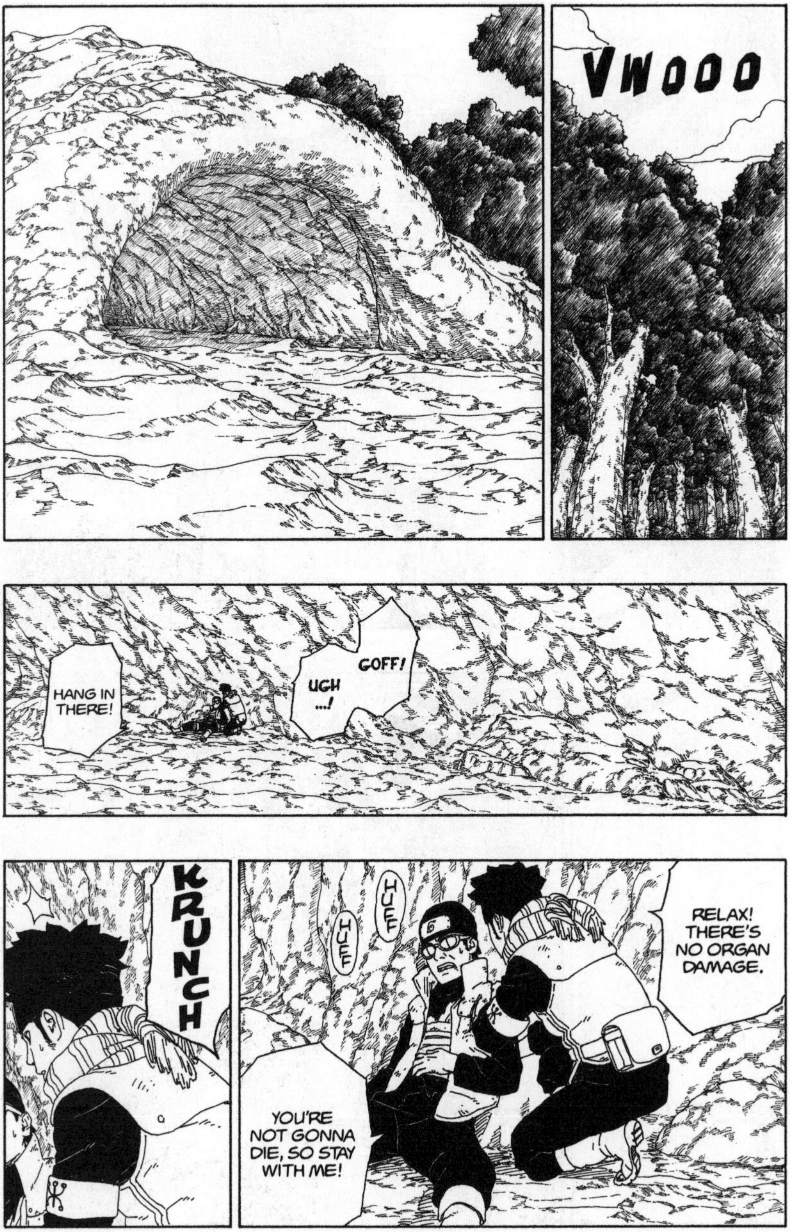
VWOOO
GOFF!
UGH ...!
HANG IN THERE!
RELAX! THERE'S NO ORGAN DAMAGE.
HUFF
HUFF
YOU'RE NOT GONNA DIE, SO STAY WITH ME!
KRUNCH

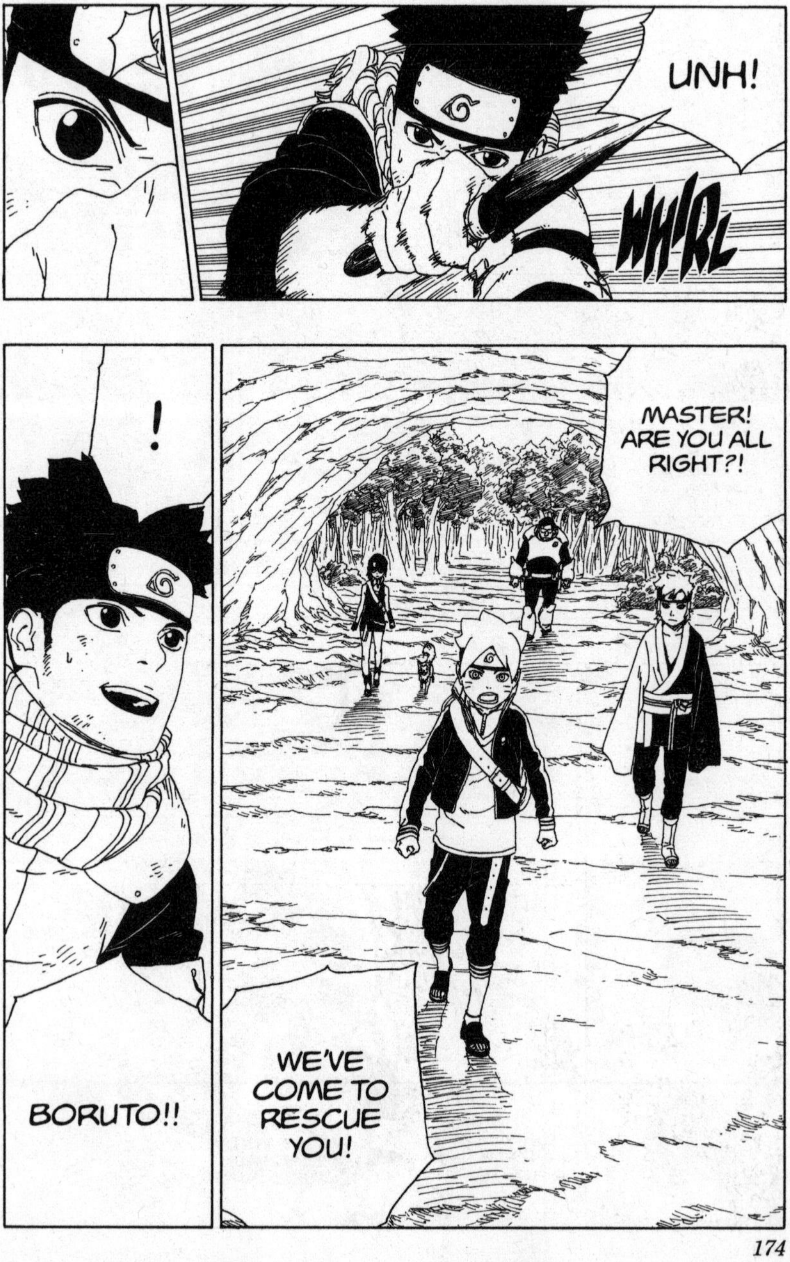
UNH!
WHIRL
MASTER! ARE YOU ALL RIGHT?!
WE'VE COME TO RESCUE YOU!
!
BORUTO!!

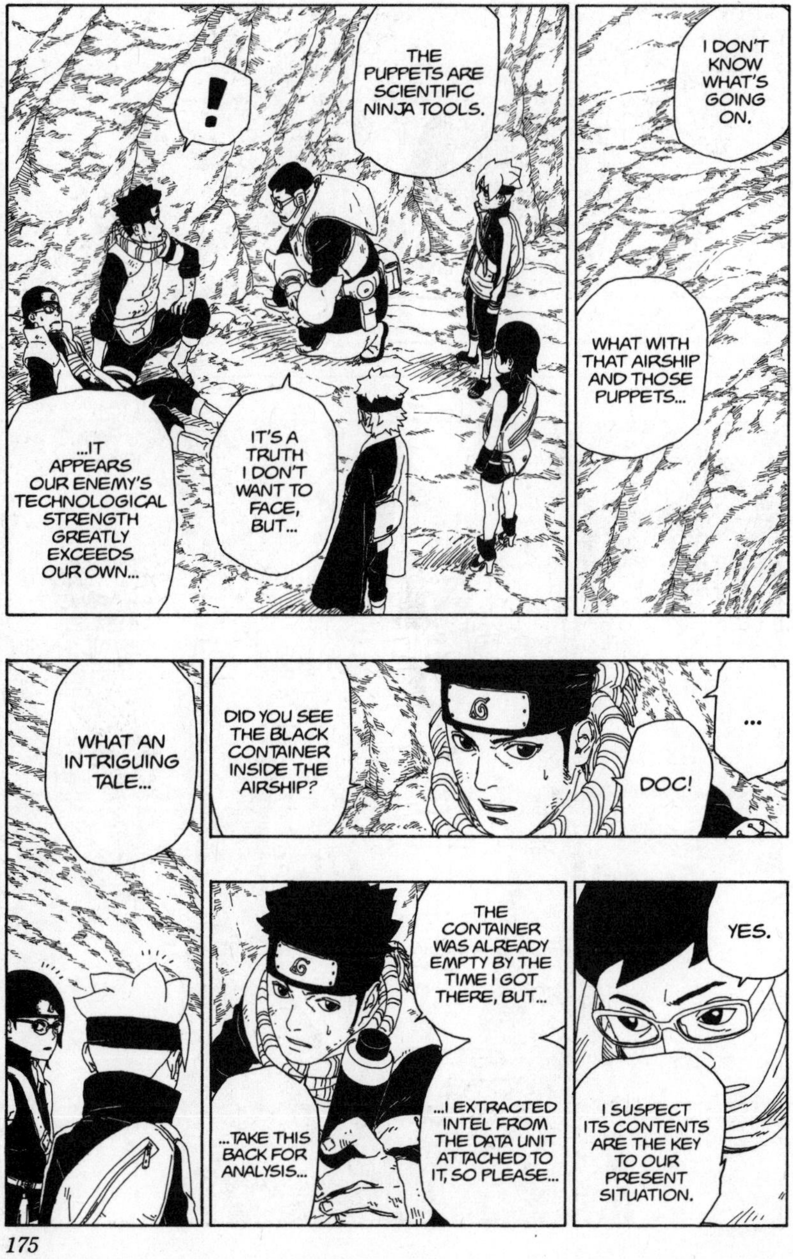
I DON'T KNOW WHAT'S GOING ON.
WHAT WITH THAT AIRSHIP AND THOSE PUPPETS...
THE PUPPETS ARE SCIENTIFIC NINJA TOOLS.
!
IT'S A TRUTH I DON'T WANT TO FACE, BUT...
...IT APPEARS OUR ENEMY'S TECHNOLOGICAL STRENGTH GREATLY EXCEEDS OUR OWN...
...
DOC!
DID YOU SEE THE BLACK CONTAINER INSIDE THE AIRSHIP?
YES.
I SUSPECT ITS CONTENTS ARE THE KEY TO OUR PRESENT SITUATION.
THE CONTAINER WAS ALREADY EMPTY BY THE TIME I GOT THERE, BUT...
...I EXTRACTED INTEL FROM THE DATA UNIT ATTACHED TO IT, SO PLEASE...
...TAKE THIS BACK FOR ANALYSIS...
WHAT AN INTRIGUING TALE...

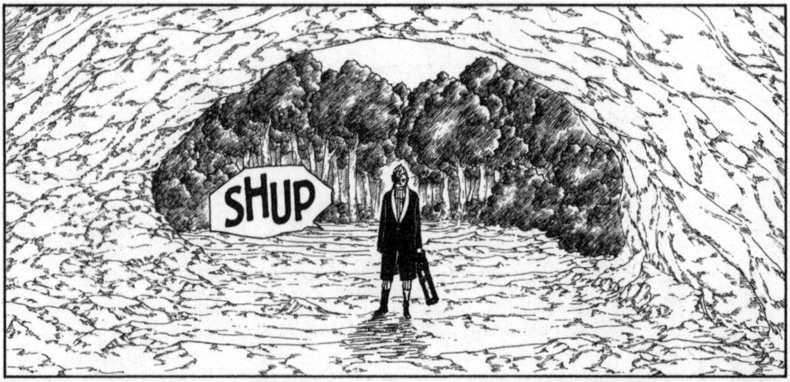
SHUP

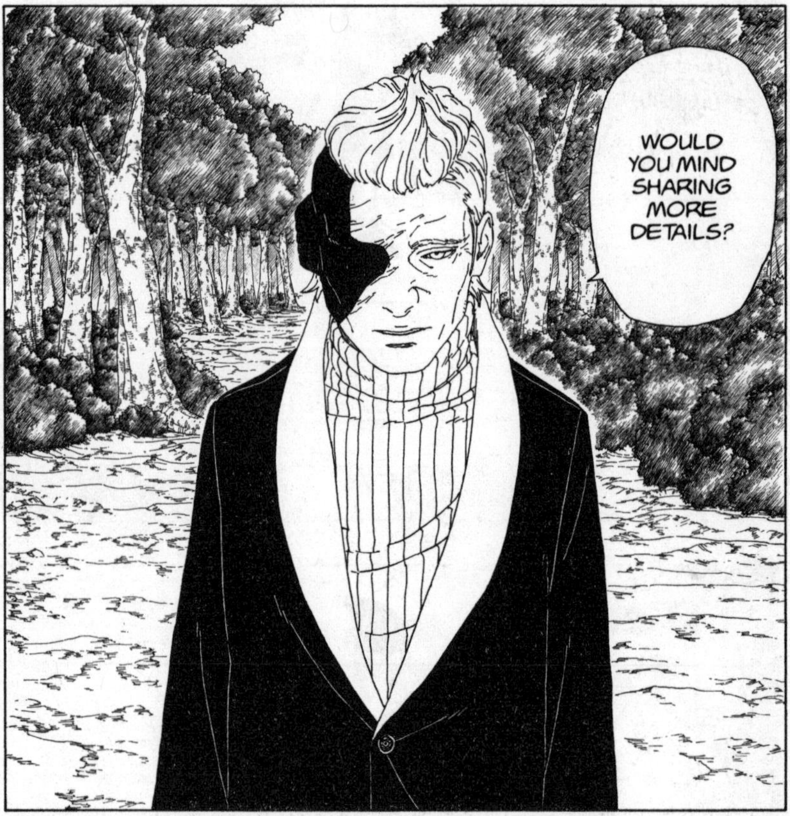
WOULD YOU MIND SHARING MORE DETAILS?

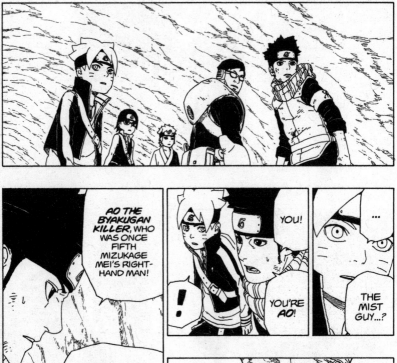

...
THE MIST GUY...?
YOU!
YOU'RE AO!
!
HO.
I'M IMPRESSED THAT YOU STILL RECOGNIZE ME.
AO THE BYAKUGAN KILLER, WHO WAS ONCE FIFTH MIZUKAGE MEI'S RIGHT-HAND MAN!
YOU WERE PREVIOUSLY LISTED IN KONOHA'S BINGO BOOK IN GOLD LETTERS. OF COURSE I STILL REMEMBER YOU.
...
AO...
...THE BYAKUGAN KILLER?!
LORD AO!

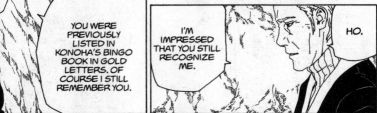

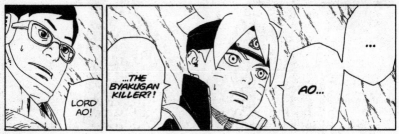

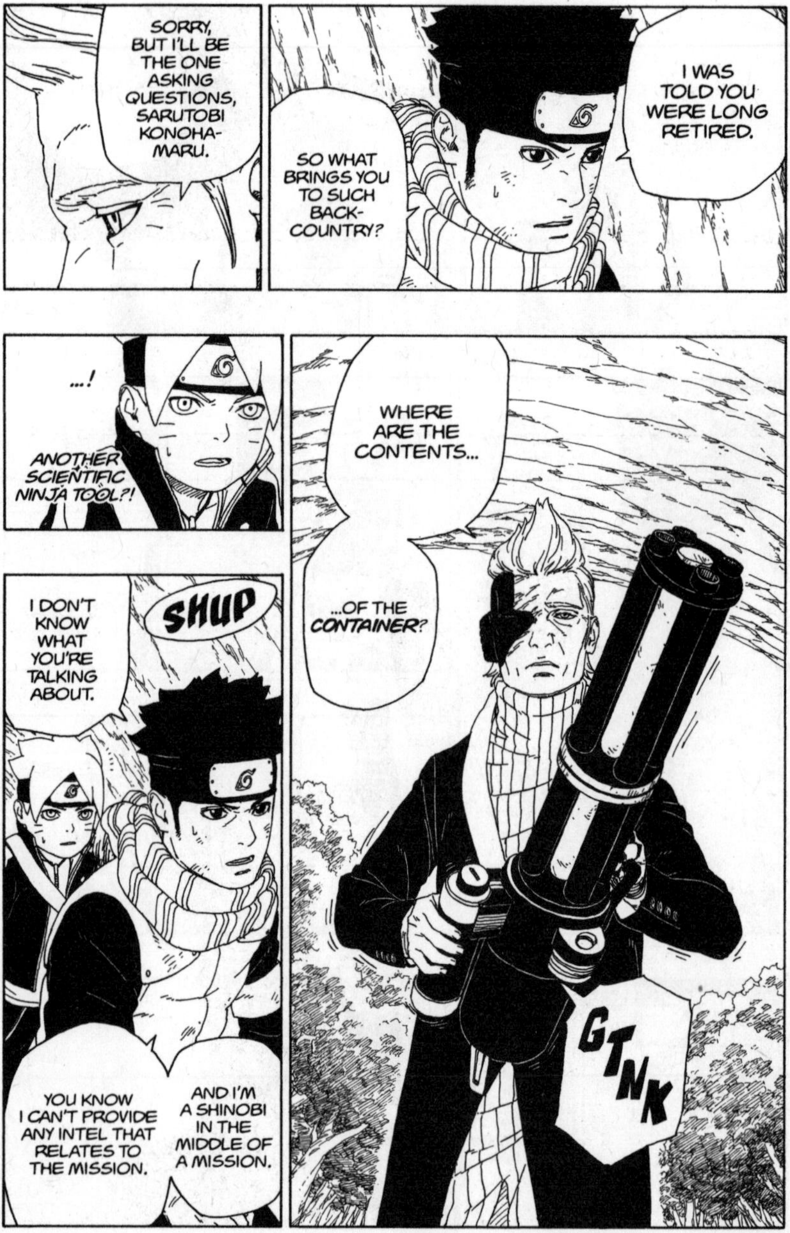
I WAS TOLD YOU WERE LONG RETIRED.
SO WHAT BRINGS YOU TO SUCH BACK-COUNTRY?
SORRY, BUT I'LL BE THE ONE ASKING QUESTIONS, SARUTOBI KONOHA-MARU.
WHERE ARE THE CONTENTS...
...OF THE *CONTAINER*?
GTNK
...!
ANOTHER SCIENTIFIC NINJA TOOL?!
SHUP
I DON'T KNOW WHAT YOU'RE TALKING ABOUT.
AND I'M A SHINOBI IN THE MIDDLE OF A MISSION.
YOU KNOW I CAN'T PROVIDE ANY INTEL THAT RELATES TO THE MISSION.

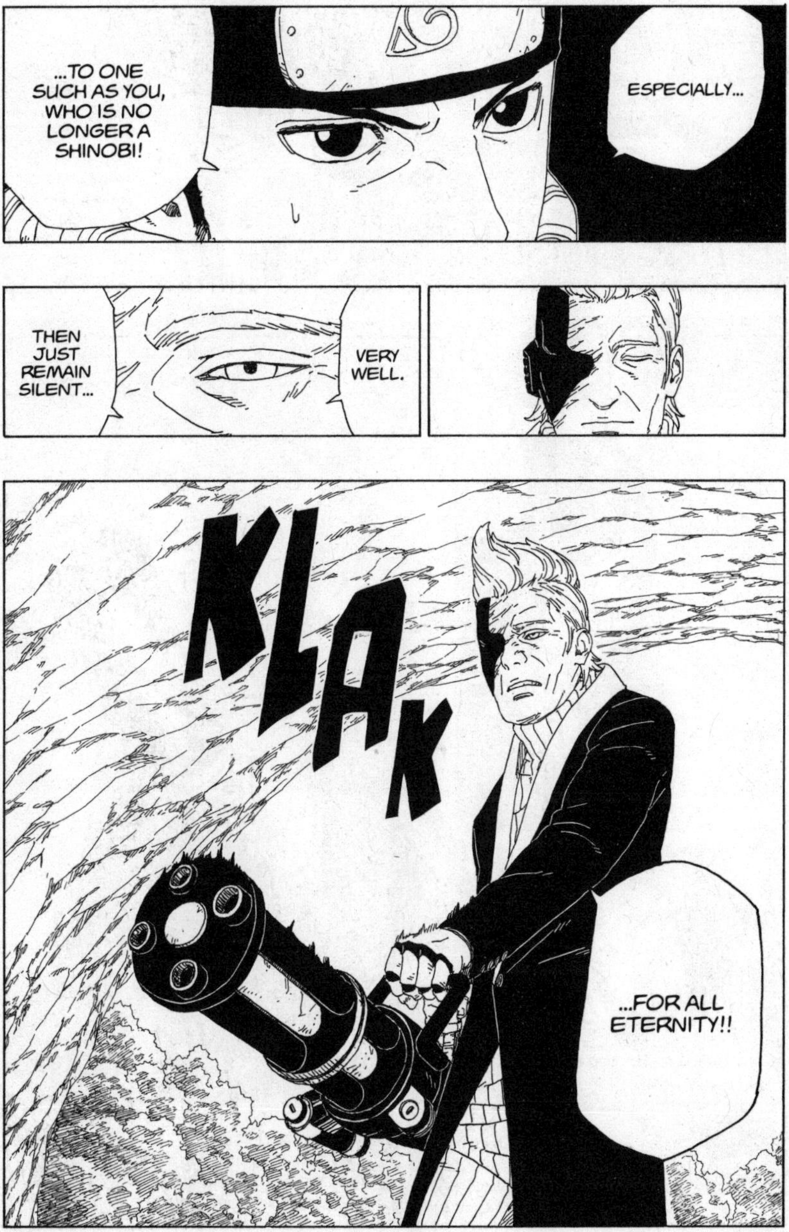
ESPECIALLY...
...TO ONE SUCH AS YOU, WHO IS NO LONGER A SHINOBI!
VERY WELL.
THEN JUST REMAIN SILENT...
KLAK
...FOR ALL ETERNITY!!

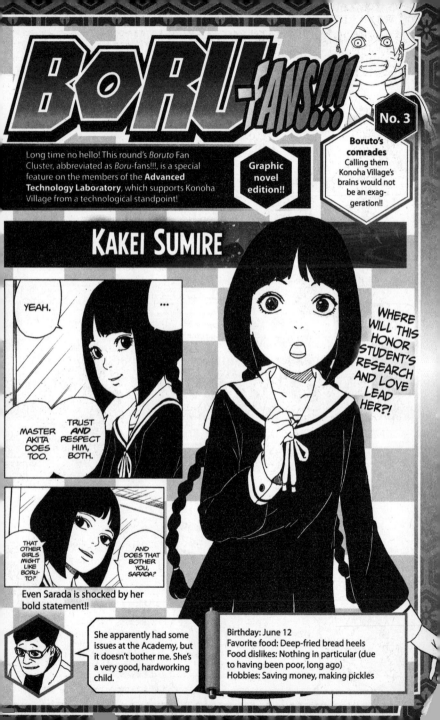

BORU-FANS!!!

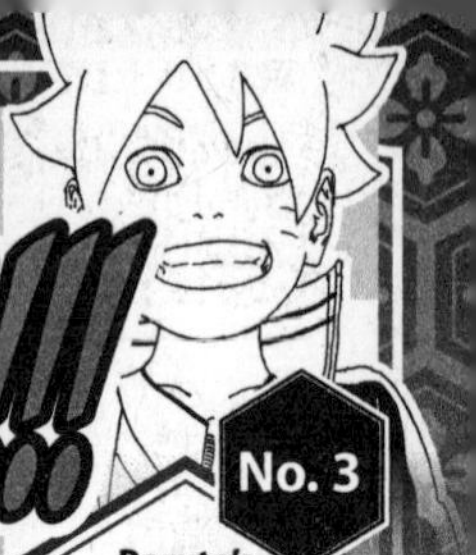

No. 3

Long time no hello! This round's *Boruto* Fan Cluster, abbreviated as *Boru*-fans!!!, is a special feature on the members of the **Advanced Technology Laboratory**, which supports Konoha Village from a technological standpoint!

Graphic novel edition!!

Boruto's comrades
Calling them Konoha Village's brains would not be an exaggeration!!

KAKEI SUMIRE

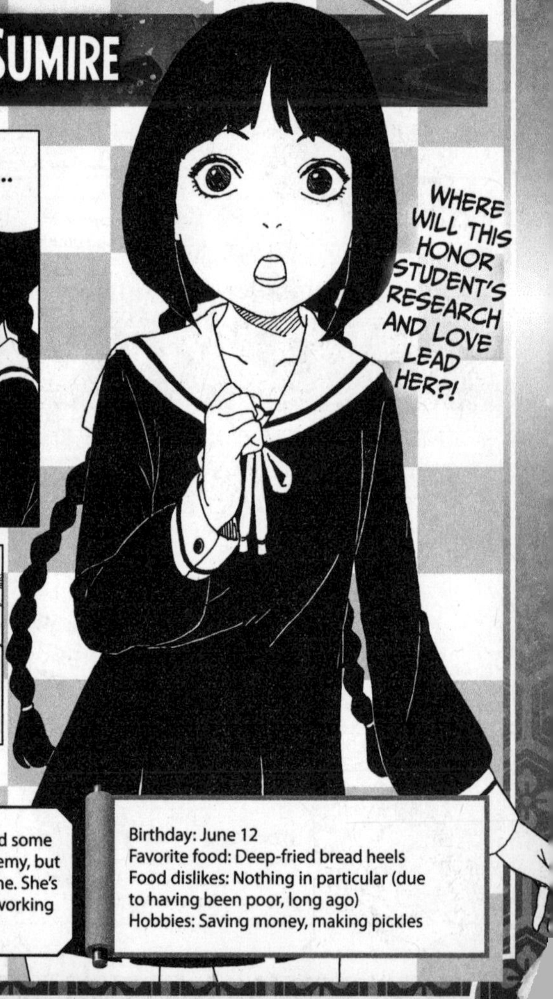
WHERE WILL THIS HONOR STUDENT'S RESEARCH AND LOVE LEAD HER?!

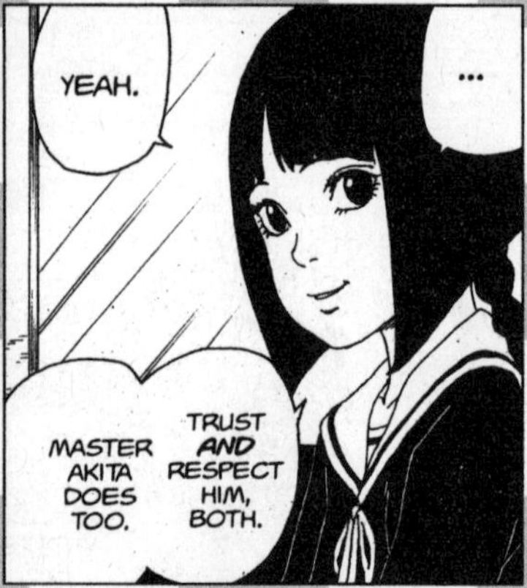
...
YEAH.
TRUST *AND* RESPECT HIM, BOTH.
MASTER AKITA DOES TOO.

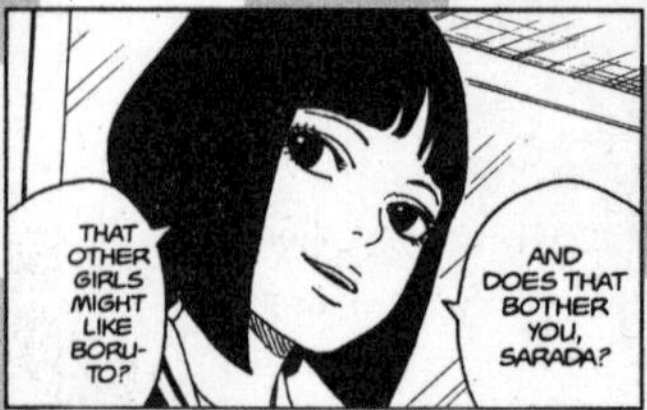
AND DOES THAT BOTHER YOU, SARADA?
THAT OTHER GIRLS MIGHT LIKE BORUTO?

Even Sarada is shocked by her bold statement!!

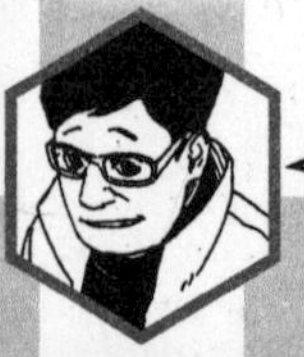

She apparently had some issues at the Academy, but it doesn't bother me. She's a very good, hardworking child.

Birthday: June 12
Favorite food: Deep-fried bread heels
Food dislikes: Nothing in particular (due to having been poor, long ago)
Hobbies: Saving money, making pickles

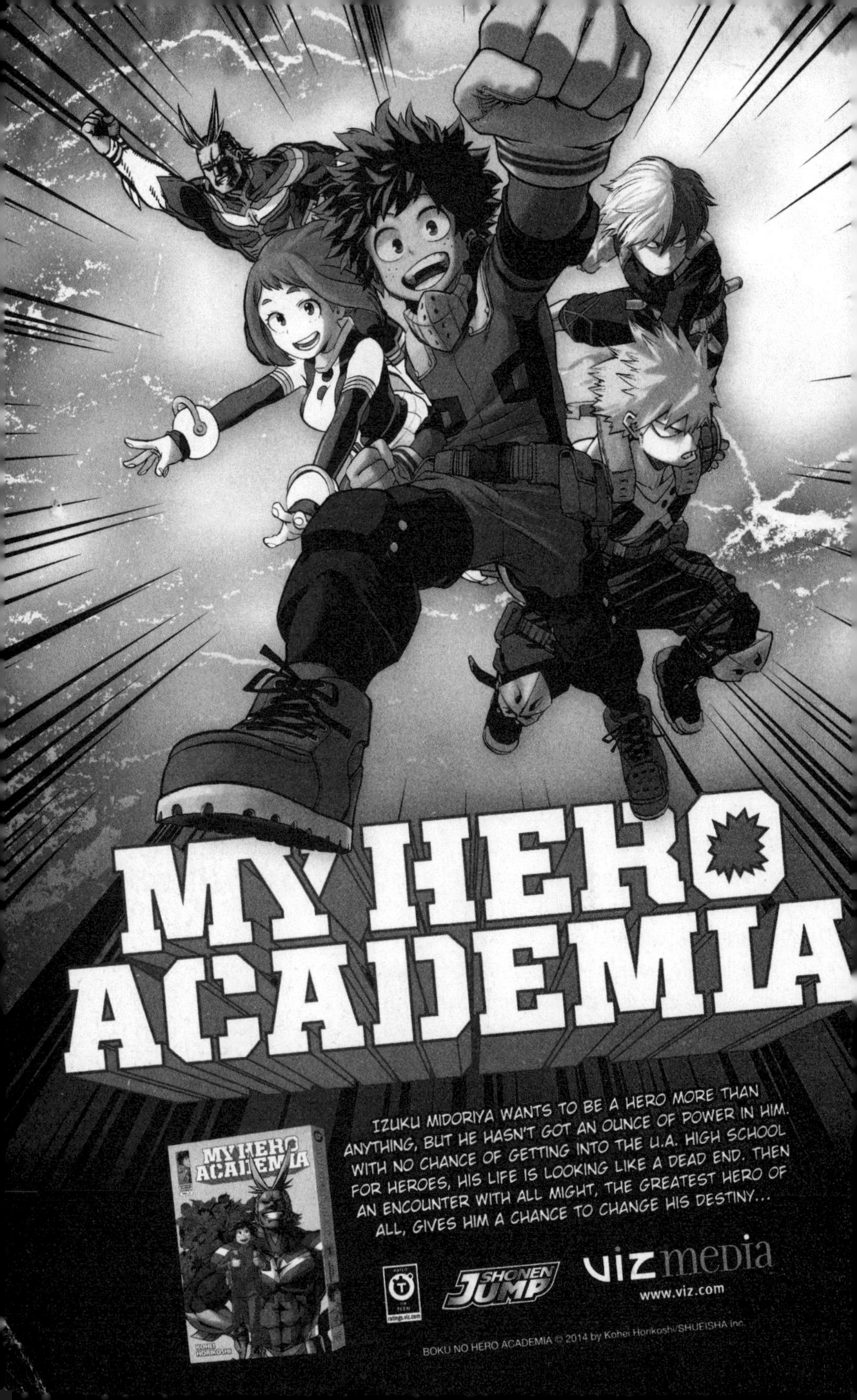
MY HERO ACADEMIA
IZUKU MIDORIYA WANTS TO BE A HERO MORE THAN ANYTHING, BUT HE HASN'T GOT AN OUNCE OF POWER IN HIM. WITH NO CHANCE OF GETTING INTO THE U.A. HIGH SCHOOL FOR HEROES, HIS LIFE IS LOOKING LIKE A DEAD END. THEN AN ENCOUNTER WITH ALL MIGHT, THE GREATEST HERO OF ALL, GIVES HIM A CHANCE TO CHANGE HIS DESTINY...
MY HERO ACADEMIA
KOHEI HORIKOSHI
RATED T FOR TEEN
ratings.viz.com
SHONEN JUMP
VIZ media
www.viz.com
BOKU NO HERO ACADEMIA © 2014 by Kohei Horikoshi/SHUEISHA Inc.

YOU'RE READING
IN THE
WRONG DIRECTION!!

WHOOPS! Guess what? You're starting at the wrong end of the comic!
...It's true! In keeping with the original Japanese format, **Boruto** is
meant to be read from right to left, starting in the upper-right corner.

Unlike English, which is read from left to right, Japanese is read
from right to left, meaning that action, sound effects and word-balloon
order are completely reversed... something which can make readers
unfamiliar with Japanese feel pretty backwards themselves. For this
reason, manga or Japanese comics published in the U.S. in English have
sometimes been published "flopped"—that is, printed in exact reverse
order, as though seen from the other side of a mirror.

By flopping pages, U.S. publishers can avoid confusing readers, but
the compromise is not without its downside. For one thing, a character in
a flopped manga series who once wore in the original Japanese version
a T-shirt emblazoned with "M A Y" (as in "the merry month of") now
wears one which reads "Y A M"!
Additionally, many manga creators
in Japan are themselves unhappy
with the process, as some feel the
mirror-imaging of their art alters their
original intentions.

We are proud to bring you **Boruto**
in the original unflopped format. Turn
to the other side of the book and let
the ninjutsu begin...!

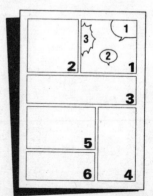

—Editor

INUZUKA AKITA

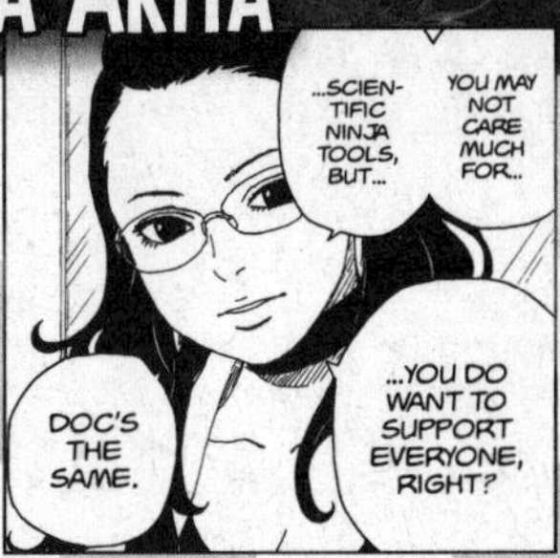
YOU MAY NOT CARE MUCH FOR...
...SCIENTIFIC NINJA TOOLS, BUT...
...YOU DO WANT TO SUPPORT EVERYONE, RIGHT?
DOC'S THE SAME.

Her feelings about Katasuke are genuine!

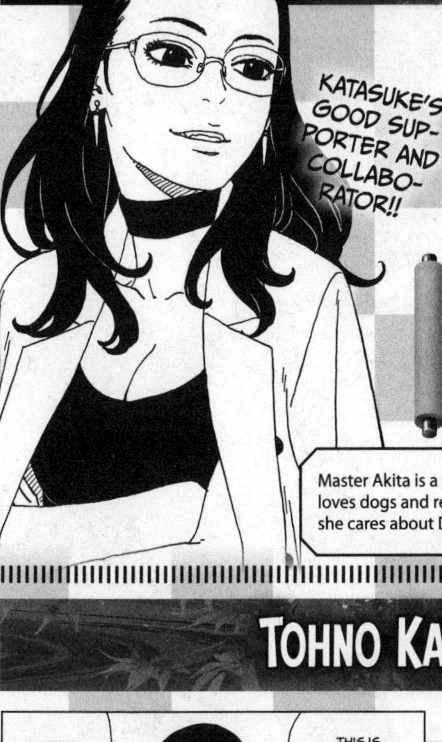
KATASUKE'S GOOD SUPPORTER AND COLLABORATOR!!

Birthday: April 20
Favorite food: Instant noodle cups, soba with tempura and egg
Food dislikes: Instant yakisoba cups
Hobbies: Eating junk food on the go

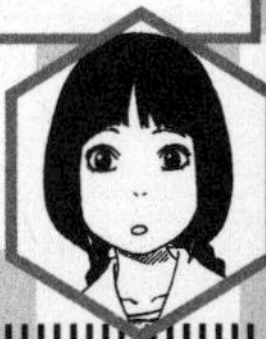

Master Akita is a really good person! She loves dogs and research...and above all, she cares about Dr. Katasuke!

TOHNO KATASUKE

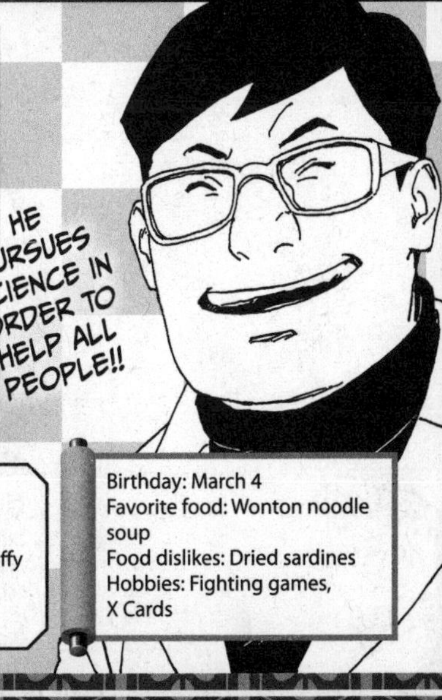
HE PURSUES SCIENCE IN ORDER TO HELP ALL PEOPLE!!

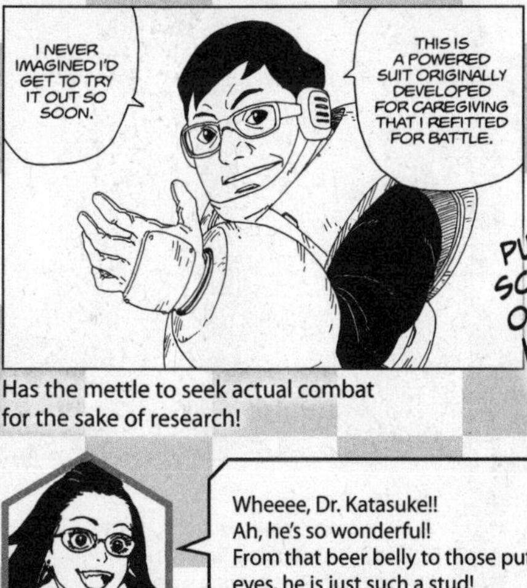
THIS IS A POWERED SUIT ORIGINALLY DEVELOPED FOR CAREGIVING THAT I REFITTED FOR BATTLE.
I NEVER IMAGINED I'D GET TO TRY IT OUT SO SOON.

Has the mettle to seek actual combat for the sake of research!

Birthday: March 4
Favorite food: Wonton noodle soup
Food dislikes: Dried sardines
Hobbies: Fighting games, X Cards

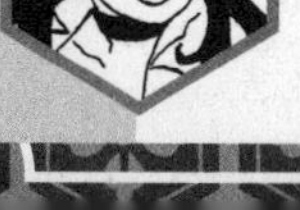

Wheeee, Dr. Katasuke!!
Ah, he's so wonderful!
From that beer belly to those puffy eyes, he is just such a stud!
Don't y'all agree?!

Black ✦ Clover

STORY & ART BY YŪKI TABATA

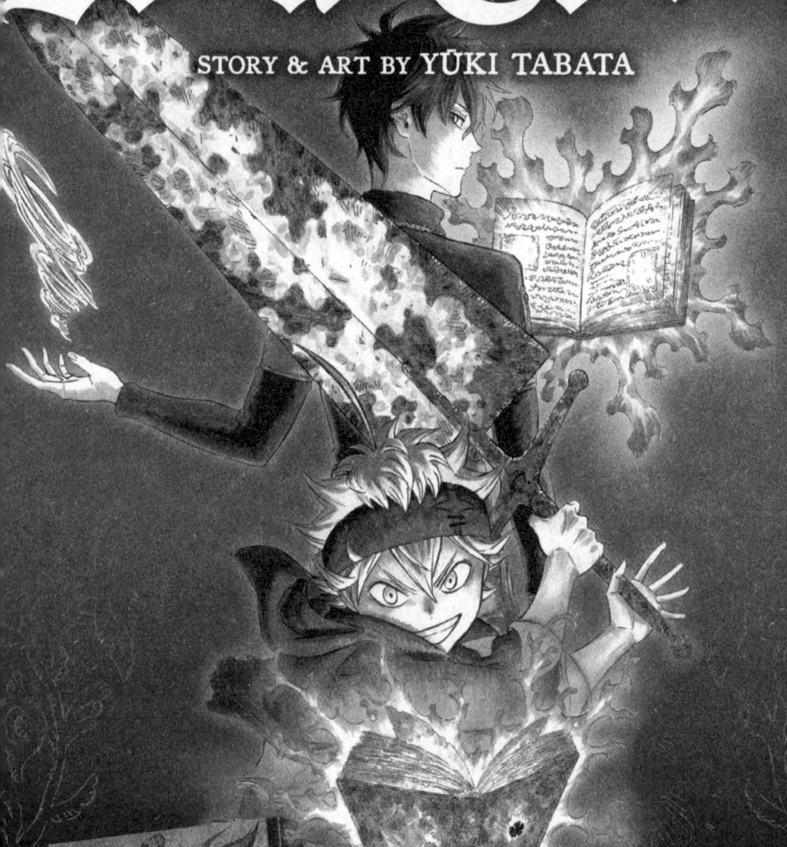

Asta is a young boy who dreams of becoming the greatest mage in the kingdom. Only one problem—he can't use any magic! Luckily for Asta, he receives the incredibly rare five-leaf clover grimoire that gives him the power of anti-magic. Can someone who can't use magic really become the Wizard King? One thing's for sure—Asta will never give up!

SHONEN JUMP   VIZ media
www.viz.com

BORUTO
=NARUTO NEXT GENERATIONS=

VOLUME 5

SHONEN JUMP MANGA EDITION

Creator/Supervisor MASASHI KISHIMOTO
Art by MIKIO IKEMOTO
Script by UKYO KODACHI

Translation: Mari Morimoto
Touch-up Art & Lettering: Snir Aharon
Design: Alice Lewis
Editor: Alexis Kirsch

BORUTO: NARUTO NEXT GENERATIONS © 2016
by Masashi Kishimoto, Mikio Ikemoto, Ukyo Kodachi
All rights reserved.
First published in Japan in 2016 by SHUEISHA Inc., Tokyo.
English translation rights arranged by SHUEISHA Inc.

Printed in the U.S.A.

Published by VIZ Media, LLC
P.O. Box 77010
San Francisco, CA 94107

10 9 8 7 6 5 4 3 2 1
First printing, March 2019

viz.com

shonenjump.com

PARENTAL ADVISORY
BORUTO is rated T for Teen and is
recommended for ages 13 and up.
This volume contains fantasy violence.

池本幹雄

Meet my cat. He's a one-year-and-ten-month-old Scottish Fold. He sleeps most of the day, moving from one favorite spot to another. But for whatever reason, every time I start working at my desk, he starts meowing at me. And always right at the moment when I've sat down with the resolve to get work done. If I end up ignoring him for a while, his meows become sharper, with an edge to them... He's so cute!

—Mikio Ikemoto, 2018

小太刀右京

Since *Boruto* started, I've received feedback from readers all across the world. Even though I'm unable to reply in most cases, I do look at every one of them.

And that is when I think to myself, "Ah, I'm glad I learned Portuguese through *Captain Tsubasa*," "I'm glad I learned Chinese through *Iron Wok Jan*," "I'm glad I learned English in order to read American comics," "I'm glad I learned French in order to read *bande dessinée* comics" and so on, making me realize how great comics are. Of course, I also appreciate comments in Japanese, and look at them as well. Please keep them all coming!

—Ukyo Kodachi, 2018